Great Trade Walls in Imperial China and Spain

I0891159

This book offers a comparative and polycentric approach to the formation of global trade networks and goods that circumnavigated China, America, and Europe in the so-called process of "early globalization" during the early modern period.

Based on a pioneering archival strategy developed by GECEM Project (Global Encounters between China and Europe, www.gecem.eu) and funded by the European Research Council (ERC), the chapters in this volume deploy innovative methodology built on the process of clustering new empirical evidence on geostrategic locations to analyse complex socioeconomic systems. Each chapter in this volume focuses on a specific case study that validates the usefulness of this methodology for a more accurate analysis of the self-regulating institutions, social networks, circulation of global goods and information, and smuggling activities that characterised the nonlinear markets of early modern China, Europe, and the Americas. These studies constitute a clear example of the new directions of global (economic) history and how a bottom-up approach through new data mining and comparative method helps to unveil big research questions. The designing of GECEM Project Database (www.gecemdatabase.eu) stands out as a cutting-edge digital humanities tool used in this book.

This book is an insightful resource for scholars of Global History and Atlantic studies, including those interested in China's trade and history, and its global encounters with the West. This book was originally published as a special issue of the journal, *Atlantic Studies*.

Manuel Perez-Garcia is tenured Associate Professor at the Department of History (School of Humanities) at Shanghai Jiao Tong University (China). He is Distinguished Researcher and Principal Investigator (PI) of GECEM Project funded by the ERC (European Research Council) Starting-Grant, ref. 679371, under the European Union's Horizon 2020 Research and Innovation Programme (www.gecem.eu); he is PI of the Global Peripheries Project funded by UMU BG22/00132. He is the founder and director of the Global History Network in China (GHN). He is the author of *Global History with Chinese Characteristics Autocratic States along the Silk Road in the Decline of the Spanish and Qing Empires 1680–1796* (2021), *Blood, Land and Power. The Rise and Fall of the Spanish Nobility and Lineages in the Early Modern Period* (2021), and *Vicarious Consumers: Trans-National Meetings between the West and East in the Mediterranean World (1730–1808)* (2013).

江漢司馬峻寫之

Great Trade Walls in Imperial China and Spain

Global goods, power struggles and bankruptcy, 1644–1840

Edited by
Manuel Perez-Garcia

Routledge
Taylor & Francis Group
LONDON AND NEW YORK

First published 2024
by Routledge
4 Park Square, Milton Park, Abingdon, Oxon OX14 4RN

and by Routledge
605 Third Avenue, New York, NY 10158

Routledge is an imprint of the Taylor & Francis Group, an informa business

British Library Cataloguing in Publication Data
A catalogue record for this book is available from the British Library

ISBN13: 978-1-032-45993-6 (hbk)
ISBN13: 978-1-032-45994-3 (pbk)
ISBN13: 978-1-003-37960-7 (ebk)

DOI: 10.4324/9781003379607

Typeset in Myriad Pro
by Newgen Publishing UK

Publisher's Note
The publisher accepts responsibility for any inconsistencies that may have arisen during the conversion of this book from journal articles to book chapters, namely the inclusion of journal terminology.

Disclaimer
Every effort has been made to contact copyright holders for their permission to reprint material in this book. The publishers would be grateful to hear from any copyright holder who is not here acknowledged and will undertake to rectify any errors or omissions in future editions of this book.

This book is dedicated to Joe McDermott, such a great friend, such an outstanding scholar. His sudden passing was shocking and sad, but his legacy as a brilliant historian and one of the best China experts will always remain, and future generations will benefit from it.

Contents

Citation Information

The chapters in this book were originally published in the journal *Atlantic Studies*, volume 19, issue 3 (2022). When citing this material, please use the original page numbering for each article, as follows:

Chapter 1

Beyond the Silk Road: Manila Galleons, trade networks, global goods, and the integration of Atlantic and Pacific markets (1680–1840)
Manuel Perez-Garcia
Atlantic Studies, volume 19, issue 3 (2022), pp. 373–383

Chapter 2

The economic "micro-cosmos" of Canton as a global entrepôt: Overseas trade, consumption and the Canton System from the Kangxi to Qianlong eras (1683–1795)
Manuel Perez-Garcia and Lei Jin
Atlantic Studies, volume 19, issue 3 (2022), pp. 384–403

Chapter 3

Compelled to import: Cuban consumption at the dawn of the nineteenth century
Nadia Fernández-de-Pinedo
Atlantic Studies, volume 19, issue 3 (2022), pp. 404–429

Chapter 4

Global trafficking and local bankruptcies: Anglo-Spanish slave trade in the Rio de la Plata, 1786–1790
Antonio Ibarra
Atlantic Studies, volume 19, issue 3 (2022), pp. 430–447

Chapter 5

The Jesuit Global networks of exchange of Asian goods: A "conflictive" musk load around the middle of the seventeenth century
Pedro Omar Svriz-Wucherer
Atlantic Studies, volume 19, issue 3 (2022), pp. 448–461

Chapter 6

Postal networks and global letters in Cartagena de Indias: the overseas mail in the Spanish empire in the eighteenth century
Rocío Moreno-Cabanillas
Atlantic Studies, volume 19, issue 3 (2022), pp. 462–480

Notes on Contributors

Nadia Fernández-de-Pinedo is Senior Lecturer at the Universidad Autónoma of Madrid (Spain). She is also a research associate of the Historical Archive of the Spanish Patent Office (EOPM) and member of the IBC Network (www.ibcnetwork.org). Her work covers a wide range consumption and distribution networks including eighteenth- and nineteenth-century Spanish and Atlantic history. She participates in various cross-disciplinary projects – GECEM project (http://www.gecem.eu) – where she has embarked on research examining technology transfer processes, institutions, fabric distribution, and material culture.

Antonio Ibarra is Full Professor of Economic History at the School of Economics, National University of México (UNAM) and the author of *Mercado e institución: corporaciones comerciales, redes de negocios y crisis colonial*; *Guadalajara en el siglo XVIII*, UNAM/ Universidad de Guadalajara, CONACyT, México, 2018, and editor with A. Alcántara y F. Jumar, of *Actores sociales, redes de negocios y corporacionesen Hispanoamérica, siglos XVII-XIX*, México, 2019.

Lei Jin is a PhD researcher at GECEM Project at the Department of History at Pablo de Olavide University (Seville, Spain). GECEM Project funded by the ERC (European Research Council) Starting-Grant, ref. 679371, under the European Union's Horizon 2020 Research and Innovation Programme (www.gecem.eu). Her PhD dissertation is on China-Europe trade relations during the Qing period. She obtained her BA degree at the University of Nottingham Ningbo, China.

Rocío Moreno-Cabanillas is Postdoctoral Researcher at the Departament of American History at University of Seville (Seville, Spain). She was Lecturer in Historiographic Sciences and Techniques, and a research fellow at GECEM Project. She has been a visiting researcher at the University of Warwick (UK), Universidad de los Andes (Colombia), Ibero-Amerikanisches Institut (Germany), Casa de Velázquez (France), and Shanghai Jiao Tong University (China). Her areas of research and publication include the Postal History of European Colonial Empires, Bourbon Reforms in the Spanish Monarchy, Caribbean History, particularly the History of Cartagena de Indias, and the Diplomatics Analysis of Spanish American Documents.

Pedro Omar Svriz-Wucherer is a Juan de la Cierva-Formación fellow at the University of Seville (Spain), member and Postdoctoral Researcher at the GECEM Project "Global Encounters between China and Europe: Trade Networks, Consumption and Cultural

Exchanges in Macau and Marseille, 1680-1840". The postdoctoral research focuses on the commercial Jesuit activities between Asia, America, and Europe during the early modern era. Svriz-Wucherer has several articles in SSCI and AHCI indexed journals (*Revista História*, 2011; *Hispania Sacra*, 2013; *Historia Social*, 2018; *Revista Electrónica de Fuentes y Archivos*, 2018; and *Atlantic Studies: Global Currents*, 2022) and presented his work in many national and international forums.

Manuel Perez-Garcia is tenured Associate Professor at the Department of History (School of Humanities) at Shanghai Jiao Tong University (China). He is Distinguished Researcher and Principal Investigator (PI) of GECEM Project funded by the ERC (European Research Council) Starting-Grant, ref. 679371, under the European Union's Horizon 2020 Research and Innovation Programme (www.gecem.eu); he is PI of the Global Peripheries Project funded by UMU BG22/00132. He is the founder and director of the Global History Network in China (GHN). He is the author of *Global History with Chinese Characteristics Autocratic States along the Silk Road in the Decline of the Spanish and Qing Empires 1680–1796* (2021), *Blood, Land and Power. The Rise and Fall of the Spanish Nobility and Lineages in the Early Modern Period* (2021), and *Vicarious Consumers: Trans-National Meetings between the West and East in the Mediterranean World (1730–1808)* (2013).

Acknowledgements

This book emanates from the successful finalisation of GECEM Project (*Global Encounters between China and Europe: Trade Networks, Consumption and Cultural Exchanges in Macau and Marseille, 1680–1840*), a project hosted by the Pablo de Olavide University (UPO) of Seville (Spain). The GECEM Project is funded by the ERC (European Research Council) Starting Grant, ref. 679371, under the European Union's Horizon 2020 Research and Innovation Programme (www.gecem.eu). The Principal Investigator (PI) is Professor Manuel Perez-Garcia (Distinguished Researcher). He is also PI of the Global Peripheries Project funded by UMU BG22/00132. In the spring term of 2022, this book was completed as part of the outcomes of GECEM Project and GECEM Database (www.gecemdatabase.eu). In addition, this research is part of the academic activities of the Global History Network in China (GHN) (www.globalhistorynetwork.com) in which Manuel Perez-Garcia is the founder and director and the contributors of this book are members of the GHN.

This research is also result of academic activities organised by the GECEM Project such as the permanent lecture series in Global and East Asian History held annually at Shanghai Jiao Tong University (SJTU) in China and UPO in Spain, as well as the international workshop "New Global Histories of Asia, Europe and the Americas in the Age of Nation-States" organised by the GECEM Project, SJTU, and the University of Leeds in Shanghai, China, September 2019. It is also part of the result of GECEM Project workshops and international conferences organised by 6th Eurasia Trajeco-GECEM international conference held in Seville, October 2018. In addition, this research has been partially presented in world academic forums in the panels organised by the GECEM Project such as "Beyond the Silk Road: The Silver Route and the Manila-Acapulco Galleons for the Global Circulation of Goods and People in China, Europe and the Americas" at the XXXVI International Congress of the Latin American Studies Association (LASA)/Latin American Studies in a Globalised World held in Barcelona (Spain), May 2018, and the panel "Social Network Analysis and Databases for New Comparative Global History Studies in China, Europe, and the Americas" at the XVIII World Economic History Conference/Waves of Globalisation held in Boston (US), July–August 2018. We thank the Delegation of the European Union to China and EURAXESS China for their constant and generous support expanding the GECEM Project academic results and actions. We also express our gratitude to academic institutions and partners of the GECEM and GHN such as Shanghai Jiao Tong University, Pablo de Olavide University, Tokyo University of Foreign Studies, the Historiographical Institute at the University of Tokyo, University of Leeds, the Beijing Center for Chinese Studies at the University of International Business and Economics (Beijing, China), the Macau Ricci Institute at the University of Saint Joseph

(Macau), the Faculty of Asian and Middle Eastern Studies at the University of Cambridge, the Center of Global History and European Studies at Pittsburgh University, the Center of Global History at the University of Warwick, the Universidad Nacional Autonoma de Mexico (UNAM), and the Center of China, Korea and Japan from the French National Centre for Scientific Research (CNRS) and L'Ecole des Hautes Etudes en Sciences Sociales (EHESS). A very important acknowledgement goes to professors Dorothea Fischer-Hornung (Heidelberg Center for American Studies, Heidelberg University, Germany) and Manuel Barcia (chair in Global History at the University of Leeds, UK) for supporting and believing in this project. We are grateful to comments and suggestions made by professors Patrick O'Brien, Lucio de Sousa, Joe P. McDermott, Mihoko Oka, Pengsheng Chiu, Hamashita Takeshi, Bartolome Yun-Casalilla, Debin Ma, Liu Shiyung (Michael), Robert Antony, and Xiangyu (Ellen) Cai. We thank reviewers and editors for their comments to improve the result of our research. Any errors are our own.

This book pays tribute to the memory of Professor Joseph P. McDermott, his sudden passing on October 2022 has overwhelmed us with grief and sadness. He was an active and close collaborator of GECEM Project, his great expertise and research on China and East Asian studies has been of great benefit for researchers of GECEM team. His intellectual curiosity, kindness, hospitality, and laugh will stay in our memories. During our visits to St John's at University of Cambridge, we will never forget the nice conversations on China experiences and anecdotes over long luncheons. The joyful meetings in Shanghai, Boston, and Seville will be missed. He and his wife Hiroko will be always remembered for their kindness, generosity, and friendship.

Manuel Perez-Garcia
Shanghai, Fall term 2022

Intertwining history(ies) in the peripheries of the Spanish and Chinese empires

Manuel Perez-Garcia

ABSTRACT
This project offers a comparative and polycentric approach to the connection of trade nodes in the Asian, American, African, and European markets in the early modern period. These analyses reevaluate the great divergence debate by presenting new case studies at the local scale and observing the impact of global goods and changes in consumer behaviour connecting local markets of the Pacific and Atlantic area. In this manner, we explore the circulation and consumption of Chinese goods in the Americas and in Europe, as well as in the African slave market through the Royal Company of the Philippines. Conversely, we also analyse the impact of the introduction of Western goods (of American and European origin) into China.

Scholarship that privileges a transnational approach to the realities of trade networks between China, the Americas, and Europe in the modern period can benefit from a methodology that foregrounds the complexity of cultural exchange as well as the role of previously overlooked participants. This volume brings together essays that deploy an innovative critical perspective, based on a pioneering archival strategy. The Global Encounters between China and Europe: Trade Networks, Consumption and Cultural Exchanges Project (GECEM), based in Seville and Shanghai and with members from Europe, Asia, and the Americas, has developed an innovative methodology built on the process of clustering new empirical evidence on geostrategic locations to analyse complex socioeconomic systems. This approach elides the paradigm of much current scholarship, based on the imprecise notion of "national borders" as principal geographical and spatial units of comparison, which has produced inaccurate conclusions.[1] Specifically, then, we examine information on port cities (particularly Canton, Macau, Manila, Buenos Aires, Cartagena de Indias, Havana) as the point of departure for this discussion of the integration of Pacific and Atlantic markets. These port cities, most of them Spanish South American-controlled territories, were arguably key sites of the complex economic and cultural realities of the time. Focus on them has been largely absent from previous scholarship.

These important entrepôts in early modern China and in South American regions were part of a complex, mostly unregulated, and not institutionally or state controlled, economic structure. This polycentric trade node system integrated Asian, American, and European markets. To understand the setting requires us to adopt a *longue durée* chronology, from 1680 when the Kangxi emperor established the custom offices in Chinese ports and French merchants took over the Mediterranean market, to 1840 and the outbreak of the Opium Wars in China.[2] The larger context included major historical events, such as the War of the Spanish Succession that ended with the arrival of the French Bourbon dynasty to the throne. Importantly as well, Seville lost its monopoly in the Atlantic market to the detriment of the port of Cadiz. In China, the arrival of the Qianlong emperor to the Beijing court marked the beginning of a period of stiff economic interventionism, that established the Canton system [*yīkǒu tōngshāng* 一口通商], which mandated that Canton could be the only port in China allowed to trade with foreign powers.[3]

Foregrounding information and new case studies about trade networks and negotiations in and around port cities allows scholars to re-envision cross-chronological and historical categories in their comparison of China and Europe. The studies included in this volume, therefore, focus on the circulation of global goods, trade networks, and circuits of information (i.e. trade letters, postal offices) in southern China, the Americas, and Europe within this historical frame, noting its influence on economic growth and the great divergence. Specifically, we focus on the diverse trade routes connecting the Mediterranean, Atlantic, and South China markets that led to the introduction of Chinese goods (i.e. silk, porcelain, and tea) into European and American markets, and of European goods (i.e. clocks, wine, and glasses, among others) into southern China.

Historical data on China comes from the Arquivo Histórico de Macau and the First Historical Archives of China (FHAC) in Beijing. These contain trade records, merchant letters, and imperial decrees, among others, that serve to analyse trade networks and the circulation of global goods in Macau, and the provinces of Guangdong and Fujian, the main coastal regions for international commerce from 1680 to 1840. The most valuable archives for information on trade in Europe and the Americas are the Archivo General de Indias (AGI) in Seville (Spain), the Archivo General de la Nación in Argentina, and the Archivo Nacional de Cuba. These key trade area of the Americas connected with the western Mediterranean, forming the main economic axis, a vital artery, of eighteenth-century Europe and the Americas that integrated Eastern and Western markets.[4]

Our methodology is not based on a simple statistical recovery of data, as with conventional scholarship over the past few decades.[5] Focusing on information about and around port cities, rather than merely on locations identified by complicated and shifting national boundaries, has allowed us to tease out previously undiscovered elements that reveal the complexity of trade at the time. Clustering data on port cities led us to ask new questions about the forms and key players in this exchange, as well as uncover important networks. A bottom-up approach to these trade networks, the so-called *jeux d'échelles* (playing with scales), blends microhistory and global history. This perspective supports the belief that global history is insufficient for explanations of events and systems beyond that of national narratives.[6] The *jeux d'échelles* approach allowed us to create clusters of new historical data and cross-references Chinese and Western sources. These clusters then served as core empirical evidence for new case studies. Social network analysis supported our examination the circulation of global goods and the formation of long-distance trade partnerships. Notable among these were the networks of Chinese merchants in the Philippines (the *sangleyes*), the merchants of Canton and Macau, Jesuits in Macau acting as traders, and South American trade groups in Argentina, Peru, or Brazil.[7]

To implement solid comparisons through a bottom-up approach, it became necessary to cluster data of diverse origins related to trader names, typologies of goods, circuits in which these goods were commercialised, and spaces and chronologies in which trade networks operated and were transformed over time. This methodology constitutes a breakthrough in the field of global (economic) history through its interdisciplinary framework (incorporating disciplines such as economics, sociology, sinology, digital humanities, international relations, among others) and possibilities to apply Big Data to historical analysis and comparative case studies between China, Europe, and the Americas for the early modern period.[8] Sources can be cross-referenced, leading to an empirically validated new global history that blends the local and the macro perspectives. This opens up the possibility of re-evaluating the great divergence debate from a local framework.

Fundamentally, this method illuminates the operations of complex systems such as the polycentric trade networks and informal institutions in South China, Atlantic regions, and western Mediterranean markets during the time of the so-called early globalisation, from 1400 to 1800.[9] Specifically, clustering data through comparisons on trade, consumption, and fiscal registers within a local scale serves to integrate and understand the diverse sources from Chinese, European, and American historical archives. As the contributors to this collection of essays argue, we have to re-examine the conventional analytical frame that contends that market integration and early globalisation began in 1820.[10] Accordingly, their research interrogates debatable and unreliable quantitative methods using macro-economic indicators and statistics such as GDP (gross domestic product) per capita.[11] The new comparisons and cross-referencing of data allowed us to re-order and analyse the historical Big Data contained in the Chinese and European archives.[12] The correction of biased historical data was enacted through proper quantification and analysis that cross-referenced historical sources of a different nature and origin.[13]

This process led to our research hypothesis: that the economic growth in South China and Europe from the late seventeenth to eighteenth century derived fundamentally from the circulation of global goods and trade networks.[14] We argue that information on the circulation and consumption of goods serves as a more valid economic indicator than the GDP traditionally used by economic historians. Each of the essays in this collection focuses on a specific case study from the clusters built out of the empirical evidence gathered from the archives. Together, they validate the usefulness of this methodology for a more accurate analysis of the self-regulating institutions, social networks, circulation of global goods and information, and smuggling activities that characterised the nonlinear markets of early modern China, Europe, and the Americas. These case studies show the advantages of introducing new comparisons and data analysis, as it foregrounds a comparison of trade and consumption information with eighteenth-century fiscal sources, trade records, and probate-inventories.

The essay by Manuel Perez-Garcia and Jin Lei analyses overseas trade and consumption in south China through the implementation of the Canton system [*yīkǒu tōngshāng* 一口通商]. This approach re-evaluates the so-called "High Qing" age [*shèng qīng* 盛清] in a period of high interventionism such as in Qianlong's reign, where the court of Beijing aimed to control trade and smuggling activities.[15] Clustering data from trade records, imperial decrees, and regulations from FHAC, and the Local Gazetteers of China [*zhōngguó dìfāng zhì* 中国地方志], revealed that the "non-state" agents and merchants who bypassed official supervision actually undermined state authority.[16] Their focus on the demand side serves as a valuable indicator of economic growth, wealth distribution, and prosperity as it identifies new patterns of consumption, mainly in the middle-low social groups.[17]

Nadia Fernández-de-Pinedo scrutinizes the demand side and trade balances by presenting a case study of consumers' purchases and choices in eighteenth-century Cuba by focusing on imported goods from Havana's balance of trade. Looking at trade statistics, her paper explores the dependence of the Caribbean markets in general, and Cuba in particular, on external markets and the introduction of Chinese goods.[18] She examines the relation supply side and trade dependency between the metropole and peripheral areas of the Spanish empire. The geostrategic position of Cuba in the Caribbean made the colony a vital entrepôt of the Spanish empire for the redistribution of goods, formation of trade networks and informal institutions, and a source for fiscal revenues. As a trade and economic linchpin that integrated Atlantic and Pacific markets, Cuba made the Caribbean a crossroad of political disputes and international relation conflicts. The Spanish empire's weakness at the dawn of the nineteenth century made it difficult for them to control trade routes and markets, leading to rampant contraband and smuggling activities. Earlier Spanish decrees on free trade in the second half of the eighteenth century had similarly been unable to regulate such activities. This intertwining of trade routes and circulation of Asian, American, and European goods made the Caribbean, and Cuba in particular, a hybrid culture and society shaped by the flow of global goods and emulation of diverse patterns of consumption.

Similarly, using trade and ship records from the AGI and Archivo General de la Nación de Argentina, Antonio Ibarra analyses the implications of the Royal Company of the Philippines in the global trade by examining the slave operations between Africa and Spanish America in the Río de la Plata slave market in the late eighteenth century.[19] Ibarra's contribution outlines the incapacity of the Spanish empire to control and regulate trade in the colonies, as well as its inability to eradicate contraband and competition with foreign powers. Enslaved persons and a wide range of goods were a valuable medium of exchange in Lima and other Peruvian regions, which Spain tried to control through the Royal Company. However, contraband persisted and competition increased in the exchange of European goods, enslaved Africans, American silver, and East Asian (Chinese) goods. Ultimately, the inefficiency of the Spanish administration in its South American colonies, stiff competition from Britain, and the growing economic power of local elites and merchants fragmented the Spanish empire, making it difficult to control the global trafficking of slaves and goods.

Omar Svriz-Wucherer's focus on Qing China and imperial Spain from the late seventeenth to eighteenth century presents a case study of Jesuit networks as the main economic agents in the circulation of musk, among other goods, in the Pacific markets through the trade axis Canton-Macau-Manila. [20] His case study is based on the examination of trade nodes of Qing China such as Macau-Canton, the Jesuits' role as "non-state" agents who participated in this global trade, and their ties with the Manila galleons.[21] Arguably, data on these "non-state" agents and complex trade networks in Manila provide key information for a micro-scale analysis of this unregulated trade system and the concomitant weakened capacity of the state for control in the peripheries of the Spanish empire. This demonstrates how "non-state" agents, such as the Jesuits, built a powerful polycentric network in peripheries of the Spanish and Qing empires, controlling trade and allowing the global circulation of Chinese goods such as silk, porcelain, and tea, but also musk and amber, among others.[22]

Since global (economic) history scholarship has largely ignored the development of trade in the Americas, comparisons between South China markets and South America stand out as unique case studies.[23] Rocío Moreno Cabanillas's essay on the postal office in Cartagena de Indias as a node connecting Pacific, Caribbean, and Atlantic markets, reveals how institutions and groups of power efficiently managed information and regulated markets. She discusses a series of postal modifications introduced by the Bourbons upon to ascension to the Spanish throne, which sought to strengthen the connection between the metropole and the periphery, which was usually disrupted by distance and the lack of reliable, regular communication. However, powerful local elites hindered the centralised Cartagena postal system because they controlled and monopolised the circulation of information. Negotiation between central powers in the court of Madrid and local elites in the colonies was crucial. The exercise of power, control of information, and its dynamic circulation through mediators and agents such as informants, bureaucrats, and correspondents became a means of domination, sovereignty, and leverage in negotiations between central and local elites.

The GECEM Project deconstructs national narratives on the New Silk Road political strategy by People's Republic of China scholarship, therefore challenging conventional processes of archival interpretation by its method, clustering data as a comparative strategy to deal accurately with large amounts of information and scattered sources. Through such comparisons, along with mining new data and examining new case studies, the circulation of global goods and trade networks can be better located within the foundations of a new global history.

Identifying and deciding before-hand what type of data we need from the sources and for what purpose has allowed us to unveil non-official trade routes, merchant networks and agents, as well as typologies of goods (mainly of Chinese origin) that fostered the accumulation of American silver in hands of south China local elites. This demonstrates the inefficiency of the Qing and Spanish empires' strategies of trade regulation. The use of new Chinese and western sources and the implementation of new methodologies, as it as has been done in this collection of essays, challenges historians as many global history studies have been negligent in comparing Chinese sources with Western (European and American) ones. In the historical sources all data cannot be used to solve historians' questions; we have identified what data are relevant and how these data can be analysed. Such interdisciplinary approach goes in line with the directions of the new global history based on the use of novel sources, methodologies and case studies.

This approach has allowed us to implement an accurate analysis of Qing China's provincial areas, focusing on markets cities such as Nanjing, Suzhou, Hangzhou, Huizhou, and Guangzhou, to investigate the connection between local markets in south China and those in the peripheries of the Spanish empire in the Philippines and the Americas. The case of silk as a key Chinese good demanded in western markets provides an important example. Our study invalidates the traditional idea that more silk was produced locally in western markets, the so-called import substitutions, than the original silk from local

Chinese markets. From small villages and towns spread around south China provinces, different types of silk of low quality were produced for export to Western markets. In the Manila galleons and ship cargoes, whose historical records can be found in abundance at the AGI, low-quality silks such as *sayas, lanquines, elefantes, cedazos* made of silk, *sayasa, pequines, segríes, tafetanes, gorgoranes, damascos, wampu* silk (commercialised from Whampoa in Canton) among other types, were distributed to American and European localities such Lima-Callao, Veracruz, Havana, Buenos Aires, Cadiz, Seville, Cartagena, and Marseille, and were identified in trade records and probate-inventories as originally from China.

These data are integrated and compared in order to identify how these Chinese original silks were traded by American and European networks and introduced in end-markets such as Cadiz, Seville, Lisbon, or Marseille, where local demand for these products rose during the eighteenth century. This examination goes on to prove the incapacity of Qing China and Bourbon Spain, respectively, to regulate trade through the Canton system and the Royal Company of Philippines. It also discovered royal decrees that forbade the introduction of Chinese goods to foster domestic production of silk, for the case of Spain, and control overseas trade and local elites for the case of China.

Notes

1. Vries, *State, economy and the Great Divergence*; Duchesne, *The Uniqueness of Western Civilization*; Goldstone, *Why Europe*.
2. Sawyer, "Time after Time"; Levi, "On Microhistory," 93–113; Burke, *New Perspectives on Historical Writing*.
3. Van Dyke, *Merchants of Canton*; González de Arce, *El Negocio Fiscal*.
4. Ibarra, "El Mundo en una Nuez," 485–518; Ibarra, Alcantara, and Jumar, eds. *Actores Sociales*.
5. Lee, and Campbell, "China Multi-generational Panel"; Broadberry, Campbell, Klein, Overton, and van Leeuwen, *British Economic Growth*; van Zanden, Baten, Foldvari, and van Leeuwen, "Changing Shape," 279–297.
6. Brewer, "Microhistory," 87–109; Berg, "Sea Otters and Iron," 50–82.
7. de Vries, "Playing with Scales," 23–36; Revel, *Jeux d'échelles*; Anderson, "Cacique Democracy," 3–31.
8. Mostern, "Historical Gazetteers," 39–46; Manning, *Big Data in History*.
9. Flynn, "Big History," 80–106; Frank, *Re-Orient*.
10. O'Brien, "Was the First Industrial Revolution," 1–53; Pomeranz, *The Great Divergence*; Ma and Rubin, "Paradox of Power," 277–294; Cox, "Political Institutions," 724–755; Broadberry, Guan, and Li, "China, Europe, and the Great Divergence," 955–1000; O'Rourke and Williamson, "Once More," 109–117.
11. Allen, Bassino, Ma, et al. "Wages, prices, and Living Standards," 8–38. Maddison, *Chinese Economic Performance*.
    Bolt, Inklaar, de Jong, et al. "Rebasing "Maddison," 1–70.
12. Kantabutra, Owens, Ames, et al. "Using the Newly Created ILE," 39–58. Codd, "A Relational Model," 377–387. Kantabutra, Owens, and Crespo Solana, "Intentionally-linked Entities," 57–78. Crespo Solana, *Spatio-Temporal Narratives*.
13. O'Brien and Deng, "Quantifying the Quantifiable," 215–223.
14. Perez-Garcia, "Consumption of Chinese Goods," 15–36.
15. Perez-Garcia, *Vicarious Consumers*. Perez-Garcia, *Global History with Chinese Characteristics*.
16. Mostern, *Dividing the Realm*; Wong, *China Transformed*.
17. McKendrick, "Consumer Revolution," 9–33; McKendrick, Brewer, and Plumb, eds. *The Birth of a Consumer Society*.

18. Fernández-de-Pinedo, "Tax Collection in Spain," 101–110.
    Andrés Ucendo and Limberger, *Taxation and Debt*.
19. Moutoukias, "Instituciones, Comercio y Globalización," 141–182.
20. Yun-Casalilla, *Iberian World Empires*. Svriz-Wucherer, *Resistencia y Negociación*.
21. Chaunu, *Les Philippines*.
22. de Sousa, *The Portuguese Slave Trade*. Díaz de Seabra, *A Misericórdia de Macau*. De Sousa, "The Jewish Presence in China and Japan."
23. Belich, Darwin, Frenz, et al. *The Prospect of Global History*.
    Riello and Tirthankar, *Global Economic History*; Riello, "Introduction," 1–15.

Acknowledgements

This research is a result of academic activities organised by the GECEM Project such as the permanent lecture series in Global and East Asian History held annually at SJTU and UPO, as well as the international workshop "New Global Histories of Asia, Europe and the Americas in the Age of Nation-States" organised by the GECEM Project, SJTU, and the University of Leeds in Shanghai, China, September 2019. It is also part of the result of GECEM Project workshops and international conferences organised by 6th Eurasia Trajeco-GECEM international conference held in Seville, October 2018. In addition, this research has been partially presented in world academic forums in the panels organised by the GECEM Project such as "Beyond the Silk Road: The Silver Route and the Manila-Acapulco Galleons for the Global Circulation of Goods and People in China, Europe and the Americas" at the XXXVI International Congress of the Latin American Studies Association (LASA)/Latin American Studies in a Globalised World held in Barcelona (Spain), May 2018; and the panel "Social Network Analysis and Databases for New Comparative Global History Studies in China, Europe, and the Americas" at the XVIII World Economic History Conference/Waves of Globalisation held in Boston (US), July–August 2018. We thank the Delegation of the European Union to China and EURAXESS China for their constant and generous support expanding the GECEM Project academic results and actions. We also express our gratitude to academic institutions and partners of the GECEM and GHN such as Shanghai Jiao Tong University, Pablo de Olavide University, Tokyo University of Foreign Studies, the Historiographical Institute at the University of Tokyo, University of Leeds, the Beijing Center for Chinese Studies at the University of International Business and Economics (Beijing, China), the Macau Ricci Institute at the University of Saint Joseph (Macau), the Faculty of Asian and Middle Eastern Studies at the University of Cambridge, the Center of Global History and European Studies at Pittsburgh University, the Center of Global History at the University of Warwick, the Universidad Nacional Autonoma de Mexico (UNAM), and the L'Ecole des Hautes Etudes en Sciences Sociales. A very important acknowledgement goes to professors Dorothea Fischer-Hornung (Heidelberg Center for American Studies, Heidelberg University, Germany) and Manuel Barcia (chair in Global History at the University of Leeds, UK) for supporting and believing in this project. We are grateful to comments and suggestions made by professors Patrick O'Brien, Lucio de Sousa, Joe P. McDermott, Mihoko Oka, Pengsheng Chiu, Hamashita Takeshi, Bartolome Yun-Casalilla, Debin Ma, Liu Shiyung (Michael), Robert Antony, and Xiangyu (Ellen) Cai. We thank reviewers and editors for their comments to improve the result of our research. Any errors are our own.

Disclosure statement

No potential conflict of interest was reported by the author(s).

Funding

This research has been sponsored and financially supported by the GECEM Project (Global Encounters between China and Europe: Trade Networks, Consumption and Cultural Exchanges in Macau and Marseille, 1680–1840), a project hosted by the Pablo de Olavide University (UPO) of Seville (Spain).

The GECEM Project is funded by the European Research Council (ERC) Starting-Grant, ref. 679371, under the European Union's Horizon 2020 Research and Innovation Programme (www.gecem.eu). The principal investigator (PI) is Professor Manuel Perez-Garcia (Distinguished Researcher at UPO). In the spring term of 2022, this book was completed as part of the outcomes of GECEM Project and GECEM Database (www.gecemdatabase.eu). In addition, this research is part of the academic activities of the Global History Network in China (GHN) (www.globalhistorynetwork.com) in which Manuel Perez-Garcia is the founder and director and the contributors of this book are the members of the GHN.

The elaboration of this chapter has been possible with the research funding granted by the Fundación Séneca (Autonomous Community of Murcia, "Jiménez de la Espada" Programme) for Visiting Professorship at Universities and Public Research Organizations (OPIS) of the Region of Murcia (Spain). Manuel Perez-Garcia is PI of the Project "Periferias globales y la 'Baker's Happiness-Theory' en China y Europa: Big Data Mining y Desarrollo Económico" carried out at the Faculty of Economics and Business, Department of Applied Economics at the University of Murcia (Spain) as Visiting Professor.

I would also like to thank the PAIDI group HUM-1000 Historia de la Globalización: Violencia, Negociación e Interculturalidad at Area de Historia Moderna (UPO), of which I am a member. The PI of the PAIDI group is Igor Pérez Tostado, funded by Junta de Andalucía (Seville, Spain).

ORCID

Manuel Perez-Garcia http://orcid.org/0000-0003-4520-3760

References

Allen, Robert C., Jean-Pascal Bassino, Debin Ma, Christine Moll-Murata, and Jan Luiten Van Zanden. "Wages, Prices, and Living Standards in China, 1738–1925: In Comparison with Europe, Japan, and India." *The Economic History Review* 64, no. 1 (2011): 8–38.

Anderson, Benedict. "Cacique Democracy and the Philippines: Origins and Dreams." *New Left Review* 169, (May/June 1988): 3–31.

Andrés Ucendo, José Ignacio, and Michael Limberger, eds. *Taxation and Debt in the Early Modern City*. London: Pickering & Chatto, 2012.

Belich, James, John Darwin, Margret Frenz, and Chris Wickham, eds. *The Prospect of Global History*. Oxford: Oxford University Press, 2016.

Berg, Maxine. "Sea Otters and Iron: A Global Microhistory of Value and Exchange at Nootka Sound, 1774–1792." *Past & Present* 242, no. Suppl 14 (2019): 50–82.

Bolt, Jutta, Robert Inklaar, Herman de Jong, and Jan Luiten van Zanden. "Rebasing 'Maddison': New Income Comparisons and the Shape of Long-Run Economic Development." *GGDC Research Memorandum GD-174* (2018): 1–70.

Brewer, John. "Microhistory and the Histories of Everyday Life." *Cultural and Social History* 7, no. 1 (2010): 87–109.

Broadberry, Stephen, Bruce M. S. Campbell, Alexander Klein, Mark Overton, and Bas van Leeuwen. *British Economic Growth, 1270–1870*. Cambridge: Cambridge University Press, 2015.

Broadberry, Stephen, Hanhui Guan, and David Daokui Li. "China, Europe, and the Great Divergence: A Study in Historical National Accounting, 980–1850." *The Journal of Economic History* 78, no. 4 (2018): 955–1000.

Burke, Peter, ed. *New Perspectives on Historical Writing*. Philadelphia: Pennsylvania State University Press, 1992.

Chaunu, Pierre. *Les Philippines et le Pacifique des Ibériques*. 2 vols. Paris: Sevpen, 1960.

Codd, Edgar F. "A Relational Model of Data for Large Shared Data Banks." *Communications of the ACM* 26, no. 1 (1983): 64–69.

Cox, Gary W. "Political Institutions, Economic Liberty, and the Great Divergence." *The Journal of Economic History* 77, no. 3 (2017): 724–755.

Crespo Solana, Ana, ed. *Spatio-Temporal Narratives. Historical GIS and Global Trading Networks (1500–1800)*. Cambridge: Cambridge Publishing Scholars, 2014.

de Sousa, Lucio. "The Jewish Presence in China and Japan in the Early Modern Period: A Social Representation." In *Global History and New Polycentric Approaches*, edited by Manuel Pérez-García and Lucio De Sousa, 183–218. Palgrave Studies in Comparative Global History, Singapore: Palgrave Macmillan, 2018.

de Sousa, Lucio. *The Portuguese Slave Trade in Early Modern Japan Merchants, Jesuits and Japanese, Chinese, and Korean Slaves*. Leiden: Brill, 2018.

Díaz de Seabra, Leonor. *A Misericórdia de Macau (Séculos XVI a XIX): Irmandade, Poder e Caridade na Idade do Comercio*. Macau: Universidade de Macau, 2011.

Duchesne, Ricardo. *The Uniqueness of Western Civilization*. Leiden: Brill Academic Publishers, 2011.

Fernández-de-Pinedo, Nadia. "Tax Collection in Spain in the 18th Century: The Case of the 'Décima'." In *Taxation and Debt in the Early Modern City*, edited by José Ignacio Andrés Ucendo and Michael Limberger, 101–110. London: Pickering & Chatto, 2012.

Flynn, Dennis O. "Big History, Geological Accumulations, Physical Economics, and Wealth." *Asian Review of World Histories* 7, nos. 1–2 (2019): 80–106.

Frank, André Gunder. *Re-Orient. Global Economy in the Asian Age*. Berkeley: University of California Press, 1998.

Goldstone, Jack. *Why Europe: The Rise of the West in World History, 1500–1850*. New York: McGraw Hill Higher Education, 2008.

González de Arce, José Damián. *El Negocio Fiscal en la Sevilla del Siglo XV. El Almojarifazgo Mayor y las Compañías de Arrendatarios*. Sevilla: Diputación de Sevilla, 2017.

Ibarra, Antonio. "El Mundo en una Nuez: de Calcuta y Cantón a Buenos Aires en una Época de Guerra. La Introducción de Efectos Asiáticos en los Mercados Suramericanos, 1805-1807." *Journal of Iberian and Latin American Economic History* 38, no. 3 (2020): 485–518.

Ibarra, Antonio, Álvaro Alcantara, and Fernando Jumar, eds. *Actores Sociales, Redes de Negocios y Corporaciones en Hispanoamérica, Siglos XVII-XIX*. México: UNAM/CONACyT/Bonilla Artigas, 2018.

Kantabutra, Vitit, J. B. Owens, Daniel P. Ames, Charles N. Burns, and Barbara Stephenson. "Using the Newly-Created ILE DBMS to Better Represent Temporal and Historical GIS Data: Using ILE DBMS for Historical and Temporal GIS." *Transactions in GIS* 14 (June 2010): 39–58.

Kantabutra, Vitit, J. B. Owens, and Ana Crespo Solana. "Intentionally-Linked Entities: A Better Database System for Representing Social Dynamic Networks, Narrative Geographic Information and General Abstractions of Reality." In *Spatio-Temporal Narratives. Historical GIS and Global Trading Networks (1500–1800)*, edited by Ana Crespo Solana, 57–78. Cambridge: Cambridge Publishing Scholars, 2014.

Lee, James Z., and Cameron D. Campbell. 2010. "China Multi-Generational Panel Dataset, Liaoning (CMGPD-LN), 1749–1909: Version 10." ICPSR - Interuniversity Consortium for Political and Social Research.

Levi, Giovanni. "On Microhistory." In *New Perspectives on Historical Writing*, edited by Peter Burke, 93–113. Cambridge: Cambridge University Press, 1991.

Ma, Debin, and Jared Rubin. "The Paradox of Power: Principal-Agent Problems and Administrative Capacity in Imperial China (and Other Absolutist Regimes)." *Journal of Comparative Economics* 47, no. 2 (June 2019): 277–294.

Maddison, Angus. *Chinese Economic Performance in the Long Run*. Paris: OECD, 1998.

Manning, Patrick. *Big Data in History*. London: Palgrave Macmillan, 2013.

McKendrick, Neil. "The Consumer Revolution of Eighteenth-Century England." In *The Birth of a Consumer Society. The Commercialization of Eighteenth-Century England*, edited by John Brewer, Neil McKendrick, and J. H. Plumb, 9–33. Bloomington: Indiana University Press, 1982.

McKendrick, Neil, John Brewer, and J. H. Plumb, eds. 1982. *The Birth of a Consumer Society: The Commercialization of Eighteenth-Century England*. Bloomington: Indiana University Press.

Mostern, Ruth. "Historical Gazetteers: An Experiential Perspective, with Examples from Chinese History." *Historical Methods: A Journal of Quantitative and Interdisciplinary History* 41, no. 1 (2008): 39–46.

Mostern, Ruth. *Dividing the Realm in Order to Govern: The Spatial Organization of the Song State (960–1276 CE)*. Harvard University Asia Center. Cambridge, MA: Harvard University Press, 2011.

Moutoukias, Zacarias. "Instituciones, Comercio y Globalización Arcaica: una Reflexión Sobre las Redes Sociales Como Objeto y Como Herramienta a Partir del Caso Rioplatense (Siglo XVIII)." In *Actores Sociales, Redes de Negocios y Corporaciones en Hispanoamérica, Siglos XVII-XIX*, edited by Antonio Ibarra, Álvaro Alcántara, and Fernando Jumar, 141–182. México: UNAM/CONACyT/Bonilla Artigas, 2018.

O'Brien, Patrick. "Was the First Industrial Revolution a Conjuncture in the History of the World Economy?" *LSE Economic History Working Papers* 259 (2017): 1–53. https://www.lse.ac.uk/Economic-History/Assets/Documents/WorkingPapers/Economic-History/2017/WP259.pdf.

O'Brien, Patrick, and Kent Deng. "Quantifying the Quantifiable: A Reply to Jan-Luiten van Zanden and Debin Ma." *World Economics* 18, no. 3 (2017): 215–223.

O'Rourke, Kevin H., and Jeffrey G. Williamson. "Once More: When Did Globalisation Begin?" *European Review of Economic History* 8, no. 1 (2004): 109–117.

Pérez-García, Manuel. *Vicarious Consumers: Trans-National Meetings Between the West and East in the Mediterranean World (1730–1808)*. London: Routledge, 2013.

Pérez-García, Manuel. "Consumption of Chinese Goods in Southwestern Europe: A Multi-Relational Database and the Vicarious Consumption Theory as Alternative Model to the Industrious Revolution (Eighteenth Century)." *Historical Methods: A Journal of Quantitative and Interdisciplinary History* 52, no. 1 (2019): 15–36.

Pérez-García, Manuel. *Global History with Chinese Characteristics. Autocratic States Along the Silk Road in the Decline of the Spanish and Qing Empires 1680–1796*. Palgrave Studies in Comparative Global History, Singapore: Palgrave Macmillan, 2021.

Perez-Garcia, Manuel, and Lucio de Sousa. *Global History and New Polycentric Approaches*. Palgrave Studies in Comparative Global History, Singapore: Palgrave Macmillan, 2018.

Pomeranz, Kenneth. *The Great Divergence: China, Europe, and the Making of the Modern World Economy*. Princeton, NJ: Princeton University Press, 2000.

Reinert, Sophus A., and Robert Fredona. "Merchants and the Origins of Capitalism." Harvard Business School Working Paper 18–021. *Harvard Business School,* 2017: 1–38 https://econpapers.repec.org/paper/hbswpaper/18-021.htm.

Revel, Jacques. *Jeux D'échelles. La Micro-Analyse à L'expérience*. Paris: Gallimard et Le Seuil, coll. Hautes Études, 1996.

Riello, Giorgio, and Tirthankar Roy, eds. *Global Economic History*. London: Bloomsbury, 2018.

Riello, Giorgio, and Tirthankar Roy. "Introduction: Global Economic History, 1500–2000." In *Global Economic History*, edited by Giorgio Riello, and Tirthankar Roy, 1–15. London: Bloomsbury, 2018.

Stephen, W. Sawyer. "Time after Time: Narratives of the Longue Durée in the Anthropocene." *Transatlantica: Revue d'Études Américaines* 1 (2015). http://journals.openedition.org/transatlantica/7344.

Svriz-Wucherer, Omar. *Resistencia y Negociación. Milicias Guaraníes, Jesuitas y Cambios Socioeconómicos en la Frontera del Imperio Global Hispánico: ss. XVII-XVIII*. Rosario: Prohistoria Ediciones, 2019.

Trivellato, Francesca. *The Familiarity of Strangers: The Sephardic Diaspora, Livorno, and Cross-Cultural Trade in the Early Modern Period*. New Haven, CT: Yale University Press, 2009.

Van Doosselaere, Quentin. *Commercial Agreements and Social Dynamics in Medieval Genoa*. New York: Cambridge University Press, 2009.

Van Dyke, Paul A. *Merchants of Canton and Macao: Politics and Strategies in Eighteenth-Century Chinese Trade*. Hong Kong: Hong Kong University Press, 2011.

de Vries, Jan. "Playing with Scales: The Global and the Micro, the Macro and the Nano." *Past & Present* 242, no. Suppl 14 (2019): 23–36.

Vries, Peer. *State, Economy and the Great Divergence: Great Britain and China, 1680s–1850s*. London: Bloomsbury Publishing, 2015.

Wong, Roy Bin. *China Transformed: Historical Change and the Limits of European Experience*. Ithaca, NY: Cornell University Press, 1997.

Yun-Casalilla, Bartolomé. *Iberian World Empires and the Globalization of Europe 1415–1668*. Palgrave Studies in Comparative Global History, Singapore: Palgrave Macmillan, 2019.

Zanden, Jan Luiten van, Joerg Baten, Peter Foldvari, and Bas van Leeuwen. "The Changing Shape of Global Inequality 1820–2000. Exploring a New Dataset." *Review of Income and Wealth* 60, no. 2 (2014): 279–297.

Interventionism and control on foreign trade in Qing China: the Canton System

Manuel Perez-Garcia and Lei Jin

ABSTRACT

Due to China's ongoing economic rise, recent studies in global (economic) history have moved away from the traditional Eurocentric view to a Sinocentric one. There is extensive literature focused on the introduction of Chinese goods to Europe, as well as on China's economic development within the framework of the great divergence debate. However, less research has centred on the introduction of European goods to Chinese markets, specifically the markets in Guangdong or other coastal regions (such as Fujian, Zhejiang and Jiangsu), before the First Opium War. This paper aims to side-step the Sinocentric approach, eschewing the current wave of national history in China, by analysing the international trade in Qing China from the Kangxi era until the Qianlong period. It provides new empirical evidence from the First Historical Archives of China (FHAC) by examining the impact on global trade of China's imperial edicts and interventionist policies.

Introduction

This essay focuses on the introduction of European goods to Macao-Canton for the period when the Canton System was established by the Qianlong emperor in 1757 in order to control western trade. The period from 1680 to 1757, which covers the reigns of Kangxi, Yongzheng and the first decades of Qianlong, was more open to international trade, putting an end to the tribute system.[1] In both periods, the opening to overseas trade by the Kangxi emperor and the control of foreign trade by Qianlong influenced merchants' drive to introduce European goods to China and to exchange American silver for Chinese goods destined for the West.[2]

This study will show how the Qing bureaucracy was inefficient in assessing and collecting customs revenues at multiple ports along the coast, a context that might explain the decision to centralise flows of exports as well as imports at Canton. However, even there the bureaucracy was incompetent, corrupt and beyond central control. Despite their anti-western rhetoric, these three emperors increased the volume of western imports into

China. As we will demonstrate, the proclaimed antipathy of these emperors to exchanges and interactions with foreigners was based far more on a policy to control local Chinese merchants than a desire for autarky, which was not sustainable once population growth accelerated and Chinese agriculture could not produce enough food.

The impact of the circulation of Asian and Chinese goods in European societies has been widely studied, whereas there has been less research dealing with the introduction of American and European goods in late Ming and Qing China.[3] In fact, there is a scholarly lacuna on the introduction of western commodities in Qing China, which arrived mainly through the Macao-Canton economic axis, and the distribution of such goods to coastal and inner areas of China.[4] The impact of global trade in regional economies of south China (mainly in the local communities of Fujian and Guangdong) and how this compared with the performance of the whole Chinese economy, along with state intervention during the Qianlong reign when the Canton System was implemented, requires further study.

To fully understand the China trade, merchants' motivations, alliances and the intervention of the state in local and international trade, it is important to analyse how the import and export trade in China was shaped by the Qing state, mainly because of the Canton System. Research that seeks out the connections, differences and similarities between European and Chinese markets could help to increase our knowledge of the China trade. Therefore, our methodology involves the use and analysis of primary sources from the First Historical Archives of China (FHAC) [*zhōngguó dìyī lìshǐ dàngànguǎn*中国第一历史档案馆], located at the Forbidden City in Beijing.

The making of the Canton System: why had Canton become the main entrepôt for foreign trade by 1840?

Chinese historians traditionally analyse the economic performance of the Middle Kingdom during the Qing period on a local level without seeking connections and/or comparisons with the rest of the world. Such scholarship conventionally takes the Opium War and/or the "Daoguang economic depression" as the catalysts for the secular economic recession in nineteenth-century China, which put an end to the prosperous economy of the eighteenth-century Qing period.[5] This transition established 1840 as the boundary between early modern and modern Chinese history.[6] The logic for this is based on the thinking of Marxist historians, who were more concerned with the country's socio-political conditions. They argued that "the outbreak of the Opium War and the signing of the Sino-British Nanjing Treaty transformed China from a feudal society to a semi-feudal and semi-colonial society."[7] In addition, the whole of the eighteenth century saw territorial expansion, frontier incorporation, economic growth, population boom, urbanisation, cultural sophistication, and intensified global trade. Commonly called the Prosperous Age of the Kangxi, Yongzheng and Qianlong, this period suddenly ended during the transition into the nineteenth century.[8]

The performance of the Chinese economy and its recession, in the transition from the eighteenth to the nineteenth century, has generally been regarded in Chinese scholarship as very susceptible to external events. They consider the interference of foreign powers, such as Great Britain, France, the Netherlands, among others, in the Chinese economy led to China's disastrous socio-economic development in mid- and late Qing China. This has also fed the sentiment of victimisation in the Chinese public psyche, which has also reached academic circles, where Westerners are seen as invaders and, therefore, as responsible for China's failure to modernise. Li Bozhong argues that "a profound inferiority complex [*qíngjié* 情结] developed in the Chinese public psyche from China's perceived backwardness relative to the West since the mid-nineteenth century."[9] This outlook became more ingrained when, more recently, scholars attempted to compare the modernisation of Qing China, under the Tongzhi reforms, with the Japan economic take-off during the Meiji Restoration.[10]

However, if we adopt a global history perspective, this description of China's economic development looks a bit narrow, as any analysis of China's economic performance should also consider the domestic economic swings and the effects of the highly interventionist Qing state, mainly during the Qianlong reign. China had been deeply involved in the world trade system since Spain reached the New World in the late fifteenth century and the Portuguese started to settle down in Macao during the sixteenth century. In this period, long before the Opium War, trade between China, south-eastern Asian regions and Europe flourished. Traditional Chinese scholarship describes the Canton System, established during the Qianlong period, as "a sign of closing the country."[11] This measure grew from the Qianlong emperor's order to the governor of Guangdong and Guangxi provinces [Liang Guang Zong Du两广总督] in 1757 to "tell foreign businessmen that in the future they only could trade in Guangdong (Canton) and are not allowed to go to Ningbo. If there is any violation, they must escort the ship to return to Guangdong."[12]

Even before Qianlong's edict, Canton was clearly the main import and export channel of Sino-European trade and occupied a strategic trade location in the Pearl River Delta, connecting with Macao where ships and their cargoes were supervised by the customs superintendents, popularly known as "hoppos."[13] The connection with Macao, where western communities (traders, diplomats, missionaries) were hosted, and southeast Asia (mainly Manila as Spanish entrepôt in the Pacific that connected the south China trade with the Americas), as well as interior provinces of China, made Canton the axis of global trade networks between European empires and the Middle Kingdom.[14] One of the most obvious reasons for restricting trade to the port at Canton was to make commerce more controllable and taxable by Qing officials as large ships could not easily navigate the narrow Canton river, which passed the Whampoa and Hanan islands, whereas in Macao ships could sail offshore and thus evade the control of the Qing authorities.[15] The Yongzheng emperor had attempted to control commerce in Canton by expelling the missionaries in 1724. However, it was the Qianlong emperor who finally established the Canton System to reinforce the overseas trade policy, eliminating the possibility for foreign ships to trade at ports outside Canton until 1840.

The evolution of the Canton System was the result of a number of factors such as the inability of the Qing state to collect customs revenues at multiple ports, the advantages of Canton's location, regional economic development, strong interventionism of the state (echoing the European mercantilist bans) and the Qing regime's political and economic strategy. Another variable to consider for imposing one single port for foreign commerce [*yīkǒu tōngshāng* 一口通商] was the desire to control trade through official institutions and channels in order to eradicate contraband and smuggling activities, which were deeply rooted in the economic activities of business elites and families controlling commerce in south China.[16] Illegal or private imports and trade were rife among the officials and Qing bureaucrats who dealt with commerce, as well as among the Huizhou traders that controlled the salt monopoly trade.[17] Therefore, while the Canton System might have seemed to be directed mainly at foreign traders, the goal of controlling the local traders in China was also a vital concern. Directly interfering with the local traders was a risky move, however, especially given that the Qing dynasty was Manchu (a foreign dynasty) and not Han (the local dynasty). Stirring up resentment among the Han could have serious consequences for the survival of the dynasty, as the threat of uprisings and rebellions was very real. Enforcement by the emperor of new polices and bans on local traders may well have provoked a violent revolt. The aim was thus to restrict all foreign trade to one location that could be controlled from Beijing.

Since 1683, the Kangxi emperor had allowed maritime trade through the Jiang/Jiangsu Customs [*jiāng hǎiguān* 江海关], Zhe/Zhejiang/Ningbo Customs [*zhè hǎiguān* 浙海关], Min/Fujian Customs [*mǐn hǎiguān* 闽海关] and Yue/Canton Customs [*yuè hǎiguān*粤海关].[18] As one of the four major customs offices opened during the early and mid-Qing dynasty, the Canton Customs had the same function as the other three, but its special feature was its connection with Macao, a strategic port for foreign trade. Thus, Canton had always been a major port for foreign merchant ships (Figure 1). The other three customs offices were also responsible for foreign trade, but they functioned with a more unstructured system. This demonstrates the incapacity of the central state, the Qing court of Beijing, to regulate foreign trade through provincial institutions.

A memorandum written by Hao Yulin 郝玉麟, governor of Fujian and Zhejiang provinces, to the Qianlong emperor in 1737 reveals the structural inadequacy of the Min Customs in dealing with foreign merchants, particularly through the negligence and lack of procedures of this official institution and its bureaucrats for tax collection.[19] A case in point: in August of 1737, a Luzon ship carrying goods such as logwood arrived to trade in the port of Xiamen, Fujian province. To determine the tax due, local officials

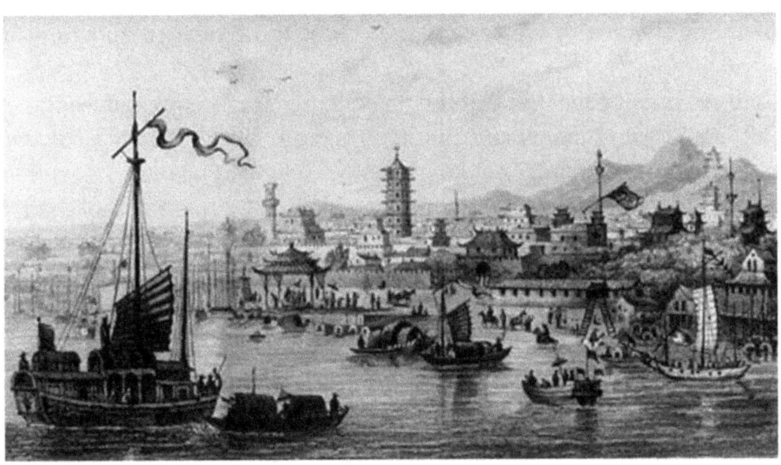

Figure 1. Canton in 1670. This small print of the city of Canton shows sailing boats and junks trading in the port between the river and walled city. Illustrations were taken from early historical sources. Courtesy of *Zhongguo tongshangtu*: 17–19 *shiji xifang renyan zhong de zhongguo*, Beijing: Beijing *Ligongdaxue chunbanshe*, 2008.

searched previous records. They found that an English ship had come to the Min Customs two years earlier, in 1735, and that the Canton Customs determined that, apart from the regular tax assigned, they should also charge 0.049 per cent per *tael* of silver of the money which foreign merchants bring to purchase goods in China, a tax called *fen tou yin*分头银. Further, 0.1 per cent per *tael* of silver, called *jiao song yin* 缴送银, should be charged along with 90 other forms of fee collection.

The Min Customs did not complete the tax report for the British ship, which sailed back to Canton. Later, in 1737, they mistakenly charged the same tax bracket as the British and European ships for the cargo that had arrived from Luzon (in the Philippines). Zhun Tai 准泰, the former governor of Guangdong and Guangxi Provinces, reported to his officials that foreign merchant ships, from neighbouring areas of south-eastern Asia, such as Luzon, should not be charged the 0.049 per cent *fen tou yin* tax. Such charges were only to be applied to ships coming from distant countries, namely ships from Europe.

Following previous research on tax collection in coastal areas of China (mainly Fujian and Guangdong provinces) we should ask whether this apparent negligence of local officials was a result of their incapacity to perform their task or because of personal alliances with local elites and foreign traders seeking to divert taxes.[20] Ultimately, the Min Customs refunded the *fen tou yin* to the Luzon ship. Similarly, in 1755 when a British ship tried to trade at the Zhe Customs, the incumbent governor of Fujian and Zhejiang provinces, Ka'erjishan 喀尔吉善, quickly reported this to the Qianlong emperor and a new tax rule was drafted.[21] Importantly, these imperial reports reflect the official situation, as they were the only channel of communication between the emperor and local officials. To obtain an accurate view of the economic system and the incapacity of the state to negotiate with local elites and manage an efficient system of tax collection, we should, as Peter Perdue suggests, observe the biographies and personal trajectories of local officials. Often these bureaucrats were involved in trade or smuggling activities, and their families made a fortune and passed the Chinese Imperial examination system as a result of their social promotion in business.[22] This local approach allows us to better understand the functioning of long-distance business partnerships between local traders of south China with westerners, as well as the global conjunctures in Chinese localities and villages.[23]

Therefore, we might conclude that the management of foreign trade was ineffectual in the coastal regions of China, where the Jiang/Jiangsu Customs [*jiāng hǎiguān* 江海关], Zhe/Zhejiang/Ningbo Customs [*zhè hǎiguān* 浙海关], Min/Fujian Customs [*mǐn hǎiguān* 闽海关] and Yue/Canton Customs [*yuè hǎiguān* 粤海关] were established by Kangxi and continued by Yongzheng, until Qianlong restricted foreign trade to Canton. Indeed, the tax system was quite disorganised, and bureaucratic negligence was common among officials, who received low salaries from the central government in Beijing.[24] An unofficial system therefore emerged, based on alliances and business partnerships between local and foreign traders who diverted funds and tax revenues to increase their personal fortunes.

It was extremely difficult for the government to control this unofficial system based on trade circuits, which then continued over generations, contributing to the status and honour of local families who displayed their economic and political power in their genealogies. This demonstrated the inability of the Qing state to create a solid system of tax collection and management of trade revenues and economic resources.[25] Canton was in a strategic geographical location for the export and import of goods, and became a major hub of foreign trade, but it was mainly seen as a way of controlling local trade and supervising the elites who made their fortunes and built their family reputations by dealing with foreign partners and accumulating highly valued American silver coins.[26]

The Qianlong emperor's 1757 decree formally blocked the entry of foreign merchant ships to the three ports in Jiangsu, Zhejiang and Fujian. But why did the emperor choose Canton? Although Guangdong had a long history of foreign trade because of its geographical location, foreign trade was concentrated in Canton mainly because the Qing state was incapable of collecting taxes in several ports, leading to the centralisation of imports and exports in one single port. When the decree was issued, foreigners were forbidden from living in Guangdong, and therefore most of them resided in Macao, making Macao the cornerstone of trade and socio-cultural exchanges between China and the West. This policy sought to control the foreign community in China, as well as to attempt to regulate the unofficial trade activities between south China gentry and foreign merchants. Central government officials, local Canton officials, as well as the Canton Customs formed a large group of interest, developing an informal network, and, ultimately, an unofficial long-lasting partnership against the state. This was rooted in the early Qing dynasty and even long before during the Ming dynasty.[27] The Canton Customs collected a large amount of tax revenue every year for the national treasury. Personnel working at the Canton Customs, such as directors, secretaries and clerks, were recruited directly by the court.[28]

From the Kangxi to Daoguang eras, which saw five emperors within nearly 200 years, the official appointments to the Canton Customs fostered an ecosystem based on unofficial trade reaching the entire Guangdong region. During Kangxi's reign, the position of customs superintendents (the hoppos) was created to eradicate corruption and to prevent the misappropriation of customs revenues. The positions of Canton Customs supervisor [*Yue Hai Guan Jian Du* 粤海关监督] and governor of the Guangdong and Guangxi provinces were known to be very lucrative and only favourites of the Emperor were appointed to these roles. Local officials and even the emperor himself pocketed part of the revenue collected. Any staff member or soldier who worked in the Canton Customs could find opportunities for corruption in foreign trade, thus boosting their personal careers and family fortunes.

According to a memorandum addressed to the Qianlong emperor in 1742, written by a Canton Customs supervisor called Yilaqi 伊拉齐, there were 47 customs ports under the jurisdiction of Canton Customs, from Guangzhou to Macao, Qiongzhou, Chaozhou, Huizhou, Gaozhou, etc. The Canton Customs supervisor – along with at least 30 subordinates – spent two months inspecting the area of his jurisdiction but he was not able to visit all the ports in person.[29] Because of the extensive bureaucracy of the Canton Customs and its reliance on clerks and sub-officials whose salaries – and skill level – were low, the whole network of Canton Customs officials was closely associated with merchants. The family wealth accumulated by those officials mainly came from trade activities.

These trade networks can be divided into three groups: Hong merchants, foreign merchants and local merchants.[30] All were under the direct supervision of customs superintendents [*hùbù* 户部 or hoppos] and the governor of Guangxi and Guangdong province [*dūfŭ* 督抚].[31] The Hong merchants were the only officially designated brokers who could trade with foreign agents. The activities of foreign merchants in Guangzhou, whether selling their own goods or buying Chinese goods, or even paying taxes, were all subject to the supervision of the Hong merchants. These Hong merchants were extremely wealthy, had close ties to the local officials and were also responsible for arranging overseas capital (through long-distance partnerships) and the import of goods. Foreign merchants introduced overseas goods to China through the Macao-Canton economic axis, which became the main channel for the trade and exchange of goods between China and southeast Asia, Japan, and the Americas, and ultimately with Europe.[32] Local Chinese merchants were the main social agents involved in purchasing goods from overseas and inland Chinese regions, serving as mediators and brokers in Guangdong and introducing foreign goods to other regions of China. This system developed a dense micro-network in south China in which a large group of people was involved in these trade activities; it was difficult for the state to control and regulate this network, which naturally established its own rules and *modus operandi*.[33] The destruction of this unofficial system would have damaged the employment and livelihoods of not only the staff of the Canton Customs, but also the wider group of related practitioners – merchants, craftsmen, deliverymen, brokers, among others.

In 1755, the English merchant James Flint 洪仁辉 arrived at the Zhejiang Customs, and while the Zhejiang officials sought to open trade with foreigners, opening trade was against the interests of the Canton group. The Qianlong emperor subsequently issued a decree stipulating that all foreign merchant ships must return to Canton for trade. Qianlong's reign was defined by rigidity and strong command; indeed, he was a paradigm of the "mercantilist ruler." He wanted to rule with a firm hand, to be seen as a good lord to his subjects, as well to protect the Han culture from western invaders, despite the fact that, as a Manchu ruler, he was himself a foreigner. Scholars consider the well-known *Flint Affair* [*Hong Renhui Shijian* 洪任辉事件] as the event that made Qianlong implement the Canton System to prevent foreign interference in China affairs.[34] However, as mentioned earlier, we believe that the real reason behind the Canton System was control of local Chinese trade – despite making foreigners the main official target of the policy.

Furthermore, the Qing government primarily sought to assure the stability and unity of the Middle Kingdom in the hands of a foreign (Manchu) dynasty. It therefore rejected many opportunities for foreign trade and avoided any possibly destabilising course of action. As a Manchu government, the Qing emperors and the nobles of the Eight Flags came from the Changbai Mountain area, located north of Shanhaiguan. They had conquered the Central Plains of China and become rulers over the (majority) Han population.[35] In order to establish their authority and rule, they had violently suppressed any resistance of the Han people and even exiled some Han overseas. The Qing government always enforced a very strict control over the people to prevent the emergence of rebellious forces.[36] Foreigners were confined to Macao and were expressly forbidden from living in Guangzhou. Migration to other regions and provinces, even in the case of Chinese businessmen bringing their foreign wives back home, was strictly regulated and required official authorisation – without which heavy penalties could be incurred.[37] The Qing rulers were also concerned that exiled Han people would collude with foreigners in order to undermine the regime.

In 1755, the British merchant ship that sailed to Ningbo, Zhejiang Province, gave the Qianlong emperor cause for concern. It was reported by local officials that there were forty boatmen on the merchant ship without pigtails.[38] Although it was confirmed afterwards that part of the ship crew were foreigners living in Macao, Qianlong might have had reason for concern. The pigtail was the traditional hairstyle of the Manchu people – most of the head was shaved, leaving a small disc of hair that was tied back. However, cutting hair was forbidden in traditional Han culture. In order to establish the rule and authority of the Manchu government, the Shunzhi emperor issued the "hair shaving order" in 1644: "Keep your hair or keep your head" [*liú tóu bù liú fà, liú fà bù liú tóu* 留头不留发, 留发不留头].[39]

Over the following centuries, small-scale uprisings and riots would occasionally occur and the Qing rulers paid special attention to this "hair identity" as a symbol of allegiance to the empire: it thus became a way of controlling the population.[40] James Flint tried to appeal to the emperor after failing in his enterprise to trade in Ningbo, although he was very likely to have had ulterior motives. He was finally convicted for his attempt to denounce corruption and was banned from Macao for three years.[41] Emperor Qianlong believed that, compared to Ningbo, Canton was far more accessible for long-distance driving into the hinterland of the Central Plains, and therefore better placed to control overseas trade and potential Han incursions.[42] For all these reasons, the Canton System continued until the Opium War erupted and the British forced the Qing government to open other ports up to trade.

The self-sufficiency of the Qing economy and the exchange of goods at the Canton Customs

The rigid implementation of rules to control trade in south China, first through the customs system established by the Kangxi emperor and continued by his son (Yongzheng), and then through Qianlong's imperial edict limiting foreign trade to Canton, had a negative impact on the state's capacity to eradicate corruption and smuggling. Despite the increasing number of officials, growing institutions, and expanding list of imperial decrees issued to supervise local and overseas trade, the state remained powerless to control the complex trade networks that had evolved. Indeed, corruption was widespread in the very institutions designed to stamp out illicit activities.[43] Despite this, Canton continued to be a major hub for foreign trade – in fact, it was the world trade centre in south China during the seventeenth and eighteenth centuries – with exports of Chinese goods to Asian and western regions and imports from the West. The accumulation of American silver in the hands of Chinese private merchants was the main driver, on a micro-scale, that boosted exchanges, allowing local traders to increase their family fortune and reputation, while escaping the control of the Qing state.

The memoranda that the local officials provided to the emperors, allow us to trace this world trade network, which connected the Guangdong region to Europe through western merchant ships (either arriving from Europe through the Indian maritime routes, or from the Americas, through the Pacific routes), bringing silver to China and exporting Chinese goods (mainly tea, silk and porcelain). These western traders also introduced goods to China's coastal regions, from which they were distributed to inland China. The goods listed in the memoranda included woollen fabrics, spices, black lead and medicinal herbs, among other commodities. During the Yongzheng and Qianlong periods, the Canton Customs would collect several hundred thousand silver *taels* in tax revenues annually. There was a commodity commercial tax [*shāngshuì* 商税] for outbound ships and a foreign tax [*yángshuì* 洋税] for overseas merchants. A report sent to the emperor in 1743 suggests that "from each foreign merchant ship we can collect an income of about ten thousand *taels* of silver, every year there will be around 10–15 foreign ships to come."[44] In the tenth year of the Yongzheng emperor's reign (1732), the Canton Customs collected 309,107 *taels* of silver. During Qianlong's fortieth year of reign (1775) the tariffs brought in 541,863 *taels* and by his 60th year (1795) income had almost doubled to 1,171,911 *taels* (Figure 2).[45]

Even though in 1757, when the Canton System was established, there was a sudden dip in the annual tax revenues of the Canton Customs, the general trend of the annual tax revenues was positive over the second half of the eighteenth century (see Figure 2). This holds particularly true during the late 1770s, when the "formal mercantile cartel of the Co-hong [*gōng háng* 公行]" was consolidated, allowing foreign supercargoes to permanently reside in Canton – which, in turn, increased the circulation of foreign goods, and therefore, the annual revenue of the Canton Customs.[46] The Canton Customs tax revenue reports were submitted on an annual basis following the seasonality of sea-faring and agricultural activities. The tax bureau could thus start the account in any month of the year and finish it twelve months later. For this reason, the annual data series was calculated with a double entry (biannual basis), but in fact the accounting system was made annually. These are the so-called "year-node divisions," which referred to the solar periods in which the Chinese lunar calendar is divided and, as the Canton Customs reports show, the month of calculation for every year was arranged randomly depending on the seasonality, forecast or predicted weather conditions for agricultural activities and maritime trade.[47]

The expansion of the global maritime trade and the growing demand for Chinese goods by western traders in the second half of the eighteenth century led to a substantial rise in China's foreign trade tariffs.[48] In contrast to Europe's enthusiasm for commodity trade, the Qing rulers, mainly the Qianlong emperor, reinforced mercantilist policies to increase tariffs

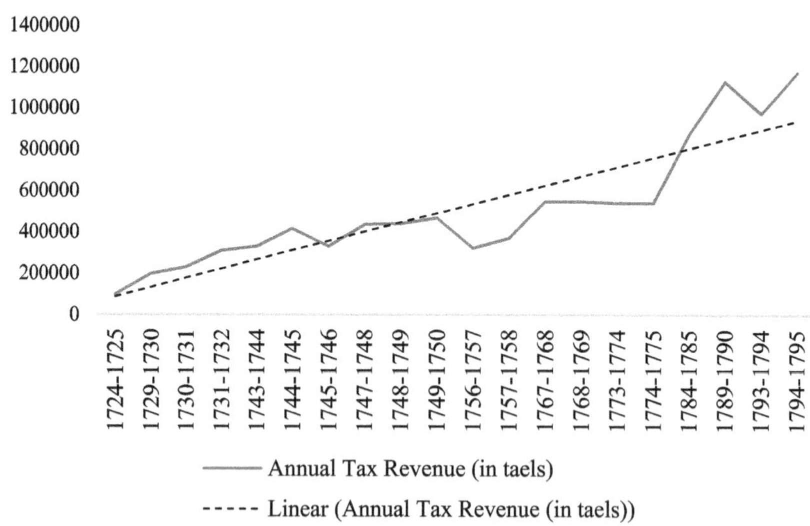

Figure 2. Annual Tax Revenue of Canton Customs from the Kangxi to Qianlong Era. The data below was collected from Zhu Pi Zou Zhe of FHAC.

on imports. Qianlong might be considered the paradigm in China of the European mercantilist ruler, even a physiocrat, because of his view of China as a self-sufficient economy and determination to foster national production. "There is nothing we don't have that we need from you," he told Lord Macartney, who had been sent on mission to China in 1792 by the British King George III.[49] The imperial policies were designed to increase capital accumulation and paid close attention to commodity exports.

During the seventeenth and eighteenth centuries, a relevant share of the state's fiscal revenues came from land tax, as well as custom duties. Most regions of China relied on agricultural production, as capitalism only really developed in the more trade-oriented south-eastern coastal regions. Overall, the economy of Qing China was primarily based on the ecological environment, which was essentially independent of – or geographically isolated from – the international trade system.[50] In the 1760s, Qianlong even restricted the export of silk products, as he believed that overseas traders were exchanging Chinese silks and introducing foreign goods that could affect the demand for local products in domestic markets.[51] This resembles the mercantilist policies issued during the same period by European monarchs.[52] Moreover, the Qing government retained stricter control over food exports. The local Hong merchants and brokers were forbidden from selling large amounts of grain to foreign traders; ship cargoes were inspected to prevent exports of large quantities of foodstuffs. Local officials were required to report regularly to the emperor that they had stringently enforced the ban on excess grain outflow.[53] These measures were surely motivated by the food shortages experienced during the Qing dynasty.

But was it really true that China needed nothing from other countries, as the Qianlong emperor had boasted to Lord Macartney? They certainly needed grain and American crops. During the Qianlong period, there was a significant population boom which set China on the path of the so-called "high level equilibrium trap."[54] The population of China had reached 400 million by the end of eighteenth century.[55] Food shortages were particularly acute in the south-eastern coastal areas, which were densely populated but had relatively little cultivated land.[56] Farm economies were heavily contingent on climate conditions. Unfavourable weather conditions (such as drought) could have disastrous impacts on the food supply of large populations.[57] The introduction and consumption of American crops (potato, maize, sweet potato), which had been introduced in China by the end of Ming dynasty through the Manila galleons, helped to mitigate such food shortages.[58]

Food shortages were also a common catalyst for public uprisings, which the Qing government was desperate to prevent. It had therefore considered various ways of averting a famine. To counteract the high-level equilibrium trap, wine prohibition became one of the measures taken to manage food shortages. Since traditional Chinese wine was made from grain, limiting cereal production for consumption as a food, not as a beverage, was a strategy to combat the scarcity of food. Farmland was therefore to be reserved for the cultivation of grain, not for viticulture.[59] Moreover, the Qing government also encouraged local merchants to trade with neighbouring Asian regions to open up a supply of food and grains to Chinese regions.

A memorandum written in 1761 by Li Shiyao 李侍尧, the governor of the Guangdong and Guangxi province, notes:

> referring to the previous case of the Fujian province, merchants who brought more than 2,000 *dan* of grain from foreign countries could get an official rank promotion. The previous year a businessman named Wang Chao, from Chenghai county, used his own capital, took the vessel of Chen Fushun, and bought 2,646 *dan* of rice from Annam. In accordance with the regulations of 2000 *dan* or more, he should be awarded with promotion to the ninth rank.[60]

The ninth rank was the lowest official rank, and while businessmen who obtained official titles acquired no special political power, they invariably experienced a rise in their wealth and reputation as a result of these promotions. This privilege was passed on to later generations. To some extent, it also helped them to forge closer relationships with local officials, shaping a dense network of socio-economic and political power. As well as buying grain, since 1745 the Qing government had also attempted to buy copper from foreign businessmen to mint coins.[61] In 1749, foreign coins were popular in the market of the Zhejiang area. Zhejiang's governor, Fang Chengguan 方承观, thought these illegal coins should be destroyed and called on other provinces to do the same. However, Qianlong believed that these coins should be recycled and re-minted.[62]

To sum up, we observe that the Qing rulers, specifically the Qianlong emperor, were keen to import food and raw materials from foreign countries, but also European luxury goods such as wool, glass, handicrafts, mirrors, clocks (indeed, the emperor was an avid collector of clocks, which he housed in one of the pavilions at the Imperial Court), as well as foreign wines and liquors. These western goods were extremely sought after, especially by the imperial family, who were the main consumers of western luxury goods, but also among the elites and Guangdong officials. This exemplifies a trickle-down effect that begins at the highest echelons of Chinese society, with the emperor himself and his court, moving down to the gentry who wanted to emulate this consumption of new and exotic luxury goods.[63] Each year, the emperor ordered Guangdong officials to purchase supplies for the Imperial Household Department, including local products from the Guangdong region and goods from foreign traders. The Kangxi emperor also asked Guangdong officials to collect information from foreigners, and even kept a group of foreigners, the Jesuits, close to the Beijing court to serve the imperial family. His son, Yongzheng, despite having officially banned Christianity from China, housed a group of Christian missionaries at the Beijing court to work as scientists, artists and technicians.[64]

The large number of historical documents that we have analysed at the FHAC, mainly relating to the policies and memoranda of different emperors, can also shed some light on the personalities and preferences of some of the emperors. For example, the Kangxi emperor (1661–1722) had a particular fascination with western culture, science and technology, as well as foreign goods. He was especially interested in astronomy and geography. He appointed the Jesuit Ferdinand Verbiest [Nan Huairen 南怀仁] as the Astronomical Bureau Officer [*qīn tiān jiān jiān zhēng* 钦天监监正] to revise the astronomical calendar and in 1674 he ordered the Great Universal Geographic Map [*kūn yú quán tú* 坤舆全图].[65] When foreign scientists came to Guangdong, Kangxi was eager to meet them, telling local government officials: "Let them come to Beijing as soon as possible."[66] The Guangdong administrators were well aware of the Kangxi's interest in western culture and in foreigners and local officials often informed him about the arrival of westerners.

The Yongzheng emperor (who reigned from 1723–1735), Kangxi's son, was more uncompromising than his father. His attitude to finances was more cautious and he was particularly concerned with the reform of China's economy. Unlike his father, he had little interest in science and western luxury goods. He issued a ban on the purchase of ivory products due to its excessive cost.[67] He believed that the Canton Customs should work to increase tariffs, and not to foster overseas trade and introduce foreign goods. Indeed, the customs duties of the Canton Customs were an important source of income for the national treasury. Nevertheless, Yongzheng relied on Guangdong officials to purchase overseas textiles and medicinal herbs for the Imperial Household Department.[68]

Yongzheng's son, Qianlong (1736–1795), inherited great wealth from his father. The Qianlong emperor – like his grandfather – had a taste for exotic goods, and he often asked local officials to procure luxury items and high-quality crafts. According to a 1758 report sent to Qianlong from the governor of Guangdong and Guangxi Provinces, Li Shiyao, the emperor had asked Guangdong officials to "purchase for me clocks, western gold beads, exotic furnishings, gold threads, new style objects, etc. Don't worry about the cost."[69] Later, Li Shiyao purchased several gold-plated decorations, striking clocks, musical clocks, wall clocks, snuff bottles, glassware, drawing tools, and pearls for him and noted that "we have spent 6,612.6 *taels* of silver on these, minus the 15,558.4 spent last year for the Duanyang festival, of the 30,000 *taels* now there are 7,828.9 *taels* left. Should I give the money to the Ministry of Revenue or the Canton Customs vault?" The emperor replied: "Keep it and use it in the future."[70]

The next year Li Shiyao submitted another report explaining that he had spent 2,503.1 *taels* looking for agate stone goods.[71] This demonstrates the conspicuous consumption fostered by the Qianlong emperor, for whom high costs was not an issue. He took great delight in acquiring rare and luxury foreign goods, despite banning their consumption for the rest of the country. Today, the museum of the Forbidden City exhibits the exquisite collection of western clocks and exotic ornaments of the Qianlong era. These items are unrivalled in quality and taste. Indeed, Qianlong was rather unenthusiastic about the *beaux gestes* offered by the British envoy, Lord Macartney, as his own collections surpassed the items the diplomat had brought to impress the emperor.

The gentry and wealthy businessmen of the Qing dynasty also showed great interest in luxury western goods. In 1743, as part of an investigation into corruption, the home of the Canton Customs supervisor, Zheng Wusai, was searched and a great quantity of antiques, jewellery, as well as western ornaments, glassware and exotic silk fabrics were discovered. The officials responsible for handling the case proposed that these recovered illicit goods should be sent to the Imperial Household Department and presented to the imperial family.[72] We might infer that the emperor's enjoyment of foreign luxury goods influenced other officials, but the thriving business of southern local officials, from Guangdong, also shaped Qianlong's desire for luxury goods. There was thus a "trickle up" effect as well as a "trickle down" effect for the consumption of luxury goods, which triggered corruption and the misappropriation of tax funds. In addition, we can assume that not only officials and gentry, but also the social elite were motivated by this drive for the conspicuous consumption of western luxury goods, which had become symbols of wealth and social distinction.

Conclusion

The body of data used for this research includes previously overlooked historical sources from the imperial archives, the FHAC, which houses very rich sources such as edicts, memoranda, imperial correspondence, among others, that constituted the main channel of communication between the emperors and local officials in China's provinces. This study uses these primary sources to analyse the rationale and foundations behind the Canton System, concentrating in particular on: 1. how Canton's unique geographical location contributed to shape a tight micro-network of local traders; 2. how it became a stable and unofficial economic system that fostered long-term foreign trade and capital accumulation, allowing local family groups and traders to thrive; 3. more specifically, how the Qing government used the Canton System not only to control foreign traders and foreigners in one single location, but also to watch the mainly Chinese local merchants whose wealth was rising through –often illicit – alliances and partnerships with foreign merchants. Behind this official system, with Canton the only port in China for foreign trade, the emperors and the entire Guangdong network of traders, local officials and gentry, as well as the Qing ruler, sought to create an economically stable regime, despite it being – in practice – run by unofficial activities, smuggling, and the widespread diverting of tax funds to line private pockets. China had a history of feudal rule for thousands of years and had formed a relatively independent and complete economic system with its own particularities. In other words, it was an economic micro-cosmos of merchants and officials who created a "system within the system."

In the early and mid-Qing period, before the outbreak of the Opium War and mainly during the Qianlong emperor's reign, the Qing government did not officially foster a large-scale foreign trade. In reality, Qianlong eagerly encouraged local officials to purchase foreign goods and luxury items which provided a high profit for the state revenues. A self-sufficient economy was the main, official, objective of the Qing rulers. Their conservative and rigid attitude aimed to maintain a stable political regime and avoid social turmoil or uprisings. They feared the possible impact of a reform of the fiscal system, which would have involved dismissing local gentry and traders from the unofficial but highly lucrative system. For this reason, as discussed, the Qianlong emperor restricted the exports of silk and grain and encouraged the imports of goods.

Qianlong was also aware of the need to import some food and natural resources to avoid environmental degradation and to preserve local economic structures. European empires had a marked maritime-trade orientation. In contrast, due to the immense geography of the Middle Kingdom (mainly through the Manchu expansion to western regions), the Qing emperors sought to unify this vast mass of land, an inland empire that was expanding westward, and to provide enough domestic supplies to the population. However, the Qing emperors still revealed their personal choices and preferences through their consumption of luxury western goods, a practice which spread throughout the upper ranks of the social hierarchy, and "trickled down" to the lower social classes, including local officials and businessmen.

By analysing the imperial edicts housed at the FHAC, we gain a better understanding of the functioning of foreign trade in China during the seventeenth and eighteenth centuries, mainly in the southern provinces such as Guangdong, from a micro-perspective, as well as why the economic Macao-Canton axis came to be a global trade hub. However, these sources have some obvious limitations, as they do not provide data on the economic circulation of these goods from suppliers to consumers. Although the total tariff incomes of the Canton System can be calculated annually, we are not able to determine the precise typologies of goods that were being taxed. Second, although we have an approximation of the kinds of luxury goods that were purchased by (or for) the emperors, it is difficult to estimate the real expenditure. However, the trend toward conspicuous consumption and the large expenditure on luxury goods can be deduced as a symbol of power. Also, a lack of data prevents us from quantifying consumption across different social groups. A further limitation is the fact that the FHAC has lost and misclassified some historical sources of the Kangxi emperor's reign, as well as some relevant foreign-politics files. Ongoing research providing data on import and export tax bills, merchant contracts and letters, local gazetteers, as well as manuscripts by scholars will help close the above-mentioned gaps and unveil a clearer picture of trade in imperial China, the Canton System and Canton as a global entrepôt.

Notes

1. According to Fairbank, the tribute system consisted of a network of informal relations, "a set of ideas and practices developed and perpetuated by the rulers of China over many centuries," which fostered trade between China and foreign territories. See: Lee, *China's Hegemony*, 28–9; Fairbank, ed., *The Chinese World Order*; Fairbank, "Tributary Trade," 129–49.
2. Von Glahn, *Fountain of Fortune*; Irigoien, "The End of a Silver Era"; Flynn and Giraldez, *China and the Birth of Globalization*.
3. Braudel, *The Wheels of Commerce*; Batchelor, "On the Movement of Porcelains," 95–121; Perez-Garcia, *Vicarious Consumers*; Gerritsen and McDowall, "Material Culture and the Other," 87–113; McNeil and Riello, *Luxury: A Rich History;* McCants, "Global History and the History of Consumption," 241–254; De Vries, *The Industrious Revolution;* Perez-Garcia, "Challenging National Narratives," 53–80; Ho, "On the Introduction, Distribution of American Crops," 21–41; Elvin, *The Pattern of the Chinese Past.*
4. Only a few studies deal with the introduction of western goods to China and they tend to focus on the supply side, mainly analysing British and Dutch trade companies such as the E.I.C. or V.O.C. There is still a lack of research on how the Qing trade policies affected international trade and how the preferences of local traders and consumers changed. See: Dermigny, *La Chine et l'Occident;* Van Dyke, *Merchants of Canton and Macao;* Ptak, *China's Seaborne Trade;* Li, *Agricultural Development*; De Souza, *The Survival of the Empire*; Perez–Garcia, "Global Goods, Silver and Market," 449–484; Perez–Garcia, "Creating Global Demand," 405–419; Perez–Garcia, *Global History with Chinese Characteristics.*
5. Wu, *Zhongguo de Xiandaihua*; Li, "The Daoguang Depression," 173–178; Ni, "Steady Customs Duties," 78–91.
6. Liu, "Ya Pian Zhan Zheng Yu Zhong Guo Jin Dai Shi Yan Jiu," 146.
7. Ibid.
8. Cao, Li and Yang, "Mt. Tambora, Climatic Changes," 597.
9. Li, *Lilun, Fangfa, Fazhan Qusi.*
10. Westad, *Restless Empire.*
11. Hsü, *The Rise of Modern China*, 4.
12. Jun Ji Chu Shang Yu Dang (JJCSYD), First Historical Archives of China (FHAC), 10th November, Qianlong 21st Year (1756).
13. Cheong, *Hong Merchants of Canton;* De Souza, *The Survival of the Empire*, 1986.
14. Blussé, *Visible Cities.*
15. Menegon, "Interlopers," 33.
16. Liang, *Guangdong shi san hang kao;* De Sousa, *The Early European Presence.*
17. McDermott, *The Making of a New Rural Order;* Zhang, *Neo-Confucianism*; Wang, "The Regulation of Sailors," 221–228.
18. Nei Ge Qi Ju Zhu, FHAC, 11th July, Kangxi 23rd Year (1684). *Qing Gong Guang Zhou Shi San Hang Dang An Jing Xuan*. 39.
19. Zhu Pi Zou Zhe (ZPZZ), FHAC, 04-01-35-0310-011.

20. Perdue, "Interlopers," 63–83; Menegon, "Interlopers," 26–62.
21. FHAC, *Ming Qing Gong Cang Zhong Xi Shang Mao Dang An,* 989–1093.
22. Peter Purdue discusses the trajectories of key social actors from Canton during the 1850s, such as Wu Jianzhang, Liu Lichuan, Fujian, and Lin Xiyuan, whose social promotion through business activities and political intrigues (ties with secret societies) were rooted in illegal activities and diverting customs funds, sometimes undermining the Qing authorities and in some cases working with them. See Purdue "Interlopers," 64–7.
23. Fairbank, *Trade and Diplomacy;* Brook, *Vermeer's hat.*
24. Ho, *Studies on the Population.*
25. McDermott, *The Making of a New Rural Order.*
26. Von Glahn, *Fountain of Fortune*; Irigoien, "The end of a silver era."
27. McDermott, *The Making of a New Rural Order*; Perdue, *China Marches West*; Miller, *State versus Gentry.*
28. Zhao, *The Qing Opening.*
29. ZPZZ, FHAC, 04–01–35–0314–007.
30. Van Dyke, *Merchants of Canton and Macao,* 7–9.
31. Ibid.
32. Perez-Garcia, "Challenging National Narratives," 53–80; Wang, "The Regulation of Sailors," 221–228; Antony, "Piracy and the Shadow Economy," 99–114.
33. Gipouloux, *The Asian Mediterranean.*
34. Schottenhammer, "The East Asian Maritime World," 2.
35. Perdue, *China Marches West.*
36. Ho-fung, "Cultural Strategies," 75–115.
37. ZPZZ, FHAC, 04–01–01–0204–003.
38. Lu Fu Zou Zhe (LFZZ), FHAC, 03–0092–060.
39. Han, *Jiang Yin Cheng Shou Ji.* Zhao, "*Jiang shang gu zhong lu,*" 3–11.
40. Zhu, "Bian Zi De Lai Li," 33–4.
41. *Ming Qing Shi Qi Ao Men Wen Ti Dang An Wen Xian Hui Bian,* FHAC, 335, 360–364, 366.
42. *Ming Qing Gong Cang Zhong Xi Shang Mao Dang An,* FHAC, 1150–1153.
43. Acemoglu, Johnson and Robinson, "The Rise of Europe," 546–579; "Reversal of Fortune," 1231–1294.
44. ZPZZ, FHAC, 04–01–35–0316–04.
45. ZPZZ, FHAC, 04–01–35–0307–030, 04–01–35–0346–028, 04–01–35–0358–040.
46. Menegon, "Interlopers," 37.
47. Elvin, *The Retreat of the Elephants.* 350; Ni Yuping, *Steady Customs Duties*, 82.
48. Flynn and Giraldez, *China and the Birth.*
49. Gentzler, *Changing China*; Waley-Cohen, "China and Western Technology," 1525–1544; Berg, "Britain, Industry and Perceptions of China," 269–88.
50. Li, *Agricultural Development.*
51. JJCSYD, FHAC, 11th May, Qianlong 27th Year (1762). LFZZ, FHAC, 03–0629–041. ZPZZ, FHAC, 04–01–01–0255–025, 04–01–01–0249–012, 04–01–01–0249–010.
52. Perez-Garcia, *Vicarious Consumers.* O'Brien, "Fiscal, Financial and Monetary Foundations," 161–168.
53. ZPZZ, FHAC, 04–01–01–0088–002, 04–01–35–1234–02.
54. Elvin, *The Retreat of the Elephants.*
55. Zhou, "Qing Dai Ren Kou Yan Jiu," 1–28.
56. Pu, "Shi Lun Qing Dai Jiang Zhe Di Qu Liang Shi Duan Que Wen Ti," 25–29.
57. Lee and Campbell, *Fate and fortune;* Cao, *The Population History of China,* 2001.
58. Perez-Garcia, "Challenging national narratives," 53–80.
59. Fan, "Qing Dai Jin Jiu Jin Qu De Kao Cha," 92–97.
60. ZPZZ, FHAC, 04–01–01–0249–011.
61. Ibid, 04–01–35–1234–027, 04–01–35–1236–020.
62. Ibid, 04–01–35–1240–012.
63. McKendrick, "The consumer revolution," 9–33.

64. Menegon, "Interlopers," 37.
65. Yan and Yuming, "Xi Fang Chuan Jiao Shi Nan Huai Ren Zai Hua Huo Dong Shu Lue," 79–82.
66. FHAC, *Kang Xi Chao Han Wen Zhu Pi Zou Zhe Hui Bian*, 439.
67. FHAC, *Yong Zheng Chao Han Wen Yu Zhi Hui Bian*, 220.
68. ZPZZ, FHAC, 04–01–30–0144–003, 04–01–35–0307–018.
69. Ibid, 04–01–01–0227–019.
70. Ibid.
71. Ibid, 04–01–14–0029–001.
72. Ibid, 04–01–01–0089–040.

Acknowledgements

We are grateful to comments and suggestions made by professors Patrick O'Brien, Joe P. McDermott, Bartolome Yun-Casalilla, Giorgio Riello, Lucio de Sousa, Debin Ma, Liu Shiyung (Michael), Mihoko Oka, Pengsheng Chiu, Hamashita Takeshi, Robert Antony and Ellen Cai. We thank reviewers and editors of this journal for their comments to improve this paper. Any errors are our own.

Disclosure statement

No potential conflict of interest was reported by the author(s).

Funding

This research has been sponsored and financially supported by the GECEM Project (Global Encounters between China and Europe: Trade Networks, Consumption and Cultural Exchanges in Macau and Marseille, 1680–1840), a project hosted by the Pablo de Olavide University (UPO) of Seville (Spain). The GECEM Project is funded by the European Research Council (ERC) Starting-Grant, ref. 679371, under the European Union's Horizon 2020 Research and Innovation Programme (www.gecem.eu). The principal investigator (PI) is Professor Manuel Perez-Garcia (Distinguished Researcher at UPO). In the spring term of 2022, this book was completed as part of the outcomes of GECEM Project and GECEM Database (www.gecemdatabase.eu). In addition, this research is part of the academic activities of the Global History Network in China (GHN) (www.globalhistorynetwork.com) in which Manuel Perez-Garcia is the founder and director and the contributors of this book are the members of the GHN.

The elaboration of this chapter has been possible with the research funding granted by the Fundación Séneca (Autonomous Community of Murcia, "Jiménez de la Espada" Programme) for Visiting Professorship at Universities and Public Research Organizations (OPIS) of the Region of Murcia (Spain). Manuel Perez-Garcia is the PI of the Project "Periferias globales y la 'Baker's Happiness-Theory' en China y Europa: Big Data Mining y Desarrollo Económico" carried out at the Faculty of Economics and Business, Department of Applied Economics at the University of Murcia (Spain) as Visiting Professor.

I would also like to thank the PAIDI group HUM-1000 Historia de la Globalización: Violencia, Negociación e Interculturalidad at Area de Historia Moderna (UPO), of which I am a member. The PI of the PAIDI group is Igor Pérez Tostado, funded by Junta de Andalucía (Seville, Spain).

ORCID

Manuel Perez-Garcia http://orcid.org/0000-0003-4520-3760
Lei Jin http://orcid.org/0000-0002-2264-6246

References

Acemoglu, Daron, Simon Johnson, and James A. Robinson. "Reversal of Fortune: Geography and Institutions in the Making of the Modern World Income Distribution." *The Quarterly Journal of Economics* 117, no. 4 (2002): 1231–1294.

Acemoglu, Daron, Simon Johnson, and James Robinson. "The Rise of Europe: Atlantic Trade, Institutional Change, and Economic Growth." *American Economic Review* 95, no. 3 (June 2005): 546–579.

Antony, Robert J. "Piracy and the Shadow Economy in the South China Sea, 1780–1810." In *Elusive Pirates, Pervasive Smugglers: Violence and Clandestine Trade in the Greater China Seas*, edited by Robert Antony, 99–114. Hong Kong: Hong Kong University Press, 2010.

Batchelor, Robert. "On the Movement of Porcelains: Rethinking the Birth of the Consumer Society as the Interaction of Exchange Networks, China and Britain, 1600–1750." In *Consuming Cultures, Global Perspectives: Historical Trajectories, Transnational Exchanges*, edited by John Brewer, and Frank Trentmann, 95–121. Oxford: Bloomsbury, 2006.

Berg, Maxine. "Britain, Industry and Perceptions of China: Matthew Boulton, "Useful Knowledge" and the Macartney Embassy to China 1792–94." *Journal of Global History* 1, no. 2 (2006): 269–288.

Blussé, Leonard. *Visible Cities: Canton, Nagasaki, and Batavia and the Coming of the Americans*. Cambridge, MA: Harvard University Press, 2008.

Braudel, Fernand. *The Wheels of Commerce, Vol. 2, Civilization and Capitalism (15th–18th Century)*. Berkeley: University of California Press, 1992.

Brook, Timothy. *Vermeer's Hat: The Seventeenth Century and the Dawn of the Global World*. New York: Bloomsbury Press, 2008.

Cao, Shuji. *The Population History of China, Vol. 5, Period of Qing Dynasty*. Shanghai: Fudan University Press, 2001.

Cao, Shuji, Yushang Li, and Bin Yang. "Mt. Tambora, Climatic Changes, and China's Decline in the Nineteenth Century." *Journal of World History* 23, no. 3 (2012): 587–607.

Cheong, W. E. *The Hong Merchants of Canton: Chinese Merchants in Sino-Western Trade, 1684–1798*. London: Routledge, 1997.

Dermigny, Louis. *La Chine et l'Occident: le commerce à Canton au XVIIIe siècle, 1719–1833*. Paris: SEVPEN, 1964.

De Sousa, Lucio. *The Early European Presence in China, Japan, the Philippines and Southeast Asia (1555–1590) – The Life of Bartolomeu Landeiro*. Macau: Macau Foundation, 2010.

De Souza, George Brian. *The Survival of the Empire: Portuguese Trade and Society in China and the South China Sea 1630–1754*. Cambridge: Cambridge University Press, 1986.

De Vries, Jan. *The Industrious Revolution: Consumer Behavior and the Household Economy, 1650 to the Present*. Cambridge: Cambridge University Press, 2008.

Elvin, Mark. *The Pattern of the Chinese Past*. London: Eyre Methuen, 1973.

Elvin, Mark. *The Retreat of the Elephants. An Environmental History of China*. New Haven, CT: Yale University Press, 2004.

Fairbank, John King, ed. *The Chinese World Order Traditional China's Foreign Relations*, Cambridge, MA: Harvard University Press, 1968.

Fairbank, John King. *Trade and Diplomacy on the China Coast: The Opening of the Treaty Ports, 1842–1854*. Stanford, CA: Stanford University Press, 1969.

Fairbank, John King. "Tributary Trade and China's Relations with the West." *The Far Eastern Quarterly* 1, no. 2 (1942): 129–149.

Fan, Jinmin. "Qing Dai Jin Jiu Jin Qu De Kao Cha." *Research in Chinese Economic History* 3 (1992): 92–97.

First Historical Archives of China (FHAC), *Kang Xi Chao Han Wen Zhu Pi Zou Zhe Hui Bian*, Vol. 6. Beijing: Archives Publisher, 1985.

First Historical Archives of China (FHAC), *Ming Qing Gong Cang Zhong Xi Shang Mao Dang An*, Vol. 2. Beijing: China Archives Publisher, 2010.

First Historical Archives of China (FHAC), Yong Zheng Chao Han Wen Yu Zhi Hui Bian, Vol. 2. Beijing: Guangxi Normal University Publisher, 1999.

First Historical Archives of China (FHAC), and Guangzhou Liwan District People's Government, *Qing Gong Guang Zhou Shi San Hang Dang An Jing Xuan*. Guangzhou: Guangdong Economic Press, 2002.

First Historical Archives of China (FHAC), Macao Foundation and Jinan University Ancient Books Research Institute, *Ming Qing Shi Qi Ao Men Wen Ti Dang An Wen Xian Hui Bian*. Beijing: People's Publishing House, 1999.

Flynn, Dennis O., and Arturo Giraldez. *China and the Birth of Globalization in the Sixteenth Century*. London: Ashgate, 2010.

Gentzler, J. Mason. *Changing China: Readings in the History of China from the Opium War to the Present*. New York: Praeger, 1977.

Gerritsen, Anne, and Stephen McDowall. "Material Culture and the Other: European Encounters with Chinese Porcelain, ca. 1650–1800." *Journal of World History* 23, no. 1 (2012): 87–113.

Gipouloux, François. *The Asian Mediterranean: Port Cities and Trading Networks in China, Japan and Southeast Asia, 13th–21st Century*. Cheltenham: Edward Elgar, 2011.

Han, Tan. *Jiang Yin Cheng Shou Ji*. Taipei: Bank of Taiwan Economic Research Office, 1968.

Ho, Ping-Ti. "On the Introduction, Distribution of American Crops and Their Influence on Chinese Agricultural Production." *World Agriculture* 4 (1979): 21–41.

Ho, Ping-Ti. *Studies on the Population of China, 1368–1953*. Cambridge, MA: Harvard University Press, 1959.

Hsü, Immanuel C.Y. *The Rise of Modern China*. New York: Oxford University Press.

Hung, Ho-fung. "Cultural Strategies and the Political Economy of Protest in mid-Qing China, 1740–1839." *Social Science History* 33, no. 1 (2009): 75–115.

Irigoin, Alejandra. "The end of a Silver era: The Consequences of the Breakdown of the Spanish Peso Standard in China and the United States, 1780s–1850s." *Journal of World History* 20, no. 2 (2009): 207–244.

Jun Ji Chu Shang Yu Dang (JJCSYD), The First Historical Archives of China (FHAC), Beijing.

Lee, Ji-Young. *China's Hegemony: Four Hundred Years of East Asian Domination*. New York: Columbia University Press, 2017.

Lee, James Z., and Cameron D. Campbell. *Fate and Fortune in Rural China: Social Organization and Population Behavior in Liaoning 1774–1873*. Cambridge: Cambridge University Press, 1997.

Li, Bozhong. "The Daoguang Depression and the 1823 Flood Economic Decline, Climatic Cataclysm and the Nineteenth-Century Crisis in Songjiang." *Shehui Kexue [Journal of Social Sciences]*, no. 6 (2007): 173–178.

Li, Bozhong. *Agricultural Development in Jiangnan, 1620–1850*. London: Palgrave Macmillan, 1998.

Li, Bozhong. *Lilun, Fangfa, Fazhan Qusi [Theory, Methodology and Developmental Trends]*. Beijing: Tsinghua University Press, 2002.

Liang, Jiabin. *Guang Dong Shi San Hang Kao [Study on Guangdong Thirteen Hongs]*. Guangzhou: Guangdong Renmin, 1999.

Liu, Chao. "Ya Pian Zhan Zheng Yu Zhong Guo Jin Dai Shi Yan Jiu." *Academic Monthly* 39, no. 6 (June 2007): 146.

McCants, Anne. "Global History and the History of Consumption: Congruence and Divergence." In *Global History and New Polycentric Approaches: Europe, Asia and the Americas in a World Network System*, edited by Manuel Perez-Garcia and Lucio de Sousa, 241–254. Singapore: Palgrave-Macmillan, 2018.

McDermott, Joseph P. *The Making of a New Rural Order in South China, Vol. 1, Village, Land, and Lineage in Huizhou, 900–1600*. Cambridge: Cambridge University Press, 2017.

McKendrick, Neil. "The Consumer Revolution of Eighteenth-Century England." In *The Birth of a Consumer Society: The Commercialization of Eighteenth-Century England*, edited by Neil McKendrick, John Brewer, and J. H. Plumb, 9–33. Bloomington: Indiana University Press, 1982.

McNeil, Peter, and Giorgio Riello. *Luxury: A Rich History*. Oxford: Oxford University Press, 2016.

Menegon, Eugenio. "Interlopers at the Fringes of Empire: The Procurators of the Propaganda Fide Papal Congregation in Canton and Macao, 1700–1823." *Cross-Currents: East Asian History and Culture Review E-Journal* 25 (2017): 26–62.

Miller, Harry. *State Versus Gentry in Early Qing Dynasty China, 1644–1699*. New York: Palgrave Macmillan, 2013.

Ni, Yuping. "Steady Customs Duties in the 'Daoguang Depression'." *Essays in Economic and Business History* 31 (2013): 78–91.

Perdue, Peter. *China Marches West. The Qing Conquest of Central Eurasia*. Cambridge, MA: Harvard University Press, 2010.

Perdue, Peter. "Interlopers, Rogues, or Cosmopolitans? Wu Jianzhang and Early Modern Commercial Networks on the China Coast." *Cross–Currents: East Asian History and Culture Review, E–Journal* 25 (2017): 63–83.

Perez-Garcia, Manuel. "Challenging National Narratives: On the Origins of Sweet Potato in China as Global Commodity During the Early Modern Period." In *Global History and New Polycentric Approaches: Europe, Asia and the Americas in a World Network System*, edited by Manuel Perez-Garcia and Lucio de Sousa, Palgrave Studies in Comparative Global History, 53–80. Singapore: Palgrave-Macmillan, 2018.

Perez-Garcia, Manuel. "Creating Global Demand: Polycentric Approaches, Crossroads of Silk and Silver in China and Iberian Empires during the Early Modern Era." *Journal of Iberian and Latin American Economic History* 38, no. 3 (2020): 405–419.

Perez-Garcia, Manuel. "Global Goods, Silver and Market Integration: Consumption of Wine, Silk and Porcelain through the Grill Company via Macao-Canton and Marseille-Seville Trade Nodes, 18th Century." *Journal of Iberian and Latin American Economic History* 38, no. 3 (2020): 449–484.

Perez-Garcia, Manuel. *Global History with Chinese Characteristics. Autocratic States along the Silk Road in the Decline of the Spanish and Qing Empires 1680–1796*. Palgrave Studies in Comparative Global History, Singapore: Palgrave Macmillan, 2021.

Perez-Garcia, Manuel. *Vicarious Consumers: Trans-national Meetings between the West and East in the Mediterranean World (1730–1808)*. London: Routledge, 2013.

Perez-Garcia, Manuel, and Lucio de Sousa, eds. *Global History and New Polycentric Approaches: Europe, Asia and the Americas in a World Network System*. Singapore: Palgrave-Macmillan, 2018.

Ptak, Roderich. *China's Seaborne Trade with South and Southeast Asia (1200–1750)*. Aldershot: Ashgate, 1999.

Pu, Xia. "Shi Lun Qing Dai Jiang Zhe Di Qu Liang Shi Duan Que Wen Ti." *Journal of Fu Zhou University, Philosophy and Social Sciences* 55, no. 1 (2002): 25–29.

Schottenhammer, Angela. *The East Asian Maritime World 1400–1800: Its Fabrics of Power and Dynamics of Exchanges*. Wiesbaden: Harrassowitz, 2007.

Van Dyke, Paul A. *Merchants of Canton and Macao: Politics and Strategies in Eighteenth-Century Chinese Trade*. Hong Kong: Hong Kong University Press, 2011.

Von Glahn, Richard. *Fountain of Fortune: Money and Monetary Policy in China, 1000–1700*. Berkeley: University of California Press, 1996.

Waley-Cohen, Joanna. "China and Western Technology in the Late Eighteenth Century." *The American Historical Review* 98, no. 5 (1993): 1525–1544.

Wang, Zhengzhong. "The Regulation of Sailors in the Maritime Trade between Jiangnan and Nagasaki in Early Qing China." In *The "Global" and the "Local" in Early Modern and Modern East Asia*, edited by Benjamin A. Elman and Chao-Hui Jenny Liu, 221–228. Leiden: Brill, 2017.

Westad, O. A. *Restless Empire: China and the World Since 1750*. Philadelphia, PA: Basic Books, 2012.

Wu, Chengming. *Zhongguo de Xiandaihua: Shichang yu Shehui [China's Modernization: Market and Society]*. Beijing: Sanlian Chubanshe, 2001.

Yan, Xiongfei, and Lei Yuming. "Xi Fang Chuan Jiao Shi Nan Huai Ren Zai Hua Huo Dong Shu Lue." *Journal of Shandong Agricultural University* 5, no. 4 (2003): 79–82.

Zhang, Yi. *Neo-Confucianism, Gentries and Lineages: The Culture and Society in Huizhou from Song to Ming Times*. Hong Kong: Chinese University Press, 2013. (revised version in Hangzhou: Zhejiang University Press, 2017).

Zhao, Ximing. "Jiang Shang Gu Zhong Lu." In *Tong Shi, Vol. 8*, edited by Sun Yuxiu, 3–11. Taipei: Guangwen Bookstore, 1968.

Zhou, Yuanhe. "Qing Dai Ren Kou Yan Jiu." *Social Sciences in China* 2 (1982): 1–28.

Zhao, Gang. *The Qing Opening to the Ocean Chinese Maritime Policies, 1684–1757*. Honolulu: University of Hawaii Press, 2013.

Zhu Pi Zou Zhe (ZPZZ), The First Historical Archives of China (FHAC), Beijing.

Compelled to import: Cuban consumption at the dawn of the nineteenth century

Nadia Fernández-de-Pinedo

ABSTRACT
One of the sources that allow us to analyse certain consumption patterns are trade balances. These documents are especially relevant in the case of island colonies, such as Cuba, that depended on the outside world for many kinds of supplies, not just the basic ones. Despite their limitations, data on imported goods from Havana's balance of trade at the dawn of the nineteenth century allow us to examine the consumer goods that were most in demand in Cuba at that time. This essay uses that information to emphasise the relationship between colony and metropole in terms of material culture, with a particular focus on the core items of food, clothing and household goods. Overall, patterns of consumption reflect patterns of production and imports.

Introduction

Cuba's insular character and its geostrategic position made it a key colony in the Americas in the early modern period. As Daylet Domínguez and Víctor Goldgel Carballo have pointed out, it was an essential hub in the Atlantic world and a central element in trans-imperial networks and rivalries.[1] It had an especially prominent role in transferring tax revenue to Spain thanks to its sustained economic growth following its insertion into the international market during the middle decades of the nineteenth century, a period in which agrarian capitalism was expanding on the island.[2] However, until its agro-industrial sector was well established, there was a struggle over whether Cuba would adopt a protectionist stance or instead seek to conquer foreign markets, given that Spain was not able to absorb all of the island's produce or act as a re-exporter in Europe. Cuba was a clear example of the struggle between protectionist and liberalising policies, which reflected the opposing interests of Cuban planters and Spanish traders respectively.

Because of Cuba's lack of a developed secondary sector at the end of the eighteenth century, and its colonial relations both with the metropole and with other countries, the island needed to be supplied with manufactured goods as well as staple foods. Although data on imported goods from the annual statements of trade have their limitations, they allow us to analyse the most relevant consumer items. Apart from the tools and machinery required to increase agricultural production, the imports into the island reflected its social pyramid and the entangled histories of imperialism, race and gender, as the goods that each social group acquired, and their eating habits, differed according to their purchasing capacity.[3] Rituals of consumption reflected the interplay of supply and demand. This essay focuses on these specific patterns, especially on the triad of "eating, clothing and dwelling."[4]

Sources and analytical framework

Scholars from different disciplines – including anthropologists, art historians, economic historians, archaeologists, folklorists and curators – have shown a great interest in material culture and diverse analytical approaches have highlighted a relevant cross-disciplinary field of enquiry.[5] This range of fields for examining material culture also uses an array of research methods from qualitative to quantitative approaches. When studying the material culture of the early modern period, historians consider tangible material objects as sources alongside more traditional textual sources in archival collections and museums, as well as probatory inventories or dowries.[6] Also of interest are fiscal and trade sources, which are less commonly explored but equally relevant. Each source offers different perspectives on how to understand the past of a society through its consumption of, for example, furniture, clothing and household goods.

Trade statistics are useful in reconstructing commercial networks, although it is true that they have significant limitations such as not including smuggling, customs fraud or fluctuations in the valuations placed on products by customs authorities. Commercial records do not reveal the uses of fabrics and apparels, but they can provide insights that help to distinguish trends and meanings of consumption. According to Loïc Charles and Guillaume Daudin, "data on external trade give fundamental insights into the material culture of Early Modern Europe and its transformations in the eighteenth and early nineteenth centuries."[7] Such statistics offer important information about shopping baskets, especially in the case of an island that was heavily dependent on its metropole.

In the case of Cuba, data on its commercial traffic are available from the end of the eighteenth century, a period in which the Royal Resolution of 18 April 1794 created a trade secretariat to record and monitor this traffic. Cuban historian Julio Le Riverend noted that figures for total trade from 1790 to 1795, from 1803 to 1815 and from 1826 onwards have been preserved.[8] However, whereas from 1826 onwards the statements of trade are printed and accessible, for the years at the end of the eighteenth century the only available printed statement is an incomplete copy of the Havana Balance of Trade of 1794.[9] This contains lists of exported and imported goods in alphabetical order, with their respective weights or volumes, but without their prices (which would have been stated in the original document).[10] It is likely that such data would have continued to be collected, although no more sources of this kind have appeared apart from the handwritten Havana balances of trade from 1803 to 1807.[11] These handwritten statements are much richer than the printed one of 1794.[12] Lists of imported and exported goods state their volume, their price in *pesos reales* and their port of origin or destination.[13] With regard to the origin of imports, it should be noted that in some cases the statements only include the last port of embarkation, whereas in others the place where the goods started their journey is also included. In value, precious metals and enslaved Africans were the most imported trade goods followed by a variety of manufactures and other supplies that reflected the needs of the island's various social groups. Certain imported goods were intended for re-export, but the statements of trade do not indicate when this was the case – as it would often have been with cotton, for example. Exports can be divided into two main categories: agricultural goods of Cuban origin, and re-exports of precious metals.

The documentation from 1803 and 1804 is particularly useful because they were years of peace immediately following the Treaty of Amiens, signed by France and Great Britain on 25 March 1802. Although the treaty was broken as early as 16 May 1803, Spain was not adversely affected until late 1804, when it went to war against Britain in support of Napoleon. When France and Spain were defeated at the Battle of Trafalgar on 21 October 1805, trade relations between Spain and its American colonies were cut until the end of hostilities between Spain and Britain on 5 June 1808. Hence, in 1806–1807, Cuba's trade had to be conducted by "neutral" countries. In the statements of trade, these countries were included under the general term of *Colonies*. At the outbreak of the war between Britain and France on 18 May 1803, the United States took advantage of the situation to establish itself as the carrier between the Americas and Europe. In the case of sugar, when Britain blocked the French ports of Martinique and Guadeloupe from January 1804, North American traders took French and Spanish products to American ports, unloaded them, and then reloaded them for European ports as if they were American exports. Therefore, the United States merchant fleet purchased sugar in the colonies of belligerent countries and sold it in the European markets. The United States became the only neutral carrier engaged in foreign trade in the Caribbean and began to focus its attention on Cuban commodities, strengthening commercial relations with the colony.[14] As Le Riverend has pointed out, the restrictive policy of monopoly interests and Spain's limited maritime power forced its colonies to take advantage of any opportunity to trade, as no navy was capable of exercising a monopoly over global trade routes.[15] The Gulf of Mexico was one of the locations where the struggle for markets between the old powers of Europe (France, Britain, Spain) and emerging powers such as the United States took place.

One of the pillars of the colonial regime was the relationship between the Spanish administration and the colonial elites.[16] Planters were expanding their productive capabilities and consumer demand for imports increased as the standard of living improved. Wider markets were needed.[17] As a result, new legislation on commerce and administration was established from the final decades of the eighteenth century onwards.

Cuba's trade was first liberalised when the Royal Instruction of 16 November 1765 authorised direct trade between eight Spanish ports and the islands of Cuba, Saint-Domingue, Puerto Rico, Trinidad and Margarita, and then further when the regulations of 12 October 1778 enacted the decrees of freedom of trade between Spain and its American colonies, making Cuba the first American colony permitted to trade with all the Spanish ports. Almost at the same time, Spain liberalised inter-colonial trade in the Americas. These liberalising measures were a reflection of Cuban economic needs (Table 1).[18]

With this new legislation, the Crown was aiming to favour Cuba – which still depended on the Mexican *situados* as currency – as the colony had become strategically important since the Seven Years' War, when the British returned Havana and Manila to Spain in exchange for Florida.[19] The measures intended to streamline trade between the metropole and its American colonies, but compliance depended first and foremost on

Table 1. Inter-colonial trade.

Supplies	• In 1796, Mexico's export custom duties to the Spanish Antilles, Guatemala, Santa Fe and Peru were reduced by 25 per cent and the silver extracted by Veracruz was made exempt from duties if it came from the profit of the sale of Antillean goods. However, the Havana Consulate also aspired to exempt silver sent from New Spain to Cuba to acquire sugar for the peninsular market. • From 1768, Cuba was authorised to import, tax-free, the food purchased in Campeche • From 1807, Spanish vessels departing from Cuba with Cuban commodities, as well as Spanish and foreign goods and effects from Spain, were permitted to unload in the ports of New Spain and Campeche, with the repeal of royal orders previously banning this.
Meat	• From 1768, Cuba was authorised to import, tax-free, meats purchased in Campeche, Veracruz and Cumaná. • From 1787, exports of salted meats from Buenos Aires to La Havana were free of duties and *almojarifazgo* for six years, a measure that was then ratified by the king. • By the Royal Order of 10 April 1793, the king removed import and export duties even 'salted or appraisal meats or to the sebum of Buenos Aires from *alcabala* and other countries of America as well for the trade of the Metropolis, as for the interior of some Provinces to another, or from port to port of the Americas' • The Royal Order of 10 April 1793, was confirmed on 20 December 1802 and 22 June 1804, and decreed that American salted meats would be free from royal, municipal and other arbitration duties.
Flour	• The Royal Cédula of 1782 exempted from *alcabalas* the Mexican flour shipped to the Windward Islands. • The Royal Order of 18 February 1784 banned foreign flour but authorised flour of Novohispanic and Spanish origin. • The Royal Order of 17 July 1790 decreed that flour from Veracruz could enter freely into La Havana. These measures sought to neutralise the presence of North American flour brought by Bostonians to Cuba.

Source: R.O. 10 May 1807, al virrey de Nueva España, AGI, Santo Domingo, 2.177; Guía o Estado General de la Real Hacienda de España, 1803 by *D. Joseph Señan, Madrid, s/a., pp. 9–10*; Expediente firmado por Garay el 31 January 1817 in Madrid in *Memoria de la Real Sociedad Patriótica* (1819).

whether Spain was militarily capable of controlling smuggling.[20] Secondly, in wartime, it was important for the purposes of trade and communication to keep open the shipping routes between Spain and the Antilles, and between the Antilles and the rest of Spain's American empire. Spain's limited naval power was not sufficient to prevent the expansion of unauthorised trade and, in wartime, allowed the neutrals to trade with Cuba. With the wars between European powers hindering, or at times preventing, the supply of Cuba by Spain and the continental American colonies, it was the neutrals that facilitated the expansion of Cuban agricultural production and provided the island with supplies and manufactured goods. It therefore became necessary for Spain to liberalise the legislation prohibiting direct trade with foreigners.

Moreover, Spain enacted special permits, such as the Royal Gracia granted in two stages on 24 December 1804 and on 1 May 1805, to various trading houses established in Philadelphia, New York, Boston and Baltimore, allowing them to ship all kinds of supplies from their ports to Havana, Veracruz, Caracas, Montevideo and Venezuela in neutral-flagged vessels, paving the way towards clandestine trade.[21] According to John R. Fisher, from 1793 on Cuba enjoyed virtually free trade with the United States, which was the dominant neutral power in the Atlantic.[22]

Population and consumption

The trade data for Havana – the principal entrepôt of the New World – is not unrepresentative of trade for Cuba as a whole. As the American consul pointed out in 1805, "eight-tenths of [Cuban trade] is exported from Havana and its dependencies and about the same proportion of the population is dependent on the city for their supplies."[23] After the British occupation of Havana, the Bourbons expanded the harbour and made the port not only one the biggest fortifications but also one of the largest cities in the Spanish Empire (Table 2).[24]

The population figures are those recorded by the official censuses and amended by Ramón de la Sagra for the years 1792, 1817 and 1827 or collected by foreign consuls on the island.[25] These statistics have their limitations – especially with regard to the large numbers of slaves, many of whom were illegally imported and therefore would not have been recorded.[26] As Michael Zeuske has noted, Spain "from 1493 to 1898 possessed the largest colonial empire in the Americas (still including Cuba and Puerto Rico after 1825), with the longest history of slavery."[27] Nevertheless, slaves constituted a smaller proportion of the total population than in any other Spanish colony in the Americas.[28]

Another problem with these early censuses is that they did not take into account the large temporary population, particularly the soldiers who came ashore from ships that might have been moored in Cuban ports for weeks and in some cases ended up staying permanently.[29] The garrison and the forced labourers working on the construction of the fortifications should also be considered. Indeed, French consular reports added 16,000 "troupes, marine, forçats" to the census numbers of 1792, increasing the total recorded population of 272,301 by 6 per cent. Almost 20 per cent of the population at that time lived in Havana.[30] By 1817 the population of Cuba would reach 553,033, an average annual rate of growth of 2.87 per cent. In fact, the population of the island increased five-fold between 1792 and 1862, an average annual rate of growth of 2.32 per cent.[31] As Franklin Knight notes "the rapid population growth affected the social structure."[32] As the population grew, a degree of miscegenation blurred the dividing lines of the social hierarchy – whites, free people of colour, and slaves – but the white and creole Spanish culture remained dominant.

The demographic expansion was the result of immigration – both voluntary and forced – and a high birth rate. The slave uprising in Haiti (1791–1804) led to an influx into Cuba of French nationals (mainly men) with their slaves, and the achievement of independence by the continental Spanish colonies brought white settlers and also favoured a white migration policy.[33] In 1796 the Marquis of Casa Peñalver proposed a limit on the number of blacks in Cuba so as to reduce the racial imbalance and avoid a rebellion like the one that had taken place in Haiti; instead he proposed the promotion of white immigration from New Spain, Campeche and the Canary Islands.[34] From 1817 the

Table 2. Cuban censuses – 1792 and 1817.

	1792 Cuba		1792 La Havana		1817 Cuba		1817 La Havana	
Population	Males	Females	Males	Females	Males	Females	Males	Females
white	72,299	61,260	12,274	11,263	130,519	109,311	20,372	17,990
negro and mixed blood – free	25,211	28,941	4,425	5,375	58,885	55,173	11,159	10,212
negro and mixed blood – slaves	47,424	37,166	7,115	10,855	124,324	74,821	12,791	11,550
total	144,934	127,367	23,814	27,493	313,728	239,305	44,322	39,752

Source: De la Sagra, *Historia física, política y natural de la isla de Cuba* and *Guía de Forasteros de la isla de Cuba*; Canga Argüelles, *Diccionario de Hacienda*,527–531; *Calendario manual para el año de 1824*, Biblioteca Nacional, Madrid, HA 12377; Affaire Etrangères, Paris, Correspondance Consulaire, La Havane, Vol. 5, 11.

Spanish government supported the settlement of foreigners in Cuba (Royal Cédula 21 October 1817; Royal Order 27 June 1821) after the continental colonies had gained their independence.[35] The sale of Louisiana and Florida undoubtedly also contributed to migratory flows to Cuba.[36] According to Jacobo de la Pezuela, Leclerc's failed 1803 expedition to Saint-Domingue resulted in the emigration of more than 27,000 people from there to Santiago de Cuba and Baracoa.[37] Two decades later, in 1823, Consul Angelucci claimed that the French constituted a third of Havana's population.[38] The absence of subsistence crises and the arrival of the smallpox vaccine in 1804 undoubtedly also had a positive demographic impact, despite the presence of yellow and dengue fever that consuls and visitors frequently referred to.[39]

Males outnumbered females in Cuba. More precisely, in 1792, males were 53 per cent of the population, and by 1817 reached 57 per cent. Even though the slave population was growing as a proportion of the total, it never exceeded the figure of 43 per cent reached in 1841 when the cultivation of sugar was expanding.[40] Whites constituted 49 per cent of all inhabitants in 1792, and 56 per cent in 1862. Essentially, therefore, although Cuba became a more racially complex society, the social structure continued to be dominated by free whites.

Most of the free white immigrants and wage-earners in Cuba from the late eighteenth century onwards were not engaged in the *zafra* (sugarcane harvest) or in other agricultural work: they were mostly working in the island's cities as artisans or estate managers, or in commercial activities such as retail merchants and small shopkeepers or in tobacco shops rolling cigars or ground snuff or in the fortifications as masons.[41] The *ingenios* (sugar mills) were also a source of employment for free whites, as they could work in roles such as *boyero* (oxen driver) or foreman in the boiling houses. At the lower strata of white society were the soldiers and sailors.[42] The vast majority of slaves, meanwhile, were engaged in low-skilled agricultural work. However, in the cities, not only whites but also free people of colour and a small minority of slaves pursued trades such as day labourers, shoemaker, tailor, baker, household servants or performed occupations related to construction as carpenter or builder.[43] It should be noted that in the eighteenth and nineteenth centuries Cuba had the largest free non-white population (free black and mulatto) in the Caribbean, because slaves could purchase their freedom under the *coartación* system.[44] As J. M. Félix de Arrate has described, the worked carried out by free people of colour included silversmithing, sculpture, painting and carving.[45]

Enslaved men and women in the cities, particularly Havana, also performed domestic tasks – as coachmen, for example – or were engaged in shipbuilding or strengthening fortifications.[46] The capital was also where the Cuban upper classes with the greatest purchasing power – including the administrators, planters, merchants and commercial agents – were concentrated.[47] According to Knight, among whites there was a greater class diversity in Cuba than in other societies in the Caribbean, with *peninsulares* (those born on the Iberian Peninsula) living alongside Cuban-born *criollos*.[48] At the top of the social ladder were the titled families and creole patriciate of wealthy planters; they were followed by the heads of government departments, functionaries of royal administration, army and navy officers.

Consumption patterns in Cuba reflected the four principal social strata: the white elite; white workers (for example shopkeepers and small farmers); *mestizos* and free people of colour; and slaves. As Rosalía Oliva Suárez has highlighted, in terms of textiles and foodstuffs the Cuban elite tended to copy the styles and eating habits of Europeans, which they gradually adapted to the local climate.[49] And to a certain extent this applied even to the lowest stratum of society, with Robert S. Duplessis noting that even "slaves and natives were rarely passive recipients of dress."[50]

Introduction of commodities into Havana

Despite the limitations of the data, the statements of imports and exports allow a better understanding of the relationship between consumption, production and trade. In order to quantify the goods in large sections their customs value in *pesos reales* has been used. Excluding metals and slaves, two groups of items stand out (Figure 1): food and clothing. Even though the island's economy was essentially agricultural during the first half of the nineteenth century, food accounted for more than 40 per cent of the customs value of imports. In the period 1803–1804, that figure reached almost 60 per cent, which probably reflects the fall in the quantity of manufactures arriving through the port – the latter were increasingly being smuggled, especially across western Cuba through Santiago de Cuba or Puerto Príncipe. By 1806–1807 the situation changed, with more manufactures (textiles) arriving through the port of Havana (that is, not smuggled) than in 1803–1804. The limited craftsmanship on the island made foreign manufactures highly valued as imports, with textiles the most important of all.

The monopoly in force during 1803–1804 is clearly reflected in Table 3, which shows the pre-eminence of Spanish ports. In the case of textiles, Cádiz and Santander stand out, while for household and personal items the ports of Barcelona, Málaga and

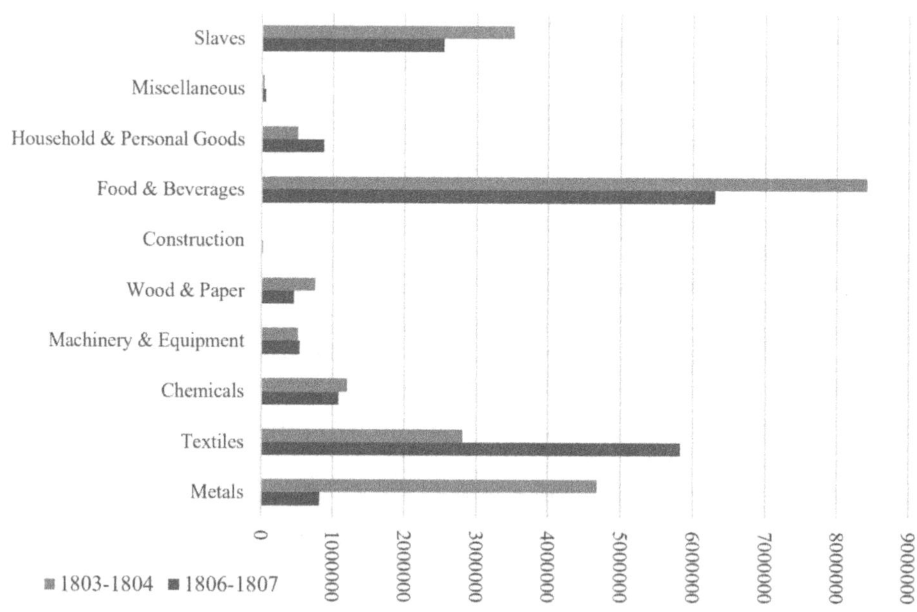

Figure 1. Imports of goods into La Havana (value in *pesos reales*) – comparison between 1803–1804 and 1806–1807. Author's own elaboration. Balanzas del puerto de la Habana 1803–1804 and 1806–1807.

Table 3. Origin of imports (textiles / food and beverages / household and personal goods).

	Textiles		Food & Beverages		Household & Personal goods	
	1803–1804	1806–1807	1803–1804	1806–1807	1803–1804	1806–1807
Port of departure	%	%	%	%	%	%
Alicante	0.01	–	0.62	–	0.18	–
Barcelona	4.82	–	5.53	–	7.46	–
Cádiz	53.36	–	14.23	–	37.54	–
Campeche	6.92	2.75	2.98	2–98	3.28	0.18
Canary Islands	1.09	–	6.63	0–00	0.21	–
Cartagena de Indias	0.69	–	0.96	0.12	0.91	0.16
Cartagena de Levante	–	–	0.01	–	–	–
Chagre	–	–	0.13	–	–	–
Colonies	2.47	94.52	21.07	91.35	8.05	98.12
Coro	–	–	0.01	–	–	–
Coruña	2.36	–	1.26	–	8.44	–
Florida	0.40	–	0.14	–	0.02	0.02
Gijón	0.29	–	0.22	–	0.09	–
Guaira	0.12	–	0.31	–	–	–
Málaga	1.81	–	6.37	–	13.66	–
Mallorca	1.27	–	0.18	–	0.24	–
Montevideo	0.42	–	13.81	0.95	0.06	0.03
Movila	0.01	–	0.00	–	–	–
Nicaragua	–	–	0.22	–	–	–
Nueva Barcelona	–	–	0.92	0.48	0.08	–
Nueva Orleans	2.31	–	4.66	–	1.00	–
Panzacola	0.01	–	0.01	–	–	–
Puerto Cabello	0.24	–	0.20	0.01	–	0.01
Puerto Rico	0.06	–	0.36	–	0.12	0.01
Puerto Velo	–	–	1.69	0.77	0.37	–
Santa Marta	0.10	–	0.02	–	–	–
Santander	14.46	–	3.45	–	6.18	–
Sevilla	0.21	–	0.51	–	1.92	–
Tarragona	0.63	–	4.65	–	3.49	–
Trinidad	–	–	0.00	0.08	–	0.01
Truxillo	0.03	0–01	0.50	0.16	0.42	0.08
Veracruz	5.58	2.36	8.24	2.81	6.26	1.18
Vigo	0.29	–	0.08	–	–	–
Villahermosa	0.02	–	0.01	–	–	–
Matanzas	–	0.34	–	0.21	–	0.20
Cumaná	–	–	–	0.07	–	–
Total in *pesos reales*	2,805,946	5,828,915	8,414,312	6,302,077	508,280	881,365

Source: Balanzas del puerto de la Habana, 1803–1807.

Coruña also played significant roles. In the case of food and beverages, Cádiz, the Canary Islands, Barcelona, Tarragona and Santander stand out.

The impact of the Napoleonic Wars significantly reduced the traffic between Spanish ports and the Americas, which led to the ships of neutral countries taking over almost all of Cuba's trade. That does not mean, however, that Spain disappeared from the trading routes in the Americas. North American ships sailed to Spain, and then set sail from there with Spanish and European products back in this case to Havana.[51] During 1805–1807, when neutral-flagged vessels virtually monopolised Cuba's trade, the quantity and variety of products arriving in Havana increased.

In the following, I analyse these three categories of goods in detail, since they are the ones that will allow us to get a better idea of the goods and foodstuffs that Cubans wanted to consume. At the same time, we will see the main differences between periods of peace and war.

Despite its economy being almost entirely agricultural, Cuba lacked some of the foodstuffs needed to feed its growing population – hence the increasing proportion of food among total imports from the 1760s on, when a greater diversification of crops (coffee, wax, indigo, mango, etc.) and a specialisation in commercial crops such as sugar, following Haiti's slave rebellion, took place.[52]

The dependence on foreign trade for basic necessities was clear, although subsistence agriculture – the cultivation of tubers (sweet potato, cassava, potato), maize, legumes and a wide variety of tropical fruits (pineapple, guava, mamei, etc.) – was practised on the plantations themselves and on the banks of rivers, and there was also livestock farming in *potreros* and *hatos* housed cattle for the considerable consumption of fresh and dried meat from the island.[53]

The shortage of basic foods was exacerbated by maritime blockades in times of war. The economic and racial dichotomy of the island was reflected in the major categories of foods and beverages that were imported. Salted fish and meat, for example, were consumed predominantly by slaves, so the quantities imported increased as the slave population expanded.[54] The relatively wealthy white population had a diet not dissimilar to the one they would have had in Spain: wheat flour, oil, wine, legumes and nuts – but also a greater quantity of fresh meat and fish than would have been the case in Spain. The troops, meanwhile, had a diet not dissimilar to that of the whites, with added *tasajo* (jerked beef), rice, legumes and wheat bread. The diet of the less wealthy classes consisted of yuca or cassava bread, tubers, salted fish and meat.[55]

Meat, particularly pork and beef, was a large part of the diet – but it is important to distinguish between the fresh and salted varieties. Cuba in the nineteenth century managed to meet the demand for fresh meat thanks to the rearing of livestock, mainly cattle and pigs, which provided fresh meat and in some cases dairy products (cheese and butter), a means of transporting goods (in the case of cattle) and also a supply of oxen and mules for export to neighbouring colonies.[56] Writings from the late seventeenth century highlight that cattle were already one of the island's principal resources – particularly the leather referred to in Europe as *cuirs de la Havane*.[57]

As Celia María Parcero Torre points out, meat was in fact one of the smuggled products that was exchanged for fabrics with the British settlers in Jamaica.[58] Fresh meat was eaten not by Cuba's slave population but by the whites, while salted meat, which the slaves did consume, was imported mainly from Río de la Plata. In the Royal Order of 10 April 1793, the king decreed salted meats from Spanish America free of rights of introduction and extraction, including the first-selling *alcabala*. In the case of Cuba, the exemption was confirmed and expanded on 20 December 1802 and 22 June 1804. As a consequence, American salted meats were decreed "free in their trafficking, not only of the royal rights but also of municipal and other *arbitriums*, whatever its origin."[59] By 1803, between 500,000 and 600,000 *arrobas* of *tasajo* were being consumed in Cuba.[60]

After the end of the eighteenth century, it was the Río de la Plata area that took the lead in exploiting its livestock for the export of leather and began to expand its salting industry.[61] Buenos Aires would begin shipping *tasajo* to Cuba, especially after American Spanish colonies start to gain their independence in 1820. Previously, as the *tasajo* records in Havana demonstrate, Montevideo had been the main export port. But these were not the only centres supplying jerked beef around the turn of the nineteenth century. New Barcelona, Campeche and Tampico also participated in this trade, although they were unable to match the low prices of the Río de la Plata. When maritime traffic was disrupted by war, Cuban planters had to resort to "buying salted meats in brine introduced by northern Americans."[62] There were two types of meats for export – both salted, but prepared in different ways:

> Some in pieces, with or without bones, preserved in brine and shipped in barrels. The rest are cut in slices then sealed in the sun and shipped without packaging. In this form, the meat is called *Tasajo* [...] it has a 40 per cent advantage in weight difference over sliced meat. The parcel is considered as defective.[63]

Cubans complained that Americans brought brine meat – lower in quality than the jerked beef because the brine extracted all the substance from it.[64] However, not everyone agreed: the French consul in Buenos Aires, for example, claimed that "brine meat [...] tastes fresher and more pleasant."[65] But South American jerked beef was cheaper than its North American equivalent, which guaranteed its pre-eminence. Demand for meat and fat ran parallel to the growth of the sugar industry. The other complement to the slaves' diet was salted cod, the main suppliers of which were the United States – whose main export ports were Portland, Boston and New York – and Newfoundland, a British colony. After the embargo of 1807 and the war of 1812, it was Newfoundland that controlled this traffic.[66]

The advantages of salted meat and fish were their high protein content, low price and the ease with which they could be conserved – which is why they became a preferred food for planters and troops (whether on land or at sea).[67] The abundance of meats of all kinds resulted in dishes such as *ajiaco*, consisting of a stew of broth with lemon juice, chilli peppers and "pork or cow meat, *tasajo*, pieces of bananas, cassava, pumpkins."[68] Sidney Wilfred Mintz and Roderick Alexander McDonald point out that the planters wanted to improve slave self-provisioning by permitting them to have a garden plot, but the reality is that masters offered a poor food allowance to their slaves.[69]

However, according to the statements of trade, flour and biscuits were the most important part of the Cuban diet. The flour from Santander, as well as the wines and oil from the Mediterranean ports, could be transported – with the appropriate tariffs – to the Americas by Spanish vessels, which would then return with colonial products and cotton (Figure 2).[70]

The commercial circuits did not merely consist of the direct exchange of these products between Spain and the Gulf of Mexico, however. To return with colonial products, Spanish Mediterranean ships had to take goods, such as wines and oils, of similar volume to the Americas (Argentina and Brazil – and especially Cuba and Puerto Rico). For traders in the Cantabrian ports of northern Spain, the only cost-effective returns consisted of importing colonial products with a similar weight and value to flour or developing a triangular circuit – hence the emphasis placed by the Santander consulate on defending its flour exports, which involved the shipping of sugar in the opposite direction. Sugar could be redistributed by cabotage, especially through the Castilian wheat network. But flour and wine, as with any bulky goods, led to the development of the fleet and generated abundant employment if their export was conducted under the Spanish flag.

The flour trade generated an abundant literature, in newspapers and reports, during the eighteenth and nineteenth centuries. While Spain's competitors were in Europe in the case of wine and oil, the rivals in the flour trade were in the Americas and close to

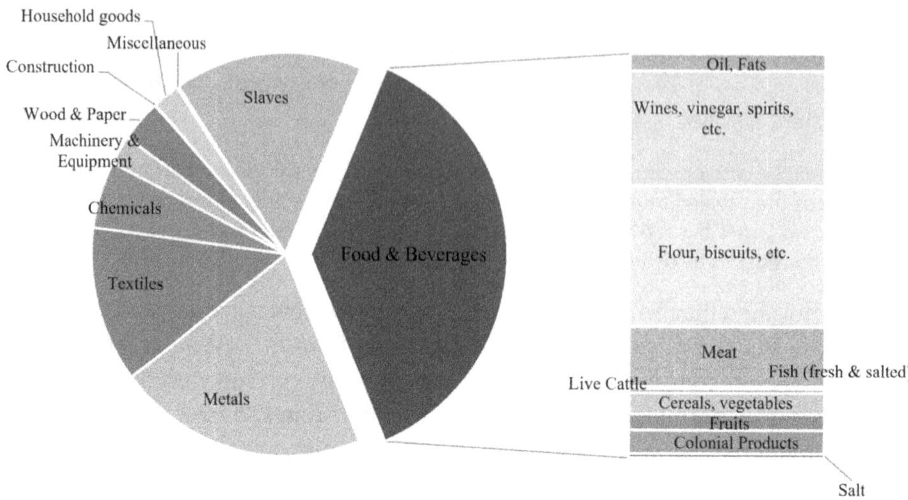

Figure 2. Imports into La Havana (in *pesos reales*), 1803–1804, with detailed breakdown of food and beverages. Author's own elaboration**.** Balanzas del puerto de La Habana 1803 and 1804.

Cuba – such as New Orleans. Higher protectionist tariffs would therefore be necessary if the interests of Spanish flour producers were to be protected. Although the supply of flour to Cuba was legally in the hands of the metropole and New Spain (Royal Cédula of 1782 and Royal Order of 1784), the frequent wars forced Spain to allow the entry of foreign flour carried by foreign ships. As Eduardo Arcila points out, the Royal Order of 25 June 1793 allowed Anglo-American ships to introduce their flour into Cuba, displacing that of New Spain.[71] Although the Royal Order of 22 January 1796 returned the flour trade to a Hispanic monopoly, in practice the United States maintained a decisive presence due to the smuggling and special licences.[72]

The supply of flour to Cuba seems to have been a complex affair. According to the *Observations on the commerce of Spain with her colonies, in time of war* (1800), even in peacetime Spain had to resort to the importation of American flour into the Iberian Peninsula and from here re-export it to its colonies:

> If we consider that the said flour of Georgia – selling at 5 or 6 dollars per barrel – was in the first instance shipped either from New York, Philadelphia or Baltimore, for a port of Spain; that previous to its embarkation it paid here the ordinary charge of 5 per cent of commission, besides other small charges; that to these must be added freight and insurance to Spain; that there fresh duties and commission were incurred, as well as new charges on the unloading and reshipment on board of Spanish vessel, that the voyage to Havana occasioned new charges, new freight and new insurance; if to this be added the fresh commission in Havana, and the profit of the speculator; if again we add those charges from thence to Florida, the price of thirty dollars in that province cannot appear to us exorbitant.[73]

When the Royal Order of 23 August 1796 granted to the Earl of Mompox and Jaruco a licence to export 9,000 cane brandy pipes from Cuba to the United States in two years, paying one *peso* per pipe, and allowed him, with the proceeds, to acquire flour for Cuba taxing the same rights as if they were Spanish, Cuban farmers and traders protested (21 November 1796).[74] Only in the early nineteenth century, as recorded by the statements of trade from 1805 to 1807, when American navigators become not only exporters of their flour but re-exporters of Cuban sugar to Europe, would the attitude of Cuban farmers and merchants change. The attitude that did not change, however, was that of the metropole.

While from 9 May 1809 foreign flour transported on a Spanish vessel would cost 45 silver *reales* of royal and municipal taxes, in the case of flour shipped on a foreign vessel it would cost 69 silver *reales*. A report from the Santander consulate to the Spanish government, dated 22 November 1814, regretted "the immense damage to the Spanish trade from foreigners [*sic*] transporting their flour directly to the Americas, without docking at the ports of the Peninsula," and complained about smuggling.[75] The Spanish tariff of 1820, and especially the Cuban tariff of 1824, would begin, as with other products, to protect Spanish flour and its transportation by Spanish vessels, but change was not evident until 1830.

Less attention has been paid to wines and oil, which also required imports of goods that the Spanish Mediterranean was not able to provide. Despite being typically Mediterranean products, they needed a very high degree of tariff protection, like the most protected manufactured products (such as certain textiles). The taxes imposed on them were surpassed only by those on flour. While the Spanish monopoly was in force (1803–1804), the wine consumed in Cuba was mostly of Spanish origin. But during the blockade (1805–1807) French wines began to arrive. It should not be forgotten that after the slave rebellion in Haiti, many French citizens took refuge in Cuba and wanted to consume their own wines (particularly the Bordeaux variety). In 1805, 70 per cent of the wine imported by Cuba (in terms of its total value in *pesos*) was of French origin; the figure in 1806 was 64 per cent, and in 1807 53 per cent. But this was an exceptional situation and would eventually change, with customs tariffs and valuations favouring Spanish wines. De La Sagra attributes the decline of exports of French wines to Cuba in the 1830s to the "increased consumption of Catalan [wine] since speculators thought of bringing to Havana the softer qualities of the principality, which against a misconception, although widespread about wines, was believed that they could not resist navigation without going bad."[76]

Besides wine, beverages such as gin, spirits, *resolí* (an aniseed-based liquor) and cider – none of which were produced locally – were also introduced into Cuba in large quantities (Table 4).

Table 4. Composition of food and beverage imports in La Havana, as a percentage of their total value in *pesos reales*.

Food & Beverages	1803 %	1804 %	1806 %	1807 %
Oils & fats	4.1	4.5	11.0	8.4
Wines, vinegar, spirits, etc.	22.8	34.0	18.4	24.9
Flour, biscuits, etc.	37.8	31.8	31.1	33.2
Meat	17.2	12.4	21.1	11.9
Fish (including salted fish)	0.8	0.4	3.5	1.0
Live cattle	0.8	1.3	–	–
Cereals, vegetables	6.5	3.9	8.4	10.5
Fruits	5.2	2.8	2.2	4.5
Colonial products	4.8	6.8	4.2	5.2
Salt	–	2.1	–	–
Ice	–	–	–	0.4
Total value, *pesos reales*	4,212,521	4,201,791	3,248,748	3,053,329

Source: Balanzas del puerto de La Habana 1803, 1804, 1806, 1807.

In addition, wines and flour also played a significant role. Since they are bulky, medium-priced products, their transport provided work for a large fleet whose profitability depended on having a similar volume of cargo for the return voyage. For wines and flour, freight costs were a significant determinant of their final price as they took up a considerable proportion of the tonnage, and in return required goods of similar characteristics – bulky and not expensive – so as to make their transport profitable.

Much of the recovery of the Spanish navy after the Battle of Trafalgar (1805) would have been based to some extent on the:

> excessive duties placed on foreign flour and wines and the big difference between the pavilion in which goods were traded. The North Americans [flour] and the French [wines] are the ones who suffer most from this state of affairs. Spain [...] almost [...] exclusively supplies Cuba with flour, and the wine of Catalonia is mostly the only kind that is consumed in the country.[77]

The consumption of dairy products, such as milk, butter, and cheese, seems also to have been very widespread in Cuba. In the case of cheese, imports in 1806–1807 came mainly from elsewhere in the Americas, in particular from the *Colonies* and Nueva Barcelona. Fats consisted mostly of butter and sebum. While fish consumption in rural areas of the island consisted mainly of salted fish (cod, herring, mackerel), in cities such as Havana packaged sardines and other fish such as anchovies, tuna and salmon were also in demand. Also noted in the statements of trade, to a lesser extent, were shrimps (*camarones*), oysters and salted turtle meat. As for fruit and vegetables, the principal imports were noodles (*fideos*), chickpeas and vegetable stew, along with raisins, olives, almonds, and garlic either from Spanish or other American ports. Some products, such as *ají* or chilli pepper, maize, beans (*frijoles*) and rice, came mainly from Campeche and Veracruz, and were part of a hybrid cuisine. Spices garnished the dishes, especially the saffron that in years of peace came through the ports of Málaga, Barcelona and Cádiz. The pepper recorded in the statements of trade was of three types: from Tabasco, Holland, and Castile. In 1807, from the *Colonies* were imported into Cuba 71,606 *pesos reales* of *pimienta fina* but without specifying the type or origin. Coffee only appeared in 1803, from the ports of La Guaira and Puerto Rico, while tea came from Cádiz and Montevideo, and cocoa was shipped mostly from Puerto Velo, Cartagena de Indias and Veracruz. As with the majority of imported foods and beverages, from 1806 onwards almost all the products arriving in Cuba came from ports in the *Colonies*.

As Earle note "the Spanish state promulgated dozens of orders, pragmatics, cédulas and other ordinances," with the aim of controlling New World attire to maintain an adequate correspondence between social position and sartorial performance.[78] In 1509 the first sumptuary law was enacted in Spanish America (Peru) to ban slaves from wearing expensive fabrics (particularly silks) and jewellery. Laws enacted in Europe or in the New World prohibited common people from wearing and spending too much by dictating a person's appearance based on moral and economic reasons. However sumptuary laws were constantly violated in both the colonies and in the metropolis, revealing the appetite for textiles and fashionable goods no matter what gender, race, or social rank in the colonial system.[79]

The range of semi-luxury and luxury goods introduced into Havana at the dawn of the nineteenth century is well known, with several authors having mentioned what Pezuela refers to as "the reputation for luxury that owners and merchants were developing" on the island, which indicates the tendency towards luxury consumption that existed in all social strata of Cuban society.[80]

Consumer goods included imported woven-fibre textiles. Although domestic weaving was widespread and every household produced clothing for their own needs, the more affluent sections of the Cuban population also purchased manufactured clothing. The popularity of buying ready-made garments can be seen in Table 5. These clothes were highly prized, to the point that, as Suárez has mentioned, a body of inspectors was created to monitor the exorbitant prices they were sold for.[81] A taste for clothing as an aspect of conspicuous consumption was not limited to the wealthy, however.[82]

Cuban fashion tended to follow European patterns – in particular those of the metropole but also, at the beginning of the nineteenth century, those of France.[83] Arrate has pointed out that the drivers of the new fashions were the Castilians who came to Cuba: "So, once the new clothing is seen it is imitated in the cut, in the good taste of colour and in the nobility of the genre, and they do not skimp on the costumes, with the finest canvases and lace, the richest garrisons and gallons, the most priced tissues and fabrics, nor the silk fabrics of more beautiful work and more delicate dyes."[84] Arrate adds that imitation and ostentation also applied to the indoor and outdoor domestic space, as with ornaments and furniture. He suggests that many Cuban families, of all social classes, were led into debt by the costly habit of seeking to emulate European consumption habits (Table 6).

As Table 6 shows, linen fabrics were the most in demand in Cuba in the early 1800s, and, in fact, they would continue to top the list of textile imports in the middle decades of the century. Wool and silk textiles, although less in demand, would maintain similar percentages over the following decades.[85] Imports of cotton fabrics, which had hardly been introduced in the early nineteenth century, would triple in value by the middle of the century, reducing the relative weight of linen. Because of the climate, woollen products were not in high demand; in 1803–1804, imported woollen fabrics consisted mainly of cloth, followed by blankets, baize, *barragán* and cashmere. According to Richard Salvucci, however, coarse woollens were commonly used for slaves' clothing during the cooler months.[86] In 1806–1807, baize accounted for 24 per cent of all imported woollen fabrics, and cloths 19 per cent. One of the main differences during wartime was the wider variety of cloths available, such as English cloth (second and third quality), fine black and fine blue varieties, and cloth from Saxony. The *paños de rebozo* (common

Table 5. Imports of ready-made dresses into the port of La Havana (quantity/value in *pesos reales*).

Year	Port of departure	Product	Units	*Pesos reales*
1794	Europe	Dresses for women and men	13	–
1803	Coruña	Embroidered muslin dresses	2	40
1804	Barcelona	Dresses for women	1	50
1803	Cádiz	Fabric dresses for Religious images	1	50
1804	Cádiz	Embroidered dresses for men	3	112
1803	Málaga	Gold-embroidered muslin dresses	20	600
1803	Barcelona	Embroidered dresses for women	52	1,560
1807	Colonies	Muslin dresses	294	2,940
1806	Colonies	Cotton and silk dresses	87	870
1806	Colonies	Silk dresses	71	1,775

Source: Balanzas del puerto de La Habana 1794, 1803, 1804, 1806, 1807.

Table 6. Imports of fabrics and textiles (percentages of total).

Fabrics & textiles	1803	1804	1806	1807
Raw materials	3.1	3.1	0.0	0.0
Textile manufactures (without indicating type of fabric)	25.5	22.8	23.4	14.7
Wool manufactures	2.7	2.0	12.0	6.8
Cotton manufactures	1.9	1.7	7.5	16.4
Silk manufactures	10.6	8.2	4.2	12.5
Linen manufactures	44.2	56.4	48.6	43.3
Furs	11.9	5.7	4.3	6.2
Value in *pesos reales*	1,427,878	1,378,068	3,771,732	2,057,183

Source: Balanzas del puerto de la Habana 1803–1804 and 1806–1807.

shawls) imported from Veracruz and the *Colonies* were common clothing "consumed in altar cloths and veils, and in coverlets and sashes" and woven by peasants in Mexico (Table 7).[87]

As for the imports of silk fabrics, they were clearly intended for the section of the Cuban population with the greatest purchasing power, capable of buying satin, taffeta, velvet and damasks. Imports of silk ribbons and stockings increased substantially between 1803–1804 and 1806–1807, while imports of taffeta diminished from 103,500 *pesos reales* in 1803–1804–18,148 *pesos reales* in 1806–1807.[88]

The origin of these products is not known, only the port of embarkation. But given the patterns of trade with New Spain, it is not entirely unreasonable to presume that some silk fabrics came from Asia. In the dowry from 1650 that Suarez has studied, there are references to a bedspread from China, dresses in black damask, red silk, silk primavera in satin, blue and pink damask from Japan, a doublet made with black damask, and patterned linen shirts in black.[89] As for changes in consumer behaviour, it should be taken into account that the presence of Chinese textiles in colonial America was not a novelty.[90] In New Spain, the arrival of Chinese silks of varying types, qualities and prices via the

Table 7. Principal imports of woollen fabrics, 1803–1804 and 1806–1807.

1803–04	Product	1806–07
pesos reales		*pesos reales*
4,160	Baize (*bayeta*)	
	Bayeta de medio ancho	15,940
	Bayeta faxuela	123,290
	Bayetas angostas	3,601
4,012	Cashmere	73,461
360	Flannel (*franelas*)	10,775
	Fresadas de lana	30,422
1,203	Etamine (*estameña*)	6,080
13,840	Woollen blankets	16,977
15,400	Cloth	
	Fine blue cloth (*paño azul fino*)	4,080
	Cloth from Saxony (*paño de Sajonia*)	13,182
	Medium-quality cloth (*paño entrefino*)	8,070
	English cloth – second quality (*paño inglés de 2ª*)	54,104
	English cloth – third quality (*paño inglés de 3ª*)	57,324
1,150	Black cloth (*paño negro*)	
	High-quality black cloth (*paño negro fino*)	1,020
	Common cloth (*paño ordinario*)	88,468
825	*Paño de rebozo o reboso*	11,808
	Serge (*sarga de lana*)	7,170

Source: Balanzas del puerto de la Habana 1803–1804 and 1806–1807.

Manila Galleon stimulated the consumption of hybridised cloth from sixteenth century on.[91] Alongside classical aesthetics and taste, a new creative and blended culture emerged. However, there is a lack of research examining whether Asian influences had the same impact in Cuba as they did in New Spain. As trade in the Gulf of Mexico was shaped by a mixture of consumer preferences, government policy and geography, it is reasonable to consider if anything similar happen with the circulation of Asian goods in the Caribbean.[92]

Imported linen fabrics were always popular in Cuba, partly because of their lightness. Even though cotton began to compete with linen, especially from the mid-1820s in the form of very fine fabrics such as *zarazas*, it did not supersede linen in Cuba until at least 1865. Between 1803–1804, *zarazas* of a total value of only 1,100 *pesos reales* appear in the statement of trade, while between 1806–1807 their total value was 363,082 *pesos reales*. The same happened with muslins, *cotines*, cotton stockings, handkerchiefs and *mahons* (a coarse durable twill-weave cotton fabric) whose imports grew between 1806–1807.

Throughout the nineteenth century, fabrics enjoyed a buoyant market in Cuba. An important aspect of this international trade were the cultural ties with Europe, in particular Spain and its colonial empire. As Pérez-García has noted, "the progressive integration of the global markets of Spanish America, such as those pertaining to the textile industry, with western Europe was a key factor in the consolidation of networks and commerce routes, as well as the flow of goods from one side of the Atlantic to the other."[93]

In the section "household and personal goods," all domestic objects, furniture and utensils have been included, while differentiating between personal objects – umbrellas, fans, shaving cases, ivory combs, razors and glasses – and jewellery. The latter includes jewellery and watches from Spain and Veracruz, and from the *Colonies* during wartime. In Havana's statements of trade we can find plentiful examples of jewellery, including necklaces and chains such as pearl chokers, rosaries (made from gold or pearls), and silver and gold crosses. There were also more sophisticated forms of jewellery, such as diamond pins, topazes, diamond rings and pearl bracelets. Timepieces included gold or silver watches along with table clocks and even fake watches (Table 8).

The "writing and reading materials" category included books, fountain pens and pencils. The increase in the quantity of notebooks and books – such as French dictionaries and guides to French grammar; Spanish books, including comedies; and fashion magazines for women – that arrived during wartime is striking. Among the imported musical instruments were pianos, violins, and large and small organs. Cards, billiards, and toys

Table 8. Household and personal goods (as percentages of total) imported into La Havana.

Household and personal goods	1803	1804	1806	1807
Personal items (canes, suitcases, brushes, etc.)	39.6	21.3	15.4	20.8
Jewellery, watches, etc.	1.7	4.1	1.8	3.3
Musical instruments, toys, sports equipment	18.5	9.2	2.3	1.9
Writing and reading materials	14.8	28.2	13.2	15.1
Household utensils – kitchen, etc.	13.0	25.2	33.6	41.0
Furniture and home furnishings	4.9	8.1	20.0	9.7
Ornaments & Decorations	5.9	3.8	12.6	4.4
Haberdashery (buttons, needles, pins, etc.)	1.5	0.2	1.0	3.8
Total value in *pesos reales*	254,126	254,154	613,909	267,456

Sources: Balanzas del puerto de La Habana 1803–1804 and 1806–1807.

for children are listed as items for entertainment and play. The objects related to domestic interiors included furnishings, tableware and decorations, along with a series of everyday household items such as kitchenware, cruets, glassware and silver knives – conspicuous consumption clearly extended to the home. Although the pottery prevalent in Havana from the second half of the seventeenth century until the late eighteenth century came from New Spain, it would be displaced by English china in the nineteenth century.[94] The use of china or porcelain was widespread in the Americas, with Havana receiving a range of British, Dutch, French and Asian varieties. In the 1794 statement of trade, the two most sought-after types of crockery were from China and Britain.[95] In 1794, crockery arrived in Cuba from ports in America and Europe, while between 1803–1804 – whether from China or elsewhere – it arrived from the Spanish ports of Cádiz, Santander, Barcelona, Tarragona, Gijon, Málaga and the Canary Islands. The most expensive crockery was British and Chinese.[96] In terms of value, in all the selected years, it is the china or *loza* that stands out.

As for other imports from China, fabrics were also notable, albeit not in large quantities; they arrived mainly via the *Colonies* after the establishment of neutrality at the end of 1804 (see Table 9).

Furnishings also reflected Atlantic networks and the consolidation of conspicuous consumption. Suarez notes that "creole artisans, *mulatos* and half-breeds began to create a style of indigenous furniture, where Cuban woods with bold proportions and rich ornamentation were enhanced."[97] After the British take-over of Havana in 1762, Cubans' taste for British-style furniture became very pronounced. Cuba seems to have also exerted an influence on production: according to David Ormrod, furniture design in Britain was influenced by the arrival of large quantities of Cuban mahogany from the 1750s on.[98] Later, according to Dena Goodman and Kathryn Norberg, the vogue for

Table 9. Chinese goods imported through La Havana (quantity/value in *pesos reales*).

Year	Loading port	Product	Quantity	Measure	Customs value *pesos reales*
1794	Colonies	Cloaks	347	pieces (*piezas*)	12,075
1794	Colonies	Blankets	328	pieces	5,248
1803	Cadiz	Asian Fabrics	249	pieces	6,225
1803	Cadiz	China	10	dozens	30
1803	Europe	China	245	dozens	735
1803	Matanzas	Handkerchiefs	32	dozens	288
1804	Colonies	China	12	dozens	36
1804	Colonies	China	23	Boxes (*cajones*)	575
1804	Colonies	China (common)	23	*guacoales*	575
1804	Veracruz	Blanket	96	pieces	1,536
1804	Veracruz	Cloak	1,002	*varas*	2,004
1805	Veracruz	Bedspread	3	unity	48
1805	Colonies	China	137	Boxes (*cajones*)	3,425
1805	Colonies	Cloak	1,469	pieces	36,725
1805	Colonies	Taffeta	1,819	pieces	45,375
1806	Colonies	Ribbons	3,853	pieces	2,408
1806	Colonies	Coffee set	18	unity	720
1806	Colonies	China	30	box (*cajones*)	750
1807	Colonies	Coffee set	5	unity	50
1807	Colonies	Satin	431	pieces	17,240
1807	Colonies	Satin	67	*varas*	83
1807	Veracruz	Satin	140	*varas*	280
1807	Colonies	Taffeta	134	pieces	4,020

Source: Balanzas del puerto de La Habana 1794, 1803, 1804,1805, 1806 and 1807.

mahogany in France "appears to have begun as a British influence."[99] Mahogany, also known as *acajou*, was much used in the Caribbean in the eighteenth century, not only due to its abundance but also because of its resistance to humidity. Although Cuba was one of the suppliers, the island also imported ready-made mahogany furniture. Referring to Saint-Domingue, Baron de Wimpffen noticed that "the wood was part of a complicated transatlantic trade network wherein mahogany was exported as raw material and imported as finished product" – and something similar seems to have been true of Cuba.[100] The imported pieces of mahogany furniture included wardrobes, linen cupboards, storage armoires, commodes, sideboards (*aparadores*) and corner cabinets (*esquineros*). This durable and expensive wood also arrived on the island in the form of beds, desks, tables, chairs and picture frames. Another common element in all homes that are also recorded in the statements of trade – without specifying the type of wood – were chests and wooden trunks used to store a multitude of items, from bedding to books, as storage was important in such a humid climate.

The importance of fashion and appearances was directly linked with interior decoration – particularly in the case of mirrors, which were shapers of people's identity and closely associated with image and hygiene. Mirrors were luxury items that proliferated from the eighteenth century onwards.[101] From 1803 to 1807, imports included looking glasses of various sizes (1/4, 1/2, 1, 1.5, 2, 2.5 *varas*). In 1807, for example, 2,728 mirrors of sizes between ¼ and ½ *varas* arrived. The largest mirrors, meanwhile, were probably destined to adorn the wealthiest homes.[102] Small mirrors and mirrors of very different sizes and frames made in gold, mahogany or even cardboard were also recorded in the statements of trade. In 1806–1807, 2,438 vanity mirrors from the *Colonies* were imported. Other objects of decoration which were imported were picture frames, paintings, crystal chandeliers, portraits (one of Napoleon Bonaparte is mentioned), vases, table clocks, wax figures, and bouquets of dried flowers. Overall, Cuban homes were stocked at the dawn of nineteenth century with a great variety of foreign imported objects, illustrating the tastes of the different social classes.

Conclusions

Despite discriminatory customs duties and tariff rates, at the beginning of the nineteenth century Cuba was a society with a distinct tendency towards conspicuous consumption.[103] The large scale imports of agricultural produce and industrial goods did not encourage the Cuban population to develop new means of manufacturing, but international prices and the size of the markets for the island's staples exports were important in creating incentives for technological innovations that succeeded in increasing production elsewhere.[104] For a colony that was essentially the hub of the Gulf of Mexico, international trade was highly important. In times of war, when communications and trade with Spain were suspended or at least sharply reduced, new opportunities emerged for the so-called neutrals, mainly the United States. In terms of imports, the main difference between times of peace and war was that the variety of commodities arriving on the island increased during conflict – especially in the case of textiles, and personal and domestic items.

At the turn of the nineteenth century, clothing, household goods and eating habits in Havana reflected the circulation within the Atlantic. Needs were met from abroad, mainly through imports from Europe and the rest of America, with galleons in turn connecting America to Asia. As a result, international networks of commodities disseminated new patterns of material culture in Cuba. As seen in the case of Havana, imports corresponded to a combination of habits and needs. On one hand, royal directives and tariff policies made possible the emulation of metropolitan habits in the colony. On the other hand, Asian objects and spices were consumed in combination with Caribbean raw materials and food. This convergence produced hybrid styles, as in the case of furniture. The resultant mix was enhanced in wartime when trade restrictions could no longer be enforced. The intermingling of influences within Cuba's material culture was spurred by economic growth and the emergence of new identities. Cuban trade was more than merely an exchange of New World commodities for metropolitan goods: it was part of an expanding world market.

Notes

1. Domínguez and Carballo, "Slavery, Mobility, and Networks," 2.
2. Pretel and Leonard, *The Caribbean and the Atlantic World Economy*; Fernández-de-Pinedo, Saiz, and Pretel, "Patent, Sugar Technology."
3. La Torre noted that "las horas ordinarias de comer hasta principios el presente siglo era las doce del día, meredándose en la tarde y cenándose de 8 à 10 de la noche" (the ordinary hours of eating, until the beginning of the present century, was twelve o'clock in the day, having snacks in the afternoon and dinner from 8 to 10 at night) to which he adds that coffee began to replace chocolate. Torre, *Lo que fuimos y lo que somos*, 120.
4. "The three basic needs of human existence: dwelling/shelter; taste/food; clothing" Bauer, *Goods, Power, History*, 1.
5. Schlereth, "Material Culture Research and Historical Explanation."
6. As noted by Duplessis, probate inventories or post-mortem inventories are the most detailed documentary sources used to study consumption even if they only can provide a record of accumulation. DuPlessis, *The Material Atlantic Clothing*, 9.
7. Charles and Daudin, "Eighteenth-Century International Trade Statistics."
8. Le Riverend, *Historia económica de Cuba*, 21.
9. Copies can be found in the Biblioteca Nacional de Madrid and in the Archivo Nacional de Cuba. For more details see Moreno Fraginals, *El Ingenio* and Fernández-de-Pinedo, *Comercio exterior y fiscalidad.*
10. It is noted that weapons, ammunition or other war equipment required by the Plaza and Arsenal are not included, nor are the construction woods consumed on the Island, nor those sent to Spain, and that 13,432,478 pesos 4 strong were drawn in silver and gold coins, jewelry and bars. *Guía de Forasteros de la Habana 1796*, 129–163.
11. Complementary information in "Estado general de los derechos reales y debidos cobrar en las administraciones generales de rentas de mar y tierra de las cantidades procedentes de comisos, de las exigidas para el vestuario de milicias, del medio por ciento de consulado, de los licores, harinas y negros introducidos, de las cajas de azúcar extraídas y de los buques de guerra, correos y mercantes entrados y salidos en 1802, 1803, 1804 y 1808." National Archives of the United States, Despatches from US. Consuls in Havana, Roll 1, December 1783 to October 1807. (hereafter NA/US/).
12. Fernández-de-Pinedo, *Las balanzas del comercio exterior de La Habana.*
13. The data in the tables do not contain the *reales*, but they have been taken into account in the calculations.
14. Schnakenbourg, "Neutral Cover and Globalised Commerce."
15. Le Riverend, *Historia económica de Cuba*, 104. Even though free trade with foreigners was legalised in 1818, non-Spanish ships still had to pay a high export duty, reinforcing protectionism.

16. Fernández de Pinedo Fernández, "Comercio colonial."
17. Pérez, "Cuba and the United States," 58.
18. Kuethe, "Havanna in the Eighteenth century," 26–18. See also Arcila, *Comercio entre Venezuela y México*, 96–97; Alonso, "Especialización mercantil y crisis de la economía rural," 63–478; Ortiz de Tablas, *Comercio exterior de Veracruz 1778–1821*, 173–174; Barbier, "Imperial policy towards the port of Veracruz," 248; Widner Sennehauser, "Veracruz y el comercio de harinas en el Caribe español," 108.
19. In addition, Spain tried to promote the Cuban internal economy by promulgating a series of regulations that sought to lower the cost of labor and the indispensable instruments for the agricultural sector such as "Utensils and tools" for Cuban agriculture that were declared free of import directly from abroad, in national vessels (Royal Cédula of 1792) and two years later, the same measure was adopted for staves and barrel arches; Royal Order of 22 April 1804. This Royal Order also exempted this sugar from *alcabalas* and the *ingenios* created from that date on from *diezmos*. The successive Royal Cédulas liberalized the importation of slaves (28 February 1789 and 24 November 1791) and allowed their traffic on foreign ships. Marichal and Souto Mantecón, "Silver and Situados." Tarragó, *Understanding Cuba as a Nation*, 9.
20. Thanks to those located in Mexico, silver circulated through Cuba, which was to be acquired through smuggling.
21. Delgado Ribas, "El Impacto de Las Crisis Coloniales," 169.
22. Fisher, *Relaciones económicas*, 211. In fact, the Royal Orders of 17 and 18 November 1797, authorised foreign goods shipped from Spanish ports in neutral ships to Spanish America. Although the Royal Order of 20 April 1799 ended this permission, the island's authorities allowed the importation of provisions and 1,800 clothes, provided they came on ships from friendly nations. Finally, the Royal Order of 8 January 1801 approved these measures. Exhibition of the Board of Commerce of Catalonia to the King, 8 December 1797 and Individual exhibitions of 6 and 13 December 1797. Archivo General de Indias, Santo Domingo, 2.177. (hereafter AGI).
23. Havana, 1 November 1805. NA/ US/ Despatches from US consuls in Havana, 1783–1807, T. 20, Washington, D.C., roll 1, vol. 1 (1805).
24. Kuethe, "Havanna in the Eighteenth century," 17.
25. De la Sagra, *Historia Física*, Vol. I, 147–227.
26. Huetz de Lemps, "Le commerce des esclaves vers Cuba."
27. Zeuske, "Historiography and Research Problems of Slavery," 88; Schneider, "African Slavery and Spanish Empire."
28. Taber and Yingling, "Networks, Tastes, and Labor," 268.
29. For this reason, Havana is described as a "foire continuelle" given the role of hub and connector it had in the Atlantic. Anonyme, *Ouvrages politiques et philosophiques*, 81.
30. Affaire Étrangères, Statistiques Extérieures d'Espagne, 1825–1853, V. 25, folio 217. (hererafter AE/SEE).
31. Maluquer, *Nación e Inmigración*, 14–15.
32. Knight, "Social Structure of Cuban Slave Society," 259.
33. Yacou, "La présence française."
34. "Expediente acerca de los perjuicios que puede ocasionar en la Isla de Cuba la introducción de negros de otras islas." Archivo Histórico Nacional, Ultramar, 1834, leg.2, 27. (hereafter AHN/ Ultramar).
35. Vázquez Queipó, *Informe fiscal*, 2; Orovio "Medio siglo de políticas poblacionistas en Cuba," 339.
36. "Observaciones sobre la región de Santiago de Cuba." 4 July 1824, NA/US/ Despatches from USA. Consuls in Santiago, 13 May 131799–27 December 1836. T 55.
37. Pezuela, *Diccionario*, Vol. II, 180.
38. Affaires Étrangères, Paris, Correspondance Consulaire, La Havane, Vol 5, La Havane, 10 March 1823, 198 and 204. (hereafter AE/CC/La Havane).
39. 10 January 1826, 235. AE/CC/La Havane; 26 July 1827, 104. AE/CC/La Havane; 11 Mai 1835, 225–227. AE/CC/La Havane.

40. Fernández de Pinedo, *Comercio exterior*, Table 2, 195.
41. Le Riverend, *Historia económica de Cuba*, 143.
42. Kuethe, "Havanna in the Eighteenth century," 19–20.
43. Fernández-de-Pinedo, *Comercio exterior*, 225–227.
44. Yelvington, Sainton, and Casimir, "Caribbean Social Structure," 327; Knight, "Social Structure of Cuban Slave Society."
45. Arrate, *Llave del Nuevo Mundo*, Chapter XIX.
46. Klein "The Cuban slave trade," 67–68; Pérez Guzmán, "Modo de vida de esclavos y forzados," 241.
47. Luzón, "Comer y beber en La Habana colonial."
48. Knight, "Social Structure of Cuban Slave Society," 262.
49. Suárez, "Los espacios domésticos habaneros," 232.
50. DuPlessis, *The Material Atlantic Clothing*, 229.
51. Fernández-de-Pinedo, *Las balanzas del comercio exterior de La Habana*, 14.
52. Le Riverend, *Historia económica de Cuba*, 113.
53. Balboa, *De los dominios del rey al imperio*, 211. Funes, *From Rainforest to Cane Field*, 331.
54. On slave diet see among others Sarmiento, "Alimentación y relaciones sociales en la Cuba colonial" and "Del 'funche' al 'ajiaco'"; Ortiz, *Los negros esclavos*; Salmoral, *Los Códigos Negros*; Florez, "La alimentación de la población esclava."
55. Parcero Torre, "La alimentación en Cuba en el siglo XVIII."
56. Moreno Fraginals, *Cuba/España, España/Cuba*, 213.
57. Anonyme, *Ouvrages politiques et philosophiques*, 30. In the statements of trade of Havana, the introduction of live animals such as birds, horses (frisons), donkeys, mules, fighting roosters or oxen also stands out.
58. Parcero Torre, "La alimentación en Cuba en el siglo XVIII," 103.
59. *Guía o Estado Genera/ de la Real Hacienda de España*, 9–10. Garay, *Memoria de la Real Sociedad Patriótica*, Madrid, 31 January 1817.
60. Letter signed by Marqués de Peñalver, A. de Arregui, M. C. de Soler and the Marqués de Santa Cruz in 1803. Archivo Nacional de Cuba, Real Consulado, Junta de Fomento, leg. 73, expediente 2.804. (hereafter ANC/RC/Junta de Fomento).
61. Fernández de Pinedo Fernández, "La recuperación del comercio español con América," 59–60.
62. Buenos Aires, 31 January 1855. AE/CC/Buenos Aires, Vol. 4, f. 6.
63. (Translation by the author). "Les unes par morceaux, avec ou sans os, conservées en saumure et expédiées dans des barils. Les autres découpées par tranches scellées ensuite au soleil et expédiées sans emballage. Sous celte forme, la viande reçoit le nom de Tasajo [...] elle présente un avantage de 40% en différence de poids sur la viande en tranches. Le colis est considéré comme tare." Buenos Aires, 31 January 1855. AE/CC/ Buenos Aires, vol. 4, fs. 6–7.
64. 21 November 1797. ANC/ Intendencia General de Hacienda, leg. 378, expediente 2.
65. (Translation by the author) "la viande en saumure ... est d'un goût plus frais et plus agréable." Buenos Aires, 31 January 1855. AE/CC/ Buenos Aires, vol. 4, fs. 6–7.
66. Ryan, *Fish out of water*, 234.
67. "However, it must be noted that saltfish was the cheapest source of a plentiful supply of protein-rich food which would not spoil in hot climates." Ryan, 251.
68. Luzón, "Comer y beber en La Habana colonial," 25.
69. Mintz, *Caribbean Transformations;* McDonald, *The Economy and Material Culture of Slaves*; Sarmiento, "Del 'funche' al 'ajiaco'"; Kiple, *Blacks in Colonial Cuba*.
70. Imports went from 121,335 pesos of olive oil in the years 1803–1804 to 47,803 in the period 1805–1807. Fernández-de-Pinedo, *Comercio exterior y fiscalidad*, 156.
71. Arcila, *Comercio entre Venezuela y México*, 93; Kuethe, "Havana in the Eighteenth Century," 29.
72. Fernández-de-Pinedo and Thépaut-Cabasset, "A Taste for French Style in Bourbon Spain."
73. *Observations on the commerce of Spain with her colonies, in time of war*, 48–49.
74. Vincent Gray, American agent in La Havana. Havana, 29 October 1802. NA/US/ Dispatches from USA. Consuls in Havana, 1783–1807, T-20, roll 1, vol. I.

75. (translation by the author) "los inmensos perjuicios que se seguían al comercio español de que los extrangeros [sic] remitiesen sus harinas directamente a las Américas, sin tocar ni adeudar en los puertos habilitados de la Península." De la Sagra, *Historia Física,* Vol. II, 107–108 and 531–532. Sierra, *Memoria sobre el estado del comercio que publica la Real Junta del de Santander*, 68–69.
76. (translation by the author) "mayor consumo que se hace del [vino] catalán desde que los especuladores pensaron en llevar a La Habana las calidades más suaves del principado, que contra una opinión equivocada, aunque muy generalizada sobre los vinos, se creía que no podían resistir a la navegación sin torcerse." De la Sagra, *Historia Física*, Vol. II, 51 and 475.
77. (translation by the author) "droits excessifs mis sur les farines et les vins étrangers et de la grande différence dans le traitement fait au pavillon espagnol el aux autres. Les américains du Nord [por las harinas] et les français [por los vinos] sont ceux qui souffrent le plus de cet état de choses. L'Espagne … presque … exclusivement fournit Cuba de farine, et le vin de Catalogne est à peu près le seul qu'on consomme dans le Pays." Havana, 11 January 1835. AE/CC/ La Havane, vol. 10, f. 4.
78. Earle, "Race, Clothing and Identity," 338.
79. Riello and Rublack, "Introduction," 1–33; Fernández-de-Pinedo and Thépaut-Cabasset, "Memoirs of the fruits of Globalization."
80. (translation by the author) "la afición al lujo que se iba desarrollando entre los propietarios y mercaderes." Pezuela, *Ensayo histórico de la isla de Cuba*, 246.
81. Suárez, "Los espacios domésticos habaneros," 233.
82. Fernández-de-Pinedo and Thépaut-Cabasset, "A Taste for French Style in Bourbon Spain."
83. Fernández-de-Pinedo and Thépaut-Cabasset "Memoirs of the fruits of Globalization."
84. (translation by the autor) "De modo que apenas es visto el nuevo ropaje, cuando ya es imitado en la especialidad del corte, en el buen gusto del color y en la nobleza del género, no escaseándose para el vestuario los lienzos y encajes más finos, las guarniciones y galones más ricos, los tisúes y telas de más precio, ni los tejidos de seda de obra más primorosa y de tintes más delicados." Arrate, *Llave del Nuevo Mundo*, Cap. XIX.
85. According to DuPlessis "the rising consumption of silks and woolens in that colony [Saint-Domingue], as well as the declining use of cottons and linens, was evidence of an emerging tropical free settler dress regime. Despite their different path, across the eighteenth century the textile cultures of Jamaica, Bahia and Saint-Domingue were converging." DuPlessis, *The Material Atlantic Clothing*, 178.
86. Salvucci, *Textiles and Capitalism in Mexico,* 59.
87. Ibid, 20.
88. Silk stocking accounted for 9,009 *pesos reales* in 1803–1804 and rose to 45,405 *pesos reales* in 1806–1807. In the case of ribbons, in 1803–1804 silk ribbons were introduced for a value of 1,270 *pesos reales* and in 1806–1807, the amount reached 52,746 *pesos reales*.
89. ANC/Protocolo: Escribanía de Regueyra, 1650, Tomo 1, f. 76, f. 0250v; f. 323v, f. 393v, f. 504. In Suárez, "Los espacios domésticos habaneros." On Peruvian inventories see Corinne Thépaut-Cabasset (https://dressworld.hypotheses.org/363).
90. Perez-Garcia, "Creating Global Demand"; Perez Garcia and Sousa, eds., *Global History and New Polycentric Approaches*; Ibarra, "El mundo en una nuez"; Bonialian, "La 'ropa de la China' desde Filipinas hasta Buenos Aires. Circulación, consumo y lucha corporativa, 1580–1620."
91. Fernández-de-Pinedo and Thépaut-Cabasset, "Memoirs of the fruits of Globalization."
92. Dobado, "The Hispanic Globalization of Commerce and Art in the Early Modern Era." As the Manila Galleon trade started in 1571 and lasted until 1815, the access to Asian commodities via Mexico had an enormous impact in the Spanish American Colonies. Priyadarshini, "Introduction," 10.
93. Perez-Garcia, "Mercados Globales de La América Española," 184.
94. Hernández Oliva, "Cerámica Mexicana," 56–61.
95. Gerritsen and Mcdowall, "Material Culture and the Other."

96. In the case of earthenwares coming from America it must be taken into account that "[i]ndeed, the earthenware ceramics from Puebla enjoyed some fame in colonial Latin America. They were exported north to the mining regions and beyond to New Mexico, east to Veracruz, south to Oaxaca, Chiapas, Guatemala, and Honduras, and to Cuba and Santo Domingo in the Caribbean." Priyadarshini, *Chinese Porcelain in Colonial Mexico*, 134.
97. Suárez, "Los espacios domésticos habaneros."
98. Ibid., 257; Ormrod, "Consuming the Orient in Britain," 4.
99. Pastore, "Mahogany as Status," 40; Goodman, Sherratt, and Lovejoy, *Consuming Habits*.
100. Pastore, "Mahogany as Status," 19–20 and 41.
101. Shrum, *In the Looking Glass*, 2.
102. Ibid., 22.
103. Knight, "Social Structure of Cuban Slave Society," 263.
104. Fernández-de-Pinedo, Saiz, and Pretel, "Patent, Sugar Technology."

Disclosure statement

No potential conflict of interest was reported by the author(s).

Funding

This chapter is part of the project of I+D+i Modalidad Generación del conocimiento, PID2021-124378NB-I00, funded by MCIN/ AEI/10.13039/501100011033/ without FEDER funding.

The research for this work was financially supported by the Spanish Ministerio de Economía, Industria y Competitividad (Agencia Estatal de Investigación)/Fondo Europeo de Desarrollo Regional (FEDER), HAR 2016-78026-P, a project hosted by the Universidad del País Vasco (UPV/EHU). I gratefully acknowledge the support of GECEM Project (Global Encounters between China and Europe: Trade Networks, Consumption and Cultural Exchanges in Macau and Marseille, 1680–1840), a project hosted by the Pablo de Olavide University (UPO) of Seville (Spain). The GECEM Project is funded by the European Research Council (ERC) [Starting-Grant, ref. 679371], under the European Union's Horizon 2020 Research and Innovation Programme (www.gecem.eu). The principal investigator (PI) is Professor Manuel Perez-Garcia (Distinguished Researcher at UPO). This work was supported by the H2020 European Research Council. This research has also been part of the academic activities of the Global History Network (GHN) in China (www.globalhistorynetwork.com). I also thank the anonymous reviewers for their feedback.

ORCID

Nadia Fernández-de-Pinedo http://orcid.org/0000-0001-6708-1480

References

Anonyme. *Ouvrages politiques et philosophiques d'un anonyme*. Londres: A Londres, aux dépens de la Société typographique dans Pall-mall, 1776.

Arcila Farias, Eduardo. *Comercio entre Venezuela y México en los Siglos XVII y XVIII*. Mexico City: El Colegio de México, 1950.

Arrate, J. M. Félix de. *Llave del Nuevo Mundo, antemural de las Indias Occidentales. La Habana descripta: noticias de su fundación, aumento y estado*. La Habana: [s.n.], 1876. http://hdl.handle.net/10347/16522.

Balboa, Imilcy. *De los dominios del rey al imperio de la propiedad privada: Estructura y tenencia de la tierra en Cuba*. Madrid: Consejo Superior de Investigaciones Científicas, 2013.

Bauer, Arnold J. *Goods, Power, History: Latin America's Material Culture*. Cambridge: Cambridge University Press, 2001.

Bonialian, Mariano. "La 'ropa de la China' desde Filipinas hasta Buenos Aires. Circulación, consumo y lucha corporativa, 1580–1620." *Revista de Indias* 76, no. 268 (2016): 641–672.

Charles, Loïc, and Guillaume Daudin. "Eighteenth-Century International Trade Statistics." *Revue de l'OFCE* 140, no. 4 (20 July 2015): 7–36.

Delgado Ribas, Josep M. "El Impacto de Las Crisis Coloniales en la Economía Catalana (1787–1807)." In *La Economía Española al final del Antiguo Régimen*, edited by Josep Fontana, 97–170. Madrid: Alianza, 1982.

Dobado-González, Rafael. "The Hispanic Globalization of Commerce and Art in the Early Modern Era." *Studies of Applied Economics* 32, no. 1 (2020): 13–42.

Domínguez, Daylet, and Víctor Goldgel Carballo. "Slavery, Mobility, and Networks in Nineteenth-Century Cuba." *Atlantic Studies* 18, no. 2 (June 2021): 1–6. doi:10.1080/14788810.2020.1783942.

DuPlessis, Robert S. *The Material Atlantic Clothing: Commerce and Colonization in the Atlantic World, 1650–1800*. Cambridge: Cambridge University Press, 2016.

DuPlessis, Robert S. "Sartorial Sorting in the Colonial Caribbean and North America." In *The Right to Dress. Sumptuary Laws in a Global Perspective, c. 1200–1800*, edited by Giorgio Riello, and Ulinka Rublack, 346–371. Cambridge: Cambridge University Press, 2019.

Earle, Rebecca. "Race, Clothing and Identity: Sumptuary Laws in Colonial Spanish America." In *The Right to Dress. Sumptuary Laws in a Global Perspective, c. 1200–1800*, edited by Giorgio Riello, and Ulinka Rublack, 325–345. Cambridge: Cambridge University Press, 2019.

Fernández de Pinedo Fernández, Emiliano. "Comercio colonial y semiperiferización de la monarquía hispana en la segunda mitad del siglo XVII." *Áreas. Revista Internacional de Ciencias Sociales*, no. *Desigualdad y Dependencia. La periferización del Mediterráneo occidental (s. XII-XIX)*. (1986): 121–135.

Fernández-de-Pinedo, Nadia. "Commercial Relations Between USA and Cuba in Times of Peace and War, 1803–1807." *Illes i Imperis: Estudios de Historia de las Sociedades en el Mundo Colonial y Post-Colonial* 4 (2001): 5–24.

Fernández-de-Pinedo, Nadia. *Comercio Exterior y Fiscalidad: Cuba (1794–1860)*. Bilbao: Servicio editorial. UPV/EHU (Economía y Empresa), 2002.

Fernández-de-Pinedo, Nadia. *Las balanzas del comercio exterior de La Habana, 1803–1807*. Bilbao: Servicio editorial. UPV/EHU (Colección Inéditos), 2000.

Fernández-de-Pinedo, Nadia, and Corinne Thépaut-Cabasset. "A Taste for French Style in Bourbon Spain: Food, Drink and Clothing in 1740s Madrid." In *A Taste for Luxury in Early Modern Europe. Display, Acquisition and Boundaries*, edited by Jon Stobart, and Johanna Ilmakunnas, 219–241. London: Bloomsbury Academic, 2017.

Fernández-de-Pinedo, Nadia, Patricio Saiz, and David Pretel. "Patent, Sugar Technology and Sub-Imperial Institutions in Nineteenth Century Cuba." *History of Technology Volume 30: European Technologies in Spanish History* 30 (2011): 46–62.

Fisher, John R. In *Relaciones económicas entre España y América hasta la independencia*. Madrid: Editorial MAPFRE, 1992.

Funes, Reinaldo. *From Rainforest to Cane Field in Cuba: An Environmental History Since 1492*. Chapel Hill: University of North Carolina Press, 2009.

Gerritsen, Anne, and Stephen Mcdowall. "Material Culture and the Other: European Encounters with Chinese Porcelain, ca. 1650–1800." *Journal of World History* 23, no. 1 (2012): 87–113.

Goodman, Dena, and Kathryn Norberg. *Furnishing the Eighteenth Century: What Furniture Can Tell Us About the European and American Past*. New York: Routledge, 2007.

Goodman, Jordan, Andrew Sherratt, and Paul E. Lovejoy. *Consuming Habits: Global and Historical Perspectives on How Cultures Define Drugs*. 2nd ed. Milton Park: Routledge, 2007.

Guzmán, Flores, and Ramiro Alberto. "La alimentación de la población esclava en Estados Unidos, el Caribe y Brasil. Comentarios sobre el estado de las cosas." *América Latina en la Historia Económica* 20, no. 2 (2013): 5–35.

Hernández Oliva, Carlos Alberto. "Cerámica mexicana." *Opus Habana* II, no. 2 (1998): 56–61.

Huetz de Lemps, Christian. "Le commerce des esclaves vers Cuba." *Les Cahiers d'Outre-Mer* 35, no. 138 (1982): 187–189.

Ibarra, Antonio. "El mundo en una nuez: de Calcuta y Cantón a Buenos Aires en una época de guerra. La introducción de efectos asiáticos en los mercados suramericanos, 1805–1807." *Revista de Historia Económica – Journal of Iberian and Latin American Economic History* 38, no. 3 (2020): 1–34.

Kiple, Kenneth Franklin. *Blacks in Colonial Cuba, 1774–1899*. Gainesville: University of Florida Press, 1976.

Knight, Franklin W. "The Social Structure of Cuban Slave Society in the Nineteenth Century." *Annals of the New York Academy of Sciences* 292, no. 1 (1977): 259–266.

Knight, Franklin W., and Peggy K. Liss, eds. Atlantic *Port Cities. Economy, Culture, and Society in the Atlantic Word, 1650–1850*. Knoxville: University of Tennessee Press, 1991.

Kuethe, Allan J. "Havana in the Eighteenth Century." In *Atlantic Port Cities. Economy, Culture, and Society in the Atlantic Word, 1650–1850*, edited by Franklin W. Knight, and Peggy K. Liss, 13–39. Knoxville: University of Tennessee Press, 1991.

Le Riverend, Julio. *Historia Económica de Cuba*. Barcelona: Ed. Ariel, 1972.

Luzón, José. "Comer y beber en La Habana colonial." *Caravelle. Cahiers du monde hispanique et luso-brésilien* 71, no. 1 (1998): 23–36.

Marichal, Carlos, and Matilde Souto Mantecón. "Silver and Situados: New Spain and the Financing of the Spanish Empire in the Caribbean in the Eighteenth Century." *Hispanic American Historical Review* 74, no. 4 (1994): 587–613.

McDonald, Roderick Alexander. *The Economy and Material Culture of Slaves: Goods and Chattels on the Sugar Plantations of Jamaica and Louisiana*. Baton Rouge: Louisiana State University Press, 1993.

Mintz, Sidney Wilfred. *Caribbean Transformations*. Baltimore, MD: Johns Hopkins University Press, 1984.

Observations on the commerce of Spain with her colonies, in time of war by a Spaniard, in Philadelphia. Translated from the original manuscript, by another Spaniard. Philadelphia: Printed by James Carey, 1800.

Ormrod, David. "Consuming the Orient in Britain, 1660–1760." Paper presented at Session 25 on "Luxury Production, Consumption and the Art Market in Early Modern Europe." International Economic History Congress, Helsinki 21–25 August, 2006.

Ortiz, Fernando. "La cocina afrocubana." *Casa de las Américas* VI, no. 36–37 (1966): 16–22.

Ortiz, Fernando. *Los negros esclavos*. La Habana: Ed. de Ciencias Sociales, 1975.

Parcero Torre, Celia María. "La alimentación en Cuba en el siglo XVIII." *Revista de humanidades: Tecnológico de Monterrey* 19 (2005): 101–116.

Pastore, Caela. "Mahogany as Status Symbol: Race and Luxury in Saint Domingue at the End of Eighteenth-Century." In *Furnishing the Eighteenth Century: What Furniture Can Tell Us About the European and American Past*, edited by Dena Goodman and Kathryn Norberg, 37–48. New York: Routledge, 2007.

Pérez, Louis A. "Cuba and the United States: Origins and Antecedents of Relations, 1760s–1860s." *Cuban Studies* 21 (1991): 57–82.

Perez-Garcia, Manuel. "Creating Global Demand: Polycentric Approaches, Crossroads of Silk and Silver in China and Iberian Empires During the Early Modern Era." *Revista de Historia Económica – Journal of Iberian and Latin American Economic History* 38, no. 3 (2020): 1–15.

Perez-Garcia, Manuel. "Mercados Globales de La América Española: El Comercio de Lana Vicuña y 'grana' Cochinilla en el Siglo XVIII." *América Latina En La Historia Económica* 23, no. 1 (2016): 184–222.

Perez-Garcia, Manuel, and Lucio De Sousa, eds. *Global History and New Polycentric Approaches - Europe, Asia and the Americas in a World Network System*. London: Palgrave Macmillan, 2018.
Pezuela, Jacobo de la. *Ensayo histórico de la isla de Cuba*. Madrid: Impr. española de R. Rafael, 1842.
Pretel, David, and Adrian Leonard, eds. *The Caribbean and the Atlantic World Economy Circuits of Trade, Money and Knowledge, 1650–1914*. New York: Palgrave MacMillan, 2015.
Priyadarshini, Meha. *Chinese Porcelain in Colonial Mexico*. New York: Palgrave MacMillan, 2018.
Salmoral, Manuel Lucena. "Leyes para esclavos: el ordenamiento jurídico sobre la condición, tratamiento, defensa y represión de los esclavos en las colonias de la América Española." In *Tres grandes cuestiones de la historia de Iberoamérica: ensayos y monografías*, edited by José Andrés-Gallego (dir.), 1–1384. Madrid: Fundación Ignacio Larramendi, 2011, 2000.
Salvucci, Linda K. "Supply, Demand, and the Making of a Market: Philadelphia and Havana at the beginning of the Nineteenth Century." In *Atlantic Port Cities. Economy, Culture, and Society in the Atlantic Word, 1650–1850*, edited by Franklin W. Knight, and Peggy K. Liss, 40–57. Knoxville: Universty of Tennessee Press, 1991.
Salvucci, Richard. *Textiles and Capitalism in Mexico: An Economic History of the Obrajes, 1539–1840*. Princeton, NJ: Princeton University Press, 1987.
Sarmiento, Ismael. "Alimentación y relaciones sociales en la Cuba colonial." *Anales del Museo de América* 11 (2003): 197–226.
Sarmiento, Ismael. "Del 'funche' al 'ajiaco': la dieta que los amos imponen a los esclavos africanos en Cuba y la asimilación que éstos hacen de la cocina criolla." *Anales del Museo de América* 16 (2008): 127–154.
Schnakenbourg, Eric. "Neutral Cover and Globalised Commerce in the Wars of the 18th Century." *Magallanica: Revista de Historia Moderna* 5, no. 10 (2019): 57–77.
Schneider, Elena. "African Slavery and Spanish Empire: Imperial Imaginings and Bourbon Reform in Eighteenth-Century Cuba and Beyond." *Journal of Early American History* 5, no. 1 (2015): 3–29.
Shrum, Rebecca K. *In the Looking Glass: Mirrors and Identity in Early America*. Baltimore, MD: Johns Hopkins University Press, 2017.
Sierra, Luis María de la. *Memoria sobre el estado del comercio que publica la Real Junta de Santander*, Santander. 1833.
Suárez, Rosalía Oliva. "Los espacios domésticos habaneros entre 1650 y 1750." PhD diss., Universidad de Granada, 2014. Accessed 23 November 2020. https://dialnet.unirioja.es/servlet/tesis?codigo=58409.
Taber, Robert D., and Charlton W. Yingling. "Networks, Tastes, and Labor in Free Communities of Color: Transforming the Revolutionary Caribbean." *Atlantic Studies* 14, no. 3 (2017): 263–274.
Tarragó, Rafael E. *Understanding Cuba as a Nation: From European Settlement to Global Revolutionary Mission*. London: Routledge, 2017.
Torre, José María de la. *Lo que fuimos y lo que somos: o, La Habana antigua y moderna*. La Habana: Imp. de Spencer y compañía, 1857.
Yacou, Alain. "La présence française dans la partie occidentale de l'île de Cuba au lendemain de la révolution de Saint-Domingue. *Outre-Mers*." *Revue d'histoire* 74, no. 275 (1987): 149–188.
Yelvington, Kevin A., Jean-Pierre Sainton, Michel Hector, and Jean Casimir. "Caribbean Social Structure in the Nineteenth-Century." In *General History of the Caribbean: The Long Nineteenth Century – Nineteenth-Century Transformations*, edited by K. O. Laurence, Vol. IV: 25–56. UNESCO: Unesco Publishing, 2011.
Zeuske, Michael. "Historiography and Research Problems of Slavery and the Slave Trade in a Global-Historical Perspective." *International Review of Social History* 57 (2012): 87–111.

Local failures of global companies: the slave trade in the Rio de la Plata, 1786–1790

Antonio Ibarra

ABSTRACT
This research focuses on the operations of the Royal Company of the Philippines in the global market, in particular on the slave trade between Africa and Spanish America, as a way to examine the local dimensions of global trade. It identifies the causes and consequences of a failed venture that, despite its failure, opened a new cycle in the Río de la Plata slave trade and its place in the global economy of the late eighteenth century.

The problem: the local scale of global commerce of the enslaved

The study of African and Afro descendants' slavery in the Río de la Plata has a long tradition. Indeed, since the 1950s attention has been drawn to the early entry of slaves into the region, who were supposed to fill the absence of the indigenous workforce, stimulate the internal market, and boost long-distance trade.[1]

New research on the volume, origins and introduction of enslaved workers, based on the work of Alex Borucki and the "Slave voyages" database, has provided more robust data for assessing the role of slavery in the Río de la Plata economy.[2]

In terms of the total volume of the slave trade, the number of enslaved workers in this region was marginal compared with the larger Atlantic world, but it had a significant impact on the local economies where slaves carried out various activities, ranging from domestic labor and agriculture to animal husbandry. Slaves were, furthermore, a medium of exchange for trade with Lima and the Alto Peru region, making their care and export particularly important.[3]

The Spanish Crown itself, however, did not directly manage or operate the slave trade, due both to its inability to compete with foreign companies and to reduce smuggling; therefore, it chose a policy of slave trade contracts (*asientos*) from the late sixteenth century to the late eighteenth century. Finally, within the framework of the new regulations on free trade (*Comercio Libre*), licenses were granted to individuals, first Spanish and later on foreigners, leading to the formation of companies dedicated to the direct importation of Africans in the late eighteenth and early nineteenth centuries.

This essay focuses on an exceptional case run, "by means of trial," by the Royal Company of the Philippines (RCP) which, through royal permissions, tried to carry out a triangular trade in European goods, enslaved Africans, American silver, and East Asian merchandise.[4] The episode attests to the complex and intricate remaking of Spanish trade across its empire, an empire segmented by corporative prohibitions, fiscal barriers and local interests. While these obstacles to freer trade significantly decreased the King's income, they gave cohesion to imperial governance.[5]

The attempt at change, in this case through the royal concession granted to a private company of monarchical interest, underlines Spanish commercial dependency on its British counterpart, the incompetence of the Crown's bureaucracy, as well as the strength of local colonial interests. Moreover, the failure of the enterprise illuminates the obsolescence of the monopoly, the fragility of the Company's management system, and the power of local actors. I am therefore interested in exploring and assessing the local conditions of global trafficking.[6]

Privileges and failures of a slaver company

On 7 September 1789, Don Martín de Sarratea, representative for the Royal Company of the Philippines in Buenos Aires, addressed a petition to the Viceroy, requesting that the Royal Company be exempted from the payment of the first-sale *alcabala* (sale tax) to the enslaved "led from Africa," at its account and risk, according to the privilege granted by the *Real cédula* (royal decree) of 28 February 1789. The concession referred to a new trade policy through which the Crown withdrew the granting of slave trade contracts to foreign companies, replacing it with the newly created Philippines Company, thereby creating a new model of direct navigation between Africa and the Río de la Plata "by means of trial."[7]

As Fernando Jumar and Alex Borucki have shown, there were three phases in the Río de la Plata trafficking from 1680 to 1780, namely: the French *asiento* between 1701 and 1712; the English *asiento* from 1713 to 1739 and, as a continuity, the long Portuguese presence in the Colonia de Sacramento, stretching from 1680 to 1777.[8] With Viceroy Cevallos' eviction of the Portuguese from Colonia and the formation of the Viceroyalty of Río de la Plata, the RCP and other Spanish subjects noticed the opportunity to take control of the slave trade to Spanish America, which, either on their own or in partnership with foreign investors, promised substantial profits.[9]

A previous, failed attempt to take control over direct trafficking through the islands of Fernando Po and Annobon in the Gulf of Guinea relinquished by the Portuguese in the Treaty of San Idelfonso, had been costly in resources and lives. Had it been successful, this sally would have allowed the embarkation of enslaved Africans from a Spanish port in Africa (*factoría*) and would have opened up a triangular trade between Cádiz and the African coast with South America and with the Philippines.[10]

The Philippines Company expeditions took place in the interim years between the taking of Colonia and the opening of the Río de la Plata market to individuals, both nationals and foreigners, in 1791. However, as Borucki has shown, the Portuguese in Brazil continued to dominate the African slave trade, as they supplied 60 percent of the laborers that forcibly entered through the ports of the Río de la Plata from 1777 to 1812.[11]

As Elena F. S. de Studer has explained in her classical study, the Bourbon strategy allowed the granting of licenses to individuals for the trade of enslaved Africans within the framework of the *Comercio Libre* policy (1789–1791).[12] However, until that moment, it had not been possible to reconcile the interests of the King with the expectations of the local American-based merchants, hence the decision to privilege the Royal Company of the Philippines.[13] In this context, this study will examine, through the RCP, the agency of local actors in the traffic, in order to explain why the RCP failed, as well as the consequences for future slave trading and the inherent contradictions of the RCP's strategy.

Business "by means of trial": enslaved Africans, partners and losses

The representative of the Royal Company of the Philippines in Buenos Aires, when assessing the new initiative, described the following in the footnote of a table that testified to the failure of the slave trade venture:

> In the preceding accounting – *Estado* – it is provable that, of the 2833 slaves that the nominated vessels took from Bonny, 656 died at sea; and that, having the Captains delivered 2177 including 3 found in Montevideo to have traveled furtively, 509 died in that place and in this capital [Buenos Aires], which, merged with the former, compose the number [of dead slaves] of 1165. Of the residual 1668 slaves, I dispatched 1073 to Lima and 594 were sold here and in Montevideo, their verified sale producing 161772 *pesos*, resting one more [unsold] due to being old and ailing.[14]

The testimony summarizes the market structures, the logic of the trafficking, and the costs that a failed slave trade venture had for the Company; a venture which, nevertheless, brought benefits to the global and local actors of trafficking.

Five components can be identified in Sarratea's description, namely: (1) The process of "production of the slave," materialized in the "appropriation and delivery" carried out by African traders, and their transportation on the "nominated vessels," belonging to a British global company; (2) The "delivery" by the "Captains" inasmuch as it was an Atlantic navigation company, subject to loading and unloading rules that implied "losses and contingencies," which translated into deaths; (3) The contraband of enslaved workers "who came furtively," who upon arrival became items of commerce and found an outlet on the market; (4) The *internación* or slave trade to the Andean region all the way to Lima, which was the provider of specie and the engine of the global circulation of the enslaved and, finally; (5) The balances of the slave market, which responded to a price structure based on the expected utility in relation to the age and the potential uses of those held captive, in concurrence with the demand effect: the "old and ailing" was the squandering of commerce and denied of humanity by trafficking.

These are the keys by which I explain the role of a mixed imperial venture, the Philippines Company, driven by the interests both of the King and of individuals in a monopolistic model that showed its limitations early on, related both to its competitive inabilities and to market failures.[15] Through this observation, I explore these statements – as a stylization of a historical process and in a specific moment – and into the position of the actors, witnesses and agents of the interests embedded in the slave trade in the Río de la Plata.[16]

When the Philippines Company decided to connect Cadiz with the Western coast of Africa, the coast of Coromandel in India and the Philippines with the coast of Canton, using American silver as the lever of global business, their global market project linked two routes that were to be complementary: the first, forcefully bringing Africans to

Spanish America, first to Buenos Aires and then from Mendoza to Chile, continuing on from the port of Valparaiso to Lima; the second, carrying silver to the East and bringing commodities that were to be financed during the first leg of the route.[17]

The circulation model that connected the Spanish American routes of the South Atlantic with the western coast of Africa was the goal of the partnership between the Company and British slave traders, an exercise both in learning and in military cunning to avoid the uncertainties of a sea ravaged by corsairs and enemy warships.[18]

To this effect, this Spanish company entered into a contract with the Baker & Dawson Company – an old acquaintance that was already transporting enslaved people to the Spanish Caribbean – to acquire two of James McTaggart's ships from the port of Bristol. The ships would embark enslaved Africans and then make the Atlantic voyage towards Spanish American ports on the account and risk of the Philippines Company, sailing first with a British flag to freely roam the seas and a Spanish one upon entry into the Rio de la Plata.[19] Another three ships were acquired in London from Fermen de Tastet (also known as Fermín de Tastet) to make the journey to Bonny (Africa) and carry slaves to Montevideo.[20]

The "Prince" or "Príncipe" – as it was called in Buenos Aires – was a 273-ton vessel, armed with six cannons and recently built in Bristol (1785), where it was registered as a slave ship (1787). The vessel set out sailing with a British flag in the same port on 28 July 1787, arriving in Buenos Aires waving a Spanish flag on 25 October 1788 under the command of Captain James Clurg and with a crew of 34 sailors. It had started with 427 Africans, but only disembarked 355 since 72 perished during the journey, a 17 percent mortality rate.[21] The ship "Princesa" was a 259-ton ship with four mounted weapons, built in Bristol (1779) and registered in the same place on the eve of its departure for Bonny, on 28 July 1787. There, it forcibly loaded 421 people, though only 350 arrived in Buenos Aires, 71 having died on the journey, again with a mortality rate of 17 percent. Its crew consisted of 27 sailors under the orders of Captain Charles Sloper.[22] Once unloaded, these ships returned with local products to Santander in July 1788, on their journey back to Bristol. The British company closed its business with the chartering of the ships and the delivery of the cargo, apparently leaving the business.

Three other British ships crossed the Atlantic with the English flag and conducted by Fermen de Tastet's company, arriving in the Río de la Plata under Spanish flag and carrying slaves for the Royal Company of the Philippines.[23] Another ship, built in Liverpool in 1784 and bought in London in 1788, was "Spanified" for further navigation.[24] The first arrivals, on 1 September 1788, docked in Montevideo carrying 688 slaves, having embarked 1072 in Africa and losing 384 in the journey. The business had been devastated by the death of so many Africans. In some cases, the mortality averages doubled from the conventional rate, as it will be shown below. The first to arrive was the *Elizabeth*, alias "El Indiano," commanded by Thomas Wallace. It was a new 240-ton ship, built in Stockton (1785) and registered in London, which began its sailing on 7 April 1788, in route to Bonny, where it forcibly shipped 470 people, disembarking in Montevideo with 241 slaves, and having 229 African deaths during the journey, that is, almost half (49 percent). Its captain returned to London after almost a year's journey, on 17 May 1789.[25] That same day, another vessel under the alias of "El Africano" arrived in Montevideo. It was a ship lower in tonnage (373), built in the shipyards of Hull (1782) and registered for sailing in London (1788), where it began its voyage to Bonny on 11 May 1788, commanded by Captain John Smith and having forcefully shipped 602 enslaved on the African coast, of which 155 perished during the journey, a death rate of 26 percent. The last ship, owned by Fermen de Tastet and leased by the Philippines Company, called "La Favorita," with capacity of up to 225 tons and under the command of Captain Joseph Banfield, forcefully carried 466 enslaved people off New Calabar, between 12 August 1788 and 12 February 1789, of which 393 arrived alive and 73 died during the journey, a mortality rate of 16 percent. The vessel returned to London, now as the "Favourite" in September 1788. The balance of the agreement with Tastet's company was particularly disastrous, with 457 enslaved Africans lost in the high seas over the 1538 shipped, averaging a 30 percent in mortality losses. At the time, the average mortality rate of slave voyages varied between 12 and 17 percent.[26]

In addition to the arrivals chartered by the Royal Company there was a "Spanified" British vessel, also named "Elizabeth," built in Liverpool in 1784 and bought in London in 1788, shipping on 27 May under the command of John Marshall in route to Bonny, where it forcibly loaded 546 enslaved Africans, of which 388 arrived alive in Montevideo on 1 September, less 158 who died aboard, a rate of 29 percent, with no difference regarding the average of the rest of the commissions.[27]

The Company of Bristol undertook ten transatlantic voyages with enslaved workers in the period stretching from 1773 to 1788. During this period, it loaded 3112 slaves and it disembarked 2682, with a death rate of 14 percent for its voyages, mainly women (52 percent) and children (24 percent). Their routes were circumscribed in the British Caribbean circuit – that is, Jamaica, Saint Lucia, Saint Vincent and Grenada – and the last two bound for Buenos Aires. Their extraction areas were Bight of Biafra, the Bight of Benin, and the Gold Coast. In this case, all arriving to Río de la Plata came from the Bight of Biafra.

It is interesting to note that the Company of Bristol is the one that best fulfilled its mission, with lower costs and shorter journeys. In contrast, the most relevant cost fell on the negotiations with Fermen de Tastet, due perhaps to the mismanagement of the captains of his vessels. This persuaded the RCP that trafficking on behalf of third parties would not yield the greatest benefit in the Río de la Plata when compared to the Portuguese traders and those who managed the supply and prices of slaves on their own.

The report that Sarratea presented to the Board (*Junta de Gobierno*) of the RCP testifies to the losses at sea and land, the sale and remission, as well as an estimate of the net value of the slaves that were negotiated based on the Company's revenue (Table 1).

Land mortality is the most significant, since it represented 77 percent of navigation deaths when the hardships increased due to diseases, mistreatment or lack of adequate living spaces. Deaths on land, for their part, showed deficiencies in the infrastructure and an incapacity to guarantee the recovery of the Africans' health, as well as a poor management of trafficking from the port of quarantine, Montevideo, to the port of sale: dysentery was lethal for the newly arrived, but so were depression, suicides, and cultural and physical violence inflicted by the slave companies.[28]

An initial conclusion points to the numbers of lost lives, both at sea and on land, as a cause of failure of the venture. Yet, a closer examination of the performance of each ship allows some additional observations. The first contract, which loaded 30 percent of the enslaved workers boarded at Bonny, had an average of sea losses of around 20 percent

Table 1. Net number of movements of slaves from boarding in Boni to remission to Lima and income per capita.

Ship	Captain	Boarded in Bonni	Delivered Montevideo	Dead at sea	Dead Montevideo	Dead Buenos Aires	Dead at land	Sold	Sent to Lima	Total Income	Cash Per cápita
Príncipe	Jayme Clourgh	427	355	72							
Princesa	Carlos Sloper	421	350	71							
Sum		**848**	**705**	**143**	**75**	**89**	**164**	**326**	**215**	**$ 88,850.00**	**$ 272.55**
Indiano	Tomas Wallace	470	241	229							
Africano	Juan Smith	602	447	155							
Favorita	José Banfield	466	393	73							
Elizabeth	Juan Marshall	446	388	58							
Sum		**1984**	**1469**	**515**	**269**	**76**	**345**	**268**	**858**	**$ 72,922.00**	**$ 126.03**
Total		**2832**	**2174**	**658**	**344**	**165**	**509**	**594**	**1073**	**$ 161,772.00**	

Note: (*) "tres recaudados en Montevideo de estas expediciones".

Source: My own elaboration based on data from "Estado general que manifiesta el numero de piezas de Esclavos que cargaron en Boni las fragatas nombradas Príncipe, Princesa, Indiano, Africano, Favorita y Elisavet (sic) de Cuenta de la R(ea)l Compañía de Filipinas: los que entregaron en Montevideo; muertos en la navegación, en d(ic)ha plaza y esta Capital; su venta; remisión con destino a Lima, existencia; total de los que me hice cargo y valor de los vendidos."AGNA, Colonia/Gobierno/Hacienda, IX 33-6-1 (2878).

Table 2. Number of slaves boarded at Boni in ships belonging to the Real Compañía de Filipinas, arrived at Rio de la Plata, 1785–1786.

Ship	Captain	Boarded at Boni	Delivered MTV/ boarded	Dead at sea/ boarded	Dead at sea/ delivered
Príncipe	James Clourgh	15.1%	83.1%	17%	20.3%
Princesa	Charles Sloper	15%	83.1%	17%	20.3%
Sum		**30.0%**	**83.1%**	**17%**	**20.3%**
Indiano	Thomas Wallace	16.6%	51.3%	48.7%	95.0%
Africano	Jhon Smith	21.3%	74.3%	25.7%	34.7%
Favorita	Joseph Banfield	16.4%	84.7%	15.3%	18.1%
Elizabeth	John Marshall	15.8%	87.0%	13.0%	15%
Sum		**70.0%**	**74.3%**	**26%**	**35%**
Total		**100%**	**77%**	**17%**	**20.3%**

Source: My own elaboration based on data from AGNA, Colonia/Gobierno/Hacienda, IX 33-6-1 (2878).

over the total delivered: Clough and Sloper fulfilled what was expected. The second consignment – which accounted for 70 percent of the business – performed more poorly, since the losses at sea were on average a third of those delivered. Here, the catastrophe that was the navigation of Wallace's *Indiano* stands out: only half of those who were loaded in Africa were delivered in Montevideo (Table 2).

At this point, the information allows me to draw some conclusions that highlight the variable luck of partnerships undertaken by the RCP. From the contract with the Baker & Dawson Company, using James McTaggart ships, the results were, according to Studer, relatively acceptable: there was a 32 percent mortality in navigation, 705 having arrived at the port of Montevideo, of which 326 were sold in that venue and 195 were sent to Lima and Chile. Of the 541 that were successfully sold, the RCP obtained 88,850 *pesos*, at a net average of 164 *pesos* per slave.[29] However, in the second contract, aboard vessels chartered in London and Liverpool, 1985 enslaved workers were loaded in Bonny and 1472 were delivered in the Río de la Plata, of which 1126 are estimated to have been sold: 268 in Buenos Aires and 858 sent to Lima. The Company reported an income from its 72,922 *pesos* sale, at a net average of 64 *pesos* and 6 *reales* per capita. In his communication to the Company's Board on 4 July 1791, Sarratea estimated a loss of 105,078 *pesos* for the death of 656 enslaved workers, at an average rate of 160 *pesos* and 1 *real* per African.[30]

The foregoing points to high operation costs since the value of the slaves' lives decreases in proportion to the increase in their price in relative terms, most notably in the second contract, when the company recovered barely 60 percent per capita in comparison to the first contract. Yet, in a closer examination it is also possible to observe the serious consequences of mismanagement on land, in addition to the losses at sea, since almost a quarter of the enslaved arrived in the ports and their effective sales were lost. Here, net estimates of the failed business in the Río de la Plata can be made, since only in the first contract 46 percent of the arrived were sold, and another 10 percent were sold in the second arrival, representing 70 percent of the business (Table 3).

Slave mortality was a factor in the failure of the venture since 41 percent of the captives died during transfer and acclimatization, considering that 2830 enslaved workers were embarked and 2174 were delivered, 656 having perished at sea, in addition to 344 more in Montevideo and 165 in Buenos Aires.[31]

Table 3. Slaves dead, sold, and sent to Lima in relation to those arrived in Montevideo in ships belonging to the Real Compañía de Filipinas, 1786–1788.

CONTRACTS/ captains	Dead in MTV/ arrived	Dead Bs As/ Arrived	Dead at land/ Arrived	Sold/ arrived	Delivered	Sent to Lima/ delivered
Clourgh/Sloper	10.6%	12.6%	23.3%	46.2%	32.4%	30.5%
Wallace/Smith Banfield/ Marshall	18.3%	5.2%	23.5%	10.2%	67.6%	58.3%
Total	**15.8%**	**7.6%**	**23.4%**	**27.3%**		**49.3%**

Source: My own elaboration based on data from AGNA, Colonia/Gobierno/Hacienda, IX 33-6-1 (2878).

According to the accounting records, 594 were sold in the ports and 1073 were sent to Lima through the western route that went to Mendoza, Santiago and Valparaiso. Of the first consignment of 907 enslaved workers sent to Lima, 27 died during transit, thus only 880 slaves were sold at a total of 322,080 *pesos,* at an average price of 366 *pesos* per capita (ppc). The transfer costs totaled 13.3 percent of the effective sale – equivalent to 42,382 *pesos*, while human losses, considering the average sale price, totaled 9882 *pesos*.

On the other hand, those who were sold in Buenos Aires and Montevideo added 89,387 *pesos* in revenue for the RCP: $61,739 from the enslaved sold in the first contract and $27,649 from the 111 enslaved sold in the second contract. The average price reached 202 *pesos* per capita, but the variance between the first (187 *pesos* per capita) and second contract (249 *pesos* per capita) represented a 33 percent increase driven by the cost of losses of the second contract.

The representative of the Philippines Company in Buenos Aires estimated, in his communication to the RCP on 4 July 1791, a loss of 105,078 pesos for the death of 656 enslaved workers, at an average rate of 160 *pesos* and 1 *real*.[32] If the sale price of the enslaved is adjusted with Sarratea's estimates, the divergence between the RCP's accounting and its *factor* is 26 percent, while the price hike between the first (+17 percent) and second contracts (+55 percent) and the sale in Lima (+128 percent), shows that, even if the business of taking slaves from Africa to Lima was a failure for the Company, the greatest benefit went to the merchants of Buenos Aires and their inland associates.[33]

In 1784, 1069 enslaved workers entered Lima by sea but, between the years of 1786 and 1789, the entry of slaves fell by half to 534, causing an increase in demand, from which the dispatch of slaves from Buenos Aires surely benefited.[34] An estimate over price sales in Lima between 1783 and 1789, based on the records of José Antonio Lavalle, show price levels between 480–550 *pesos* for men and 380–400 *pesos* for women.[35] In Lima, the Conde de San Isidro, one of the largest shareholders of the Company and resident in the city, was the one who received the preference of the *factores* – commercial representatives – and the advantages of prices, having in 1789 acquired a total of 140 slaves dispatched by the Company in his vessel, named "San Juan Nepomuceno," from Valparaiso.[36]

After 1791, trafficking in Buenos Aires returned to individual initiative, national and foreign, making way for the more dynamic cycle of the entry of enslaved workers, both by the Portuguese of Brazil who brought the enslaved from Bahia and Río de Janeiro, and from the African coast by merchants of the Río de la Plata, Brazil, and the United States.

The second shareholder of the Company in the Rio de la Plata, Antonio de Letamendi, confided to his partner in Cordoba (inland Argentina), Ambrosio Funes, who was also committed to the business of introducing enslaved workers, the following diagnosis of the situation:

> The Negroes still maintain their high price at 270–280 *Spanish pesos*, but with the many that have arrived, and who will not be sent to Chile, it follows that in this winter we will have more equity.[37]

A month later, Letamandi informed Funes in another letter that expectations had changed, thanks to the effect of the "*invernada*" (wintering) and the direct trade that generated confidence in better purchases and good sales:

> Negroes are in abundance, but their price is not declining: In this winter it is believed that they will be much cheaper, because some expeditions that have departed from here to bring them from the coasts of Africa are still to come: If this were to happen, of course, it was a business that promised utility, selling them to Peru in spring after the wintering here.[38]

For the people of the Río de la Plata, the logic of trade was buying low and selling high, something the Company was not able to understand on a global dimension; it considered that the instruments of fiscal privilege and the monopoly would be enough to penetrate the local market in Buenos Aires, lower the costs of entry and to finance their business in East Asia with Spanish American silver obtained from the "infamous trade." They were mistaken.

The organization of the business and its results

The privilege granted to the Royal Company of the Philippines for trafficking in South America, as I have described, was committed to generating capital that would provide liquidity to trade with the East. The Company's goal, as Borucki has pointed out, had its interest set on seizing tax revenue in Buenos Aires and Lima, which would later be used in negotiations in the Philippines.[39]

This global business model, based on shipping enslaved workers to America and on taking American silver to East Asia, implied that the organization was necessarily subjected to a complex chain of wills. The first will was, naturally, the "royal favor" and, later on, the acquiescence of the Assembly of Shareholders (Asamblea de accionistas) run by Minister Soler in agreement with the Conde de Galvez in Madrid. In its internal structure, the board – which responded to the Assembly of Shareholders, or *Junta de accionistas* – reached agreement on all important decisions with Soler and enforced them through their representatives in various loading and unloading points, in this case in Buenos Aires, Lima and Manila.

Among its duties, the Board (Junta de Gobierno) had to present account statements by transaction and by localities, attending to the reports of their representatives. But the case at hand must have seriously concerned the shareholders and Martin Antonio de Huizi, promoter for the business in London, was asked to prepare a balance of the "black trading account," in 1789.[40]

The general balance of 30 September of that year showed losses of 2,100,156 *reales de vellón* and 22 *maravedíes*, around 105,008 Spanish *pesos*. This included not only the deficit of slaves lost at sea and on land, but specifically the engineering that involved the deployment of resources and actors to mobilize the institutional apparatus, the partners and the employees, the seamen, the stranded costs of a company without a sufficient fleet of its own, without competent personnel, and enmeshed in a dense net of relationships with local actors, which privatized the benefits and transferred the losses to the RCP.

I focus on three internal elements to understand the failure of the "slave trade sally" in the Río de la Plata: first, the cost of navigation as a proportion of the expected and actual profits through the sale of enslaved people; second, the logistics chain of the management of trafficking, from the partnership with British merchants to operating expenses in the local scale of the transfer and sale of enslaved people; third, the stranded costs of the shipping operation and the fiscal pressure brought on by prolonged and costly negotiations with local American actors. In Huizi's accounting, the result shows a liability of "balance by loss" that barely reached 18 percent of the difference between the Debit and Credit columns. This accounting was designed to buffer the net impact of the losses in the company's finances, where what mattered most were the arguments in favor of the expected profits in future ventures.

An examination of the categories of expenses, separated from the returns, may help to establish a different margin of losses and their possible causes: firstly, the global navigation cost should be considered, trying to distinguish the two contracts separately and a total estimation; secondly, the series of expenses associated to the logistical chain and its stranded costs should be considered; thirdly, the number and value of the sold slaves must be computed according to Huizi's estimates of the business as a whole.

An inspection of the categories of navigation, using the distinctions given by the sources, shows that the cost of the ships considering their charter, habilitation, *rancho* (provisions) expenses and cargo effects, added up to 67,645 British pounds, equivalent to 500,022 Spanish *pesos*: 60 percent corresponded to "cargo effects," which are not specified as their own. The ships also transported cargo and operational resources for the Spanish Crown, which did not generate proceeds, but constituted a political obligation due to the benefits and privileges that had been granted.[41]

In net terms the cost of the fleet added up to 210,247 Spanish *pesos*: $83,011 for the cost of six ships, $107,012 for their habilitation and *rancho* – provisions – in addition to $20,195 for management expenses of the venture. Shipping, according to Huizi, entailed other additional operating expenses equivalent to 17,864 *pesos*, divided among many categories: (1) "Préstamos y gastos de los individuos españoles en Londres" [Loans and expenses of Spanish individuals in London]; (2) "Corretajes, portes de cartas y sellos de letras en Londres" [Brokerage, bill of lading shipping charges, and letter seals in London], (3) "Por asignaciones pagadas en San Sebastián y Cádiz de los individuos españoles que fueron en estas Expediciones" [Allowances paid in San Sebastián and Cadiz to Spanish individuals who went in these trips]; (4) "Por Bestuario (sic) y otras provisiones remitidas desde la Coruña a Buenos Aires" [Clothing and other provisions sent from La Coruña to Buenos Aires].

The first category included the expenses of the Spanish officials and sailors sent to Britain with the purpose of becoming involved in the knowledge of navigation, since they would be in charge of future Spanish slave voyages. These were the men who would receive stipends for their performance on the travels, which could be considered as costs of apprenticeship (*costos de instrucción*).

More interesting are the costs associated with the financial management of the expeditions since the RCP was forced to resort to a simulated issuance of debt, operating as a company financed from Madrid but involved in the circulation of securities in London. Hence, the expenses for brokerage and acknowledgement of debt were relevant to expectations for the success of the venture.

The value of the load represented 58 percent of the total amount that was executed in the set of contracts: 39,202 British pounds, equivalent to an estimate of 289,775 Spanish *pesos*. On this basis, expenses were accumulated in the habilitation and *rancho* – provisions – of the ships (21 percent), while extra expenses (4 percent) totaled more than ten million *reales de vellón*, equivalent to over 500,000 Spanish *pesos*.[42] These were the calculations presented by Huizi to inform the shareholders.

Additionally, other operating expenses show the financial management of the venture: 105,554 Spanish *pesos* were added for items ranging from loans and expenses on the way from London to Buenos Aires ($38,171) to stopover and unloading expenses in Cadiz ($1387), Montevideo ($23,729), and in "disassembling and adjustment" in Cádiz and at the end of the journey ($42,267). The total costs of the venture had risen to 685,025 Spanish *pesos*, equivalent to more than thirteen million *reales de vellón*.

The accountants of the Company were only able to cover a sale total for 126,135 Spanish *pesos*: $89,387 from the sale of slaves, 70 percent of which correspond to the first sale and the rest to the second one, which turned out to be disastrous. The freight recovery of 14,238 *pesos* represented just over 11 percent, and a load of pelts sold in London accounted for 12 percent of the Company's income. If this was so then, as of 30 September 1790, 25 percent of the original investment had been recovered.

A confidential report to the Spanish Finance Minister clearly reveals the problems with the business model, questioning both its aims and its results and, specifically, the debts to the Real Hacienda over amounts advanced and unfulfilled taxes:

> As the Company needed funds in Lima and Buenos Aires, the Direction thought that the exclusive commerce of blacks for Peru and the provinces of the Rio de la Plata would be an efficient way to acquire them. The King agreed if this were to be a trial so that the Nation could over time make this direct commerce from the coasts of Africa. The Permit was issued requesting an economy regarding the sale of Negroes *a costo y costas*, demanding an exact account to present to the Ministry justified with the respective collection of its consignments taken by the Superintendents or Royal Ministries of America. The expeditions would be carried from the ports of Spain in national vessels. The Direction later obtained a license to buy the vessels and dispatch them from their ports to sell *peso fuerte por sencillo* [spanish dollars for common currency] at the price that was calculated and marked by the respective Superintendents of the Royal Treasure and the commissioners of the Company, setting the approximate calculation al *costo y costas*. Also, it was granted that four of the six expeditions that were made to Buenos Aires returned with freight to the ports of England.[43]

As noted earlier, the contracts were disadvantageous, the handling of the "merchandise" was messy, the infrastructure was inappropriate, the management and cost of British financing was expensive, as were the navigation and liquidation costs, the port sales were inconsistent, and the forceful transfer of people was advantageous only for the local merchants in Buenos Aires and further inland. From the viewpoint of the Ministry of the Royal Treasure (Ministerio de Real Hacienda), the business model – paid at its expenses and without any fiscal return – was disastrous for the King's finances:

> There have been no savings. The Negroes have been of very bad quality and have been sold at excessive prices. All the political goals of the Ministry have been frustrated. Nothing of what was stipulated was achieved. The Royal Treasure has not been reimbursed for the supplements that had been made to the Company in Lima and Buenos Aires as it was offered by the Direction with the sales product of the Negroes, on the contrary it [the Royal Treasure] is owed the rights of these [sales] and of the returns that ascend to 72,432 *pesos*.[44]

Thus, it is possible to return to the starting point. The dispute between the *Real Hacienda* and the Philippines Company revolved around the tax privileges and the exemption of taxes, but it also involved the monopoly on sales and its insolvency to comply with the charges made to the King's finances in the Royal Treasury (*Reales Cajas*) of Buenos Aires and Lima. These were issues that were not settled until years later. At any rate, slave trafficking on behalf of the Company had a premature end. The conclusion of the confidential report to the Finance Minister was definitive:

> It is said however that the Direction [of the RCP, AI] undertook this commerce driven by the Ministry to contribute to its goals and administration. Administration without fulfilling any of the conditions of its permit and trial dispatching of course six expeditions in which ten million were spent, are two things that are not understood.[45]

Conclusions

Enmeshed in an imperial logic of trafficking, this episode testifies to the complexities and disruptions of the global strategy adopted by the Royal Company of the Philippines and, more clearly, the obsolescence of monopolistic practices which had dominated trade with Spanish America from the 1590s to 1780s. After the imperial rearrangement of the Seven Years' War, the moment of commercial globalization throughout the world showed Spanish decline, British hegemony and the repositioning of actors in the Americas who were in the control of global businesses on a local scale.

The nature of the slave trade market, imposed by British control over the sale and shipment of slaves in the transatlantic world and demand of forced labor on plantations (particularly in the Caribbean) as well as the irruption of Anglo-Americans and their plantations into the business, led to the end of price regulation through the competitive advantages of the monopoly.[46] The episode is particularly meaningful for the Río de la Plata, since it shows the changes within an era and in the sense of the benefits of American trafficking, which rested on local actors as managers of its benefits.

The Philippines Company showed its shortcomings in the organization of trafficking, the financing of shipping, the lack of infrastructure and the high costs of provisioning, in crew remuneration and in the negotiations with British ship-owners and shipping companies. Mortality at sea and on land did not compensate for the investments, nor did sales and the prices of the internal slave trade to Lima; instead, this operation transferred the benefits to the local market and to American logistics. In short, the failure of the venture is an eloquent episode revealing the complexity of the global market on a local level, testifying at the same time to the archaism of privilege: a new era in business made the efforts to preserve monopolistic practices costly at a time when the benefits of free trade were increasingly manifest.

In his defense of the Philippines Company's privilege, Sarratea made rhetorical arguments which had been already been presented to the King to authorize the venture and facilitate its financing with resources from the *Real Hacienda* in order to omit sanctions and avoid bankruptcy:

> Which graces and which freedoms are not presumable in favor of the Royal Company that made its first attempts at its own cost, with six large expeditions in times in which it lacked the knowledge that are acquired with practice and experience? [...] it was the first and only that risked its assets in the draft of Negroes, the one that, at the expense of immense losses, served as stimulus to other nationals and that, therefore, has better backings to expect a total liberation of fees.[47]

This was the stance Sarratea maintained for more than a decade in the dispute with Juan José Núñez, administrator of the Royal custom office in Buenos Aires, since Sarratea requested the exemption of duties in September 1789, up until September 1800, when he won the conflict. The royal decree confirmed the privilege of exemption to the RCP and the validity of the benefits granted to the trafficking of the enslaved, in addition to ordering the return of forty thousand *pesos,* pawned as a security bond for the payment of taxes, closing the institutional chapter of a commercial failure in 1800.

The local actors who staged a legal fight backed by their corporate representations – the *Real Hacienda* and the RCP – concluded a series of confrontations that involved Viceroy Arredondo, the *Tribunal de cuentas,* the Judge for civil matters, Marqués de la Plata, and the prosecutor for the *Real Hacienda,* Don Ángel Izquierdo, who brought forward the possibility of the King deciding over the resolution of the conflict. The King's determination favored the RCP, strengthened Sarratea's local position, and established a precedent for the privilege that the Company enjoyed.

Future research will entail exploring the purchase-sale contracts that followed the introduction of the Company in order to identify its beneficiaries.

It is already known that the costs of the failed company fell to the Royal Treasury (*Real Hacienda*), but the benefits were diluted in the commerce of the Río de la Plata. Perhaps this failure allowed the people of the Río de la Plata to remake their strategies and obtain the institutional grant of permits to become the new slave traders. They reaped the greatest benefits of the Crown's bad business, as well as inaugurating a good project for future business in the following decade. Trafficking in the Río de la Plata experienced a new boom from 1790 until 1812. In fact, after the revolution of independence in Buenos Aires, the local merchants would leave the infamous commerce and turn to privateering with their Anglo-American partners, precisely against Spanish slaver ships. Thus, swirls the loop of History.

Notes

1. Classical studies of slave trade in Buenos Aires and Córdoba were Molinari, *La trata de negros*; Studer, *La trata de negros*; Molina, *Las primeras experiencias*; and Assadourian, *El tráfico de esclavos*. Here I will refer primarily to studies on the Atlantic slave trade and the circulation of slaved workers in the internal market. While they fall beyond the scope of my research, I acknowledge the value of the contributions made by Garavaglia, "The Economic Role"; Gelman, "Sobre esclavos, peones"; and Amaral, "Rural Production," to understand the ways in which slaves were included in the Rio de la Plata economy.
2. At the end of his exhaustive research, Borucki concludes that 70,000 people were forcibly introduced to the Río de la Plata between 1777 and 1812, of which about 40 percent arrived directly from Africa and the rest from Brazil, through Montevideo and Buenos Aires.

The largest repository of information regarding trafficking is available in https://www.slavevoyages.org. For a periodization of regional trafficking, see Borucki, Eltis and Wheat, "Atlantic History," 433–461. Research done by Maximiliano Camarda at the Buenos Aires archives focuses on the perspective of local actors of the slave trade. See Camarda, "Una aproximación," 43–71, and more extensively his PhD dissertation, *La Región Rio de la Plata*.

3. For an evolution of the subject, in a wide spectrum of interests, see the account of Vela, "Encuentros intelectuales," 199–211. Regarding Afro-descendants, Rosal's book offers a broad description of the life of "Afroporteños" in the eighteenth and nineteenth centuries.
4. The venture was studied by Díaz-Trechuelo, *La Real Compañía*, 222–226, in her study of the Company and by Studer, *La trata de negros*, 244–246, in his exhaustive book on African slavery in the Rio de la Plata; however, due to the approach taken and the scale of his research – a general study of the company and the flow of slaves – he did not focus on the significance of this episode. The approach of my own research, considering the "trial" as part of a global market strategy, makes other contours of the problem visible.
5. As Díaz-Trechuelo's classic study explains, the Royal Company of the Philippines was a partnership between the Crown and merchants who sought competitive advantage in royal privilege, once the Royal Guipuzcoan Company of Caracas had been liquidated. Strictly speaking, the RCP intended an integration of the circulation of Asian goods that would overcome the power accumulated by the *Consulado de Comercio de Mexico*, which had controlled the transit between the Philippines and Europe. It also aspired to create an organization equivalent to its English, Dutch, and French counterparts that would corporatize global control of colonial trade. In this context, trafficking was a "trial" in a broader business strategy. Díaz-Trechuelo, *La Real Compañía*, 33–58.
6. For an updated view on global history, from a Latin American perspective, see the work of Hausberger, *La globalización temprana*.
7. This was made known to the Viceroy of the Rio de la Plata, in a communication from the Marques de Sonora of 2 June 1787, answered on 27 September of the same year, instructing him "para su inteligencia y gobierno, y a fin de que al arribo de los Buques de este comercio a cualquiera de los puertos de la comprensión de ese Virreinato los admita, proteja y procure despachar con la brevedad posible para evitar gastos en su demora que han de recaer forzosamente en el valor de los Negros cuyo comercio se procura fomentar" ["for his intelligence and government, and with the aim that, upon arrival in any of the ports of this Viceroyalty, the ships of this commerce are to be admitted, protected, and dispatched soon in order not to incur in expenses by the delay, expenses which may forcefully fall on the value of Negroes whose commerce is to be encouraged."] Archivo General de Indias (hereafter AGI), *Reales Ordenes* 1787–1788. Reproduced in Molinari, *La trata de negros*, 511–512.
8. Jumar, "El comercio rioplatense," 22–98; Borucki, "Notas sobre el tráfico," 7–28.
9. Regarding the French *asiento*, see Jumar's Ph.D. thesis "Le commerce atlantique au Río de la Plata," as well as Jumar and Paredes, "El comercio rioplatense," 33–98. See a panoramic vision of trafficking in the Rio de la Plata in Borucki, *De compañeros de barco*; see also Crespi's vision, "El comercio de esclavos," 237–252, on sources and themes.
10. Studer, *La trata de negros*, 239–253; Berquist, "Early Anti-Slavery Sentiment," 188.
11. Borucki, "The Slave Trade," 81–107. A global vision for Luso-Spanish America, in the classic text by Klein, *The Atlantic Slave Trade*.
12. Studer, *La trata de negros*, 255–270.
13. Borucki, "Notas sobre el tráfico," 20; Medeiros, *O trafico de escravos*, 80–85.
14. "Estado general que manifiesta el numero de piezas de Esclavos que cargaron en Boni las fragatas nombradas Príncipe, Princesa, Indiano, Africano, Favorita y Elisavet (*sic*) de Cuenta de la R(ea)l Compañía de Filipinas: los que entregaron en Montevideo; muertos en la navegación, en d(ic)ha plaza y esta Capital; su venta; remisión con destino a Lima, existencia; total de los que me hice cargo y valor de los vendidos." Archivo General de la Nación Argentina, Buenos Aires (hereafter AGNA) IX, 33-6-1. The translations are mine, and I hope the readers will excuse any errors on my part, considering the difficulties that the Spanish formal documents present even for Spanish speakers. I have tried to remain as faithful as possible to the original

meaning and have kept the Spanish expressions between brackets when I could not find a satisfying translation.

15. The case has already been addressed in Studer's classic study *La trata de negros*, 274–277, with a more anecdotal than analytical intention, about the failure of the Royal Company of the Philippines.
16. Thus, were the terms used to refer to slaves. For a critical appraisal of the "infame comercio," see Medeiros, *O tráfico de escravos*.
17. The route was comprised of 370 leagues and the Andean crossing, through the Uspallata Pass, the great obstacle of the journey. Crespi, "El comercio de esclavos," 243. See also Sobarzo's recent work on this, "La garganta del comercio," 345–384.
18. In the report of the project it was said that "On the 4th of this month two slave '*negreras*' vessels of 350 tons each were to depart Bristol to Bonny owned by the Company, even if in appearance English, in which several young Spaniards that have some training in Commerce and Sailing are embarked in order to be instructed in this traffic and navigation and [thus] become capable of directing by themselves similar expeditions in the future. In this [venture] the Classified Plan has been followed, a plan that was communicated to the Company by the illustrious zeal of His Excellency Count de Floridablanca by way of His Excellency Deceased President the Marquis of Sonora" in "Memoria de las primeras operaciones de la Real Compañía de Filipinas y su estado actual" 1787. AGI/Filipinas, 986. I thank Alex Borucki for the generous transmission of the summary of the text.
19. It was the English vessels *Prince* and *Pilgrim*, respectively named "El Príncipe" and "La Princesa" upon their arrival in Buenos Aires. Studer argues that the *Príncipe* entered under the alias of *Alexandro*. Studer, *La trata de negros*, 274.
20. Two named *Elizabeth*, one registered upon arrival as "El Indiano" and another as "El Africano," while the third *Favorite* was named "La Favorita."
21. The English vessel's name is "Prince." https://www.slavevoyages.org, voyage no. 18008. Bonny was located in the region known Bight of Biafra, the region with the highest mortality rate in all of transatlantic trafficking.
22. https://www.slavevoyages.org, voyage no. 18275.
23. Fermín de Tastet would be the "broker" between the PRC and the British slavers of the East Indian Company, thanks to his political ties and commercial agency. He offered shipping, commercial and financial services: he was an intermediary who, along with his brother Antonio, formed companies involved in trafficking and Asian trade. His services to the RCP surely brought him a good income. "Fermin Tastet – says Aragón in his study about the brothers – served as the representative of the Royal Company of the Philippines in London from at least 1783. In 1788 Fermín Tastet, who had been designated plenipotentiary by the Spanish Crown on 9 June of that same year, met with the chairman, Nathaniel Smith, and the secretary, Thomas Morton, of the East India Company with a view to entering into trade negotiations. Although a commercial treaty authorizing the East India Company to supply the Royal Company of the Philippines with goods was indeed drafted in 1788, the changes proposed by Fermín Tastet were not accepted." Aragón Ruano, 13–15. I thank Alex Borucki for this information.
24. https://www.slavevoyages.org, voyage no. 81208. It was also named "Elizabeth."
25. https://www.slavevoyages.org, voyage no. 81203.
26. The calculations for the period can be made in https://www.slavevoyages.org, by region and by slavery ship's flag.
27. https://www.slavevoyages.org, voyage no. 81208.
28. "The Viceroy says that the Caste of Negroes shipped is so unknown that none among the many that there are there knows their language, [they are] so arrogant, untamed and cruel even for themselves, and so barbarian that they rather eat rats and raw meat than have any condiment. They have arrived very sick, at sea there have been 64 deaths in the first remittance and 71 in the second." AGI/Filipinas 991. I thank Alex Borucki for the generous sharing of this document.
29. Studer, *La trata de negros*, 275.
30. Studer, *La trata de negros*, 276.

31. Borucki agrees with these figures. "Notas sobre el tráfico," 19.
32. Studer, *La trata de negros*, 276. Our sales figures do not match the author's, since the sources I work with preceed the accounts we have described.
33. Borucki explains that the slaves were taken to Lima because they could not be sold in Buenos Aires because of their high price, compared to the price of slaves after the arrival of several Portuguese ships in 1782–1783. Borucki, *De compañeros*, 33–34. Díaz-Trechuelo argues that there were no buyers in Buenos Aires, *La Real Compañía*, 224–225.
34. Mazzeo, *Los comerciantes limeños*, Table III, 167.
35. Ibid., 167–168.
36. Ibid., 153n, and Table II, 163. In his study on the III Conde de San Isidro de Lima, Flores Guzmán testifies to the Company formed by the Conde, his brother and Angel Izquierdo to import slaves from Brazil through Buenos Aires, for which they designated Martin de Sarratea as their representative. Flores Guzmán, "El destino manifiesto," 111–113. An extension of the topic is available in his valuable thesis: I thank the author for sharing it.
37. Letter from Letamendi to Funes, 26 March 1800, Martínez Paz, *Papeles*, 37.
38. Letter from Letamendi to Funes, 26 April 1800, Martínez Paz, *Papeles*, 38.
39. According to his source, 200 thousand *pesos* were taken from Lima and 1 million from Buenos Aires (AGI/ Filipinas, 987). However, I did not find this evidence in the accounts of the RCP, probably because it could not extract the amount in cash or because it was prorated for the following years, with predictable delays. Borucki claims that the price of slaves went from 200–250 in Buenos Aires to an average of 400 in Lima, with a 63 percent benefit. Borucki, "Notas sobre," 19 Vid AGI, Filipinas 986; AGI, Filipinas 987.
40. AGI/Filipinas 984. I thank Alex Borucki for his kindness in sharing the document.
41. For the value of the *pesos* of Carlos III at 8 *reales* – the universal currency for foreign trade changes, equivalent to 20 reales of vellon – as I have standardized the amounts, see Muñoz Serrulla, *La moneda castellana*, 153–156.
42. AGI/Filipinas 984.
43. AGI/Filipinas 990. "Minuta sobre la trata de negros, por vía de ensayo entre Londres, África y Buenos Aires." Undated, *circa* 1790.
44. Ibid. Underlined in the original.
45. Ibid. Underlined in the original.
46. Borucki, in "The U.S. slave ship," shows that the Angloamerican trade that exchanged slaves for leather, jerky meat and silver between Mozambique, the Rio de la Plata, the Caribbean region and North-America, consolidated their role as "neutral" intermediaries during the Napoleonic wars and made them occupy a significant place in intra-American commerce.
47. Sarratea to Royal Treasury Prosecutor Velasco, 18 July 1798. AGNA, IX, 22-6-1, ffs. 24–25. Emphasis added, AI.

Acknowledgements

Many thanks to Stefan Rinke, for his hospitality, and Alex Borucki for his support. I would also like to thank the anonymous reviewers for their helpful comments and suggestions, and to Thomas Passananti for his observations.

Disclosure statement

No potential conflict of interest was reported by the author(s).

Funding

This research has been sponsored and financially supported by GECEM Project (*Global Encounters between China and Europe: Trade Networks, Consumption and Cultural Exchanges in Macau and*

Marseille, 1680–1840), a project hosted by the Pablo de Olavide University (UPO) of Seville (Spain). The GECEM project is funded by the ERC (European Research Council) Starting-Grant, ref. 679371, under the European Union's Horizon 2020 Research and Innovation Program, www.gecem.eu. The P.I. (Principal Investigator) is Professor Manuel Pérez García (Distinguished Researcher at UPO). This work was supported by H2020 European Research Council, and the National University of Mexico/DGAPA during my sabbatical research at the Latin American Institut, Freie Universität Berlin, in 2019. This research has also been part of the academic activities of the Global History Network in China www.globalhistorynetwork.com, in which I am a member of the steering committee.

Bibliography

Amaral, Samuel. "Rural Production and Labour in Late Colonial Buenos Aires." *Journal of Latin American Studies* 19, no. 2 (1987): 235–278.

Aragón Ruano, Álvaro. "French Basque and Béarnaise Trade Diaspora from the Spanish Basque Country During the Eighteenth Century." *Atlantic Studies* 16, no. 4 (2019): 452–481.

Assadourian, Carlos Sempat. *El tráfico de esclavos en Córdoba, de Angola a Potosí*. Córdoba: Universidad Nacional de Córdoba, 1966.

Berquist, Emily. "Early Anti-Slavery Sentiment in the Spanish Atlantic World." *Atlantic Studies* 31, no. 2 (2010): 181–205.

Bonialian, Mariano, and Bernd Hausberger. "Consideraciones sobre el comercio y el papel de la plata hispanoamericana en la temprana globalización, siglos XVI–XIX." *Historia Mexicana* 68, no. 1 (2018): 197–244.

Borucki, Alex. "The U.S. Slave Ship *Ascension* in the Río de la Plata: Slave Routes and Circuits of Silver in the Late Eighteenth-Century Atlantic and Beyond." *Colonial Latin American Review* 29, no. 4 (2020): 630–657.

Borucki, Alex. *De compañeros de barco a camaradas de armas. Identidades negras en el Río de la Plata, 1760–1860*. Buenos Aires: Prometeo Libros, 2017.

Borucki, Alex. "Notas sobre el tráfico de esclavos al Río de la Plata durante el siglo XVIII." *Revista Latino-Americana de Estudos Avançados I* 1 (2016): 7–28.

Borucki, Alex, David Eltis, and David Wheat. "Atlantic History and the Slave Trade to Spanish America." *American Historical Review* 120, no. 2 (2015): 433–461.

Borucki, Alex. "The Slave Trade to the Río de la Plata, 1777–1812: Trans-Imperial Networks and Atlantic Warfare, 1777–1812." *Colonial Latin American Review* 20, no. 1 (2011): 81–107.

Camarda, Maximiliano. "Una aproximación a la participación de los rioplatenses en el comercio de esclavizados a fines del siglo XVIII." *Revista de Historia Americana y Argentina* 51, no. 2 (2016): 43–71.

Camarda, Maximiliano. "La Región Río de la Plata y el comercio ultramarino durante las últimas décadas del siglo XVIII: circulación comercial, mercancías y actores." Ph.D. diss., Universidad Nacional de La Plata, Argentina, 2010.

Crespi, Liliana. "El Comercio De Esclavos En El Río De La Plata. Apuntes Para Su Estudio." *Cuadernos De Historia. Serie Economía y Sociedad* 3 (September 2020): 237–252.

Díaz-Trechuelo, María Lourdes. *La Real Compañía de Filipinas*. Sevilla: Escuela de Estudios Hispano-Americanos, 1965.

Flores Guzmán, Ramiro. "El destino manifiesto de un mercader limeño a fines del siglo XVII: de comerciante a consignatario. La vida y negocios de don Isidro Abarca, Conde de San Isidro." In *Los comerciantes limeños a fines del siglo XVIII. Capacidad y cohesión de una elite, 1750–1825*, edited by Cristina Mazzeo, 89–130. Lima: Pontificia Universidad Católica del Perú, 1999.

Flores Guzmán, Ramiro. "Un proyecto comercial borbónico: la Real Compañía de Filipinas en el Perú (1786–1820)." Licenciatura en Historia diss. Pontificia Universidad Católica del Perú, Lima, 1998.

Garavaglia, Juan C. "The Economic Role of Slavery in a Non-Slave Society: The River Plate, 1750–1860." In *Slavery and antislavery in Spain's Atlantic empire*, edited by Josep Maria Fradera and Christopher Schmidt-Nowara, 74–100. New York: Berghahn, 2013.

Gelman, Jorge. "Sobre esclavos, peones, gauchos y campesinos: El trabajo y los trabajadores en una estancia colonial rioplatense." In *El mundo rural rioplatense a fines de la época colonial*, edited by Juan C. Garavaglia and Jorge Gelman, 44–83. Buenos Aires: Biblos, 1989.

Hausberger, Bernd. *La globalización temprana*. México: El Colegio de México, 2018.

Jumar, Fernando. "El comercio ultramarino por el complejo portuario rioplatense y la economía regional, 1714–1778." *Magallánica. Revista de Historia Moderna* 3, no. 5 (2016): 166–259.

Jumar, Fernando, and Isabel Paredes. "El comercio rioplatense intrarregional en el complejo portuario rioplatense: el contrabando visto a través de los comisos, 1693–1777." *América Latina en la Historia Económica* 15, no. 12 (2008): 31–98.

Jumar, Fernando. "Le commerce atlantique au Río de la Plata, 1680–1778." PhD diss., Ecóle des Hautes Études en Sciences Sociales, París, 2000.

Klein, Herbert S. *The Atlantic Slave Trade (New Approaches to the Americas)*. Cambridge: Cambridge University Press, 2010.

Martínez Paz, Enrique. *Papeles de Don Ambrosio Funes*. Córdoba: Universidad Nacional de Córdoba/ Bautista Cubas editor, 1918.

Mazzeo, Cristina, ed. *Los comerciantes limeños a fines del siglo XVIII. Capacidad y cohesión de una elite, 1750–1825*. Lima: Pontificia Universidad Católica del Perú, 1999.

Mazzeo, Cristina. "Esclavitud y acumulación mercantil: El tráfico negrero en el contexto de las reformas borbónicas." *Histórica* 17, no. 2 (1993): 149–178.

Medeiros dos Santos, Corsino. *O tráfico de escravos do Brasil para o Rio da Prata*. Brasilia: Senado Federal, 2010.

Molina, Raúl A. *Las primeras experiencias comerciales del Plata: el comercio marítimo 1580–1700*. Buenos Aires: Talleres gráficos Dorrego, 1966.

Molinari, Diego Luis. *La trata de negros. Datos para su estudio en el Río de la Plata*. Buenos Aires: Universidad de Buenos Aires, 1944.

Moutoukias, Zacarías. *Contrabando y control colonial en el siglo XVII. Buenos Aires, el Atlántico, y el espacio peruano*. Buenos Aires: CEAL, 1990.

Muñoz Serrulla, María Teresa. *La moneda castellana en los reinos de Indias durante la Edad Moderna*. Madrid: UNED, 2015.

Rosal, Miguel Ángel. *Africanos y afrodescendientes en el Río de la Plata. Siglos XVIII–XIX*. Buenos Aires: Editorial Dunken, 2009.

Schultz, Kara. "'The Kingdom of Angola is not Very Far from Here': The South Atlantic Slave Port of Buenos Aires, 1585-1640." *Slavery and Abolition* 36, no. 3 (July 2015): 424–444.

Sovarzo, José. "La garganta del comercio suramericano. Las relaciones comerciales terrestres entre la región del Rio de la Plata y los mercados del Pacífico suramericano a fines de la dominación hispánica en América." *El Taller de la Historia* 11, no. 11 (2019): 345–384.

Studer, Elena F. S. de. *La trata de negros en el Río de la Plata durante el siglo XVIII*. Buenos Aires: Universidad de Buenos Aires, 1958.

Vera, María Elena. "Encuentros Intelectuales y epistémicos: Los Argentinos Conocen y Estudian África y a Los Afroargentinos." *Cuadernos De Historia. Serie Economía y Sociedad* 9 (2007): 199–211.

Jesuits, exchanges, and Asian goods: a shipwreck and a cargo of musk in the seventeenth century

Pedro Omar Svriz-Wucherer

ABSTRACT
In 1648, a Portuguese ship that left Macau sank off the coast of the Philippines. The local authorities in Manila confiscated and sold all of its goods. This led to a dispute with the Jesuits, who claimed a certain amount of musk belonging to the Vice Province of China, the sale of which would support their religious mission. This article offers an analysis of this event, focusing on the dispute between the mentioned parties, but also as an example of the complex global networks of goods exchanges and economic interests in these regions of Southeast Asia in the middle of the seventeenth century.

Introduction

Global History is currently experiencing both a great boom and a period of self-reflection.[1] However, there is still a historiographical debate about its definition, field of study, and methodology.[2] The focus of this article does not permit a detailed examination of the various proposals framed within this Global History discussion.[3] However, a brief overview of some of the key ideas is necessary to situate the analysis of this 1648 event which follows.

Some researchers have developed analyses connecting various parts of the world to comprehend the early modern globalization in more depth.[4] Other scholars have made comparisons on a large scale.[5] At the same time, historiographic development exposed the limitations of these approaches. Some perspectives point to the Anglo-Saxon origin of Global History and therefore often neglected, or placed on the periphery, the cases of Latin America and Africa in their analysis.[6] Attending to these critiques will allow us to avoid making similar mistakes.

From a methodological point of view, several studies chose to reduce the focus of analysis in order to understand this global world based on local phenomena from the fifteenth to the eighteenth centuries.[7] This article will move forward in this direction, adopting a micro view to understand the macro.[8] I consider it necessary to reduce the object of analysis to a specific point, and from there to understand more complex and connected global processes. In this way I hope to overcome this frequent opposition between Microhistory and Global History,[9] understanding them as "two brothers in constant conflict, but inseparable."[10]

Therefore, I will make a "play with scales" that links the circulation and exchange of specific Asian goods (musk in this case), with the role played by certain non-state agents (Jesuits) who participated in this process.[11] I want to explore the idea that the Jesuits played a key role in the exchange circuits of Asian goods and that their intervention was vital for these products' circulation and consumption, both in Latin America and Europe.

Many studies have analyzed the circulation and consumption of goods, and have incorporated methodologies from Global History when examining the early modern era.[12] Bartolomé Yun-Casalilla and Bethany Aram, for example, have examined the impact that various types of goods of Latin American origin had on European societies in this period.[13] Along these lines, substantial research devoted to specific goods, analyzing their circulation and overall consumption, such as sugar, silk, porcelain, wine, among many others has been published.[14]

Furthermore, several studies have also analyzed the trade and good exchange circuits of specific interest for this article, especially between Macau and Manila. Some of them have focused on the role of the Jesuits in those regions. Dauril Alden's study about Jesuit economic activities in the Portuguese Empire is significant, especially because of its emphasis on Macau.[15] In the same way, Charles Boxer studied in depth the so-called "Black ships" that linked Macau and Nagasaki in the early seventeenth century. Other studies have focused on the role played by the Jesuit procurator fathers in these exchanges, as well as the disembarkation of goods and their packaging,[16] which allows for a better understanding of these exchanges and for finding similar strategies on the Macau-Manila route. Benjamin Videira Pires's study and others specifically on Jesuit activities in the Philippines, such as Eduardo Descalzo Yuste's research, are fundamental to understanding the Jesuit role on the Macau-Manila route. They are also important because they provide a context for the following case study, indicating the mechanisms carried out by the Jesuits to exchange and disseminate Asian goods, while also connecting spaces in Southeast Asia and Latin America during the early modern era.

The Macau-Manila route, goods exchanges around the middle of the seventeenth century

The Iberian Empires established various routes for the exchange of people, goods, and ideas across the globe in the early modern period, which has been analyzed from a number of perspectives in an array of studies.[17] However, this study focuses on the economic activities that were developed by "non-state actors" such as the members of the Society of Jesus.[18] Specifically, I will focus on the activities of the Jesuits on a particular shipping route which linked the ports of Macau (China) with those of the Philippines, mainly Manila and Cavite. This route was developed between 1565 and 1815.[19] The sources refer to the fact that two ships were used on the outbound Macau-Manila route, and two or three ships for the return voyage. From the beginning of the eighteenth century, when the so-called *Naos de China* managed to transport more than 1,000 tons, only one ship was required.[20] I examine the case of the Portuguese ship called *Nossa*

Senhora da Conceição (called *Nuestra Señora de la Concepción* in the Spanish sources), which was on this route in 1648 when it became the protagonist in a serious conflict.

During this period, the region was experiencing the results of historical transformations that altered trade exchanges in Southeast Asia. The first was the definitive closure of Japanese ports to Portuguese traders from 1639 and the subsequent persecution of Christians (1640–1641). This situation forced the Jesuits of Macau to locate new exchange sites from which to economically support their mission in China, the establishment of a "new Japan" in the region.[21] In this context, Father Adriano de las Cortes sought to carry out "a certain business of consideration" by undertaking his journey from Manila to Macau on 25 January 1625, in an attempt to consolidate this exchange route.[22]

The second event was the arrival of the Dutch to Macau in the first decades of the seventeenth century. The Dutch altered (and attacked) many of the Portuguese commercial circuits and ports, with the Goa-Macau route being particularly affected. At the same time, the Dutch were the only Europeans who managed to maintain the Japanese trade link from their post on the island of Dejima. Simultaneously, the Portuguese began to focus their trade mainly on the Atlantic, particularly in Brazil, with the Cape route between Macau-Brazil and Lisbon becoming progressively stronger.[23]

The third catalyst for change stemmed from the confrontation between Spain and Portugal. After Portugal's independence in 1640, a global conflict, that lasted more than two decades, affected the various possessions of these empires unequally. The Thirty Years' War impacted South-East Asia and all its trade connections. During this period, the Dutch and the English made several incursions into the possessions of the Iberian empires. The former managed to invade Pernambuco and consolidate their power in Brazil, while simultaneously founding New Amsterdam on what is now the island of Manhattan. Thereby, they became the strongest European empire in Asia from 1617 onwards, managing to establish numerous forts in the region. Two years later, the Dutch finally controlled Batavia, from where they consolidated their commercial power. In 1641 they took Formosa, snatched Malacca from the Portuguese, and established a trade monopoly with Japan on the aforementioned island of Dejima. In the following decade, the Dutch expelled the Portuguese from Ceylon and Cochin. The British, for their part, succeeded in replacing the Portuguese in Surat in 1612, and obtained trading privileges from the Grand Mongol in 1618.[24]

In light of the complexity of this situation, it is necessary to briefly characterize the main commercial ports of this route: Macau and Manila. *Nome de Deus de Macao* was founded by the Portuguese on 14 August 1556, at the mouth of the Pearl River, very close to the city of Canton or Guangzhou. Macau began as a stopover on the Portuguese merchants' journey to Canton.[25] Father Adriano de las Cortes mentioned that the Macanese port was a city inhabited "by *fidalgos* and Portuguese merchants" and that it was 180 leagues from Manila.[26] Other testimonies detail the main characteristics of this port and its dependence on the sea. In 1652 he asserted that "here [Macau] there are no goods from scratch, nor any other way of life, but that to embark on trade."[27] A century later, this dependence on the sea persisted. One account in 1775 states, "as this land lives on nothing else (but the sea), the more ships there are, the better the people can live, who cannot occupy themselves in this city in any other place."[28]

On the one hand, sources agree that Macau was small in area and did not have the possibility of developing sufficient agriculture or industry, and therefore the wealth of this city was based on its role as an intermediary between the various trade circuits nearby. Thus, Macau's ships and inhabitants developed key trade routes to Manila, Nagasaki, Timor, Batavia, Malacca, Madrasa, Calcutta, Goa, and Surrate throughout the early modern period.[29]

On the other hand, the city of Manila, founded on 24 June 1571 by Miguel López de Legazpi, from the beginning, this port sought to act as a commercial link between Asian and Latin American territories for the Spanish monarchy. Abundant scholarship has focused, therefore, on the so-called "Manila Galleon" and the commercial links that were established.[30] However, fewer studies have focused on the Manila-Macau route.[31] Father Pedro Murillo Velarde highlights the international character of that city, noting that just spending an hour in that port one would see people from all nations of Europe, Asia, America, and Africa.[32] This testimony provides an idea of the global connections that were developing in this port.

We must bear in mind that these exchanges of products on a global scale, i.e. from Asia to the European ports of Seville or Lisbon, were only profitable with products that did not occupy much space on a ship but which could be sold at very high prices.[33] Thus, this traffic included spices such as cinnamon and pepper and aromatic substances like grey amber and musk, the latter being the focus of this essay.

Musk made the Fathers of the Society of Jesus key agents since it was easier for them to participate in a trade with goods that were small in volume, easy to transport, and for which they received important privileges. Further, geographical distance and delays in communication contributed to the development of new instruments of government and more autonomy in the Jesuits' hands in these Asian regions. Studies by Markus Friedrich and Fabian Fechner recently show the influence of the structure of Jesuit government in different overseas missions, and the important role of communication in this religious expansion.[34] In balance, all these studies show how the order's central authorities left a certain degree of freedom to its members in matters of economy and trade to solve the day-to-day economic problems of their missions. The musk trade provides a very good example.

With regard to privileges, numerous documents highlight the needs Jesuits faced in this context, for which they requested exemption from the payment of certain taxes.[35] Thus, for example, the Jesuit procurator Baltasar de Lagunilla asked the crown to enable him to send eight crates of medicines and gifts from the port of Acapulco to the Philippine Islands without having to pay duties. The authorities granted him exemption for four crates. Interestingly, the clarification made in their report by the members of the *Casa de la Contratación* on this matter added the condition that this father procurator "swears that they are for the said religious [order] bought with his money and that he does not touch or have any part in them in particular."[36]

The Jesuit fathers clearly played a key role in trade exchanges in South East Asia. Analyzing the sinking of the Macanese ship off the Philippine coast around 1648 and how the Jesuits were involved in their later disputes highlights the economic role they played.

A shipwreck and a conflict: Jesuits and a cargo of musk

Sometimes an "exceptional" circumstance can mark the "normality" of a period. allowing us to identify certain common practices in the trade of goods at the Iberian frontiers.[37] In

1648 a Portuguese ship from Macau, *Nuestra Señora de la Concepción*, was shipwrecked off the coast of Manila.[38] The ship's captain, Diego de Mendoza Furtado, and its Portuguese crew members were arrested and their property seized by the royal officers of the Philippines. The confiscation was carried out by the *oidor* fiscal Cavallero de Medina, on the basis of an order from Governor Diego Fajardo. For the next fifteen days, this Portuguese ship was guarded by Juan Muñoz and twelve soldiers.[39] Then the notary public Juan de Campos y Rojas carried out the inventories and the corresponding storage of the confiscated goods over a period of twenty-seven and a half days.[40]

The ship was carrying goods for a total value of 54,473 pesos, 4 tomines, and 3 grains, which were placed in the royal box on 29 July 1648.[41] Father Andrés de Ledesma, Procurator General of the Society of Jesus in the Philippines, stated that he had given Antonio Rodrigues de Lagos, master and scribe of the ship, "in one of his boxes, twenty-seven *cates* of musk belonging to the Province of China."[42] We know that this "finissimo" musk was sent by Manuel Figueredo, a Jesuit father who was the procurator of the mission in China, "so that he could use the profit expected from its sale to support the fathers who worked in China."[43] These words come from a letter written by Ferdinand III of Habsburg, in Vienna and dated 17 November 1654, consulting his cousin Philip IV, King of Spain, about this musk confiscation, six years after the incident. Ferdinand III also mentioned that "just as in Macau there are no goods from the countryside that the Supreme Pontiff has granted under certain limits, so too the religious may exert some kind of merchandise for their sustenance."[44]

The following year, King Philip IV ordered by royal decree that this amount be returned to the Portuguese. However, the then governor Sabiniano Manrique de Lara only gave the Portuguese a total of 4,600 pesos, arguing "the needs of the R[e]l Caxa." The governor mentioned that among the goods seized were "28 musk buyones [*sic*], which is much more than the amount that the father procurator of the province of China claims to belong to him." He affirmed that "despite the fact that neither the *imbentarios* [*sic*] nor the *almonedas* were seized, he neither reasoned nor declared that any part of this musk belonged to the procurator or his province."[45] On 23 July 1662, after being consulted by the Council of the Indies, the public prosecutor decided that the excess should be applied to the Royal Treasury, since Father Martín Martínez "can only claim that what is contained in his report should be handed over to him."[46] Finally, on 9 September 1662, the *Consejo de Indias* decided that Father Martinez should be given back "the amount of musk or the value of its proceeds."[47]

A long process began in which the Jesuits demanded from the crown and the Philippine authorities the return of the value of those twenty-seven pounds of musk, equivalent to 2,430 pesos in eight reals, which belonged to the vice-province of China. A royal charter was finally issued on 18 June 1662 to return this amount to the Jesuit procurator in China, Martin Martinez.[48] However, this payment was not made, and the Jesuits filed a claim again in 1672, even requesting that the payment come out of Mexico's royal coffer, given the Philippine authorities' limited income.[49]

We do not know precisely if this payment was eventually made. This case, however, serves to point out the importance of the commercial networks developed by the Jesuits in these regions, and at the same time highlights the conflicts that could arise with the local and imperial authorities. It also sheds a light on a product that was very valuable to the Jesuits, namely musk.

The trade in musk became very important in Manila. For example, the historian Antonio García Abásolo highlights the figure of Captain Pedro de Alas Marrón, whom he describes as "the greatest merchant of musk and ambergris." [50] In his will, this captain gave 16 musk pots and 46 ounces of ambergris for sale in Seville. Other references to this product can be found in various sources from the sixteenth and seventeenth centuries. Friar Martin Ignatius of Loyola, in his journey through China, mentioned "there are many musk animals, which are the size and appearance of a small dog, which they kill and bury for a few days and after all the flesh and blood has rotted, it becomes those smelly powders."[51] Sebastian de Covarrubias, around 1611, highlighted the particularities of musk, with its "very fragrant smell" and "a very mild, uplifting smell."[52]

Years later, the Jesuit Adriano de las Cortes wrote that during his journey he crossed paths with Chinese hunters who used dogs to harass the "musk animal." This Jesuit then provided details about the animal and drew an image of how the musk was obtained; "in the navel it has a pocket and through it purge a blood or humour that is curdled by the musk."[53] The inventory of goods belonging to Governor Alonso Fajardo de Tenza, carried out between 12 and 16 July 1624, includes 126 musk swords. Later, in the celebrated *almoneda*, the 4 pounds and 4 and a half ounces of musk sold for 76 pesos.[54]

Overall, the presence of musk was frequent in commercial exchanges between the territories of Southeast Asia, particularly in Manila. This commodity was equally important in Macau. Around 1600, Macanese ships took two musk *picos* to Japan, which they bought for 8 *reais* for the *cate* in Canton, and it was sold in Japanese lands for 14, 15, or 16 *reais*, depending on the demand.[55] In July 1618 a similar quantity of musk (2 *cates*) was shipped by the Jesuits to Japan.[56] At the same time, 6 or 7 *picos* of this product were taken by Macaense ships to India, where it was used by the natives.[57] Towards the middle of the seventeenth century, the Senate of Macau included musk among the products that had to pay duties (3 percent), indicating the importance that its trade had acquired in that port.[58]

Based on these descriptions, we have a general idea of this particular product and how it was obtained and traded in the region. We know that one of musk's most frequent uses was as a perfume.[59] However, a reference from the middle of the eighteenth century states that "it was widely used in Chocolate" because it managed to "exalt the virtue of any drink."[60]

Jesuits and trade

Members of the Society of Jesus were directly or indirectly involved in commercial trafficking from Macau and the Philippines. The Jesuits had their own vessels in the Macau port with which they carried out trade missions to various points. Thus, in the 1630s, the Macau school owned two junks and participated in the activities of other vessels in the city.[61] Significantly, the Jesuits of Macau not only participated in the Macau-Philippines route; there are references to numerous activities on other exchange routes with territories near the Macau port. Without a doubt as noted earlier, the great route of exchange is that which united that port with Japan and which they dominated until the first decades of the seventeenth century.

In 1661, the Jesuits of the Macau School acted as partners of the Portuguese merchant Francisco Vieira de Figueiredo in trade using the *Nossa Senhora da Conceiçao e Sao*

Domingos Suriano. We know that this ship officially carried "sappan and sandalwood" but that it unofficially transported gold and sugar to Goa. These products were confiscated by the Dutch when this ship was captured in October 1661 in Batavia. Finally, these goods were recovered, and the journey could be completed in March 1662.[62] This is a very good reference of the Jesuit Fathers directly involved in the transport and trade – and also smuggling – of Asian goods in this area.

In the early years of the eighteenth century, a new "exceptional" case points to these links of the Macau Jesuits to trade. Sources state that Father Manuel Queirós Pereira was one of the owners of the ship *Jesús, María e José*. This ship, captained by Francisco Leite Pereira, was captured during its return journey from Batavia in February 1712[63] by the French corsair Henry Bouynot, who later sold it in the port of Manila to Aleixo Pessoa.[64] The following year, the Treaty of Utrecht, which put an end to the War of the Spanish Succession, was signed. In May 1714, this led to the Portuguese Vice-Royalty of India ordering the return of the ships from Macau that traded with Manila. This prompted Leite Pereira to travel to Goa in May 1716 to personally discuss the return of *Jesús, María e José*, which eventually transpired in 1719.[65] Two years later, the Senate of Macau wrote to Jesuit Father Antonio Soares, who was in the Kingdom of Siam, asking him to "guide and direct in everything" the captain sent from the city for the "conservation of the treatment and trade" between Macau and that Kingdom.[66]

In the early decades of the eighteenth century, the governor of the Philippines, Fernando Manuel Bustillo y Bustamente, sent grey amber and musk to New Spain with the Jesuit fathers. The sale of these products could cover the 4,400 pesos he owed Manuel López Pintado for his passage to the islands: "I have resolved that a small box is being taken into the care of father Marcelo de Valdivieso."[67] Once again the Jesuits were directly involved in the transport and trade of Asian goods on the Manila Galleon route.

Furthermore, Peter Borschberg cites as an example the cargo of two Portuguese carracks among which we find "several hundred ounces" and "eighteen boxes of musk-balls."[68] However, beyond the weight estimate of the cargo, Borschberg' calculation of the profit margin for musk is noteworthy. Initially he states that the simple calculation may lead us to think that the profit exceeded 1,500 percent, noting that "that calculation is of course very hypothetical and ignores other important factors such as loss and damage incurred during the voyage."[69] Borschberg then analyzes the sources by the United Dutch East India Company (VOC), which reflects the "[g]enuine profits of say 300–500 percent on the original investment were achieved in exceptional circumstances and only from the purchase and sale of prime quality musk."[70] This comparison allows us to understand the significance of musk in the commercial exchanges in those regions for different empires. Therefore, and given the need to sustain their mission in Eastern lands, the Jesuits themselves included musk as one of the products they could trade. Considering the Macau *Congregatione* of 1620 said the goods for trade were limited to raw silk, gold, musk, and ambergris, it is not surprising that musk occupied a significant place in the cargo carried by the Jesuits to Japan.[71]

Conclusions

As I have argued, Global History offers theoretical and methodological challenges to the understanding the world of early modern times – understanding local phenomena and/or precise junctures may allow us to find answers for questions about occurrences and situations in a global context

Thus, I have drawn attention to a very specific fact, a case of musk confiscation in Philippines around 1648, but one that, seen from a broader perspective, allows us to shape those global responses: the role that the Jesuits played as commercial agents in both Macau and the Philippines. They acted as direct transporters of Asian goods to other destinations, but they also collaborated in the logistics of this trade (ships). We also observe the particularities in the trade of a product such as the musk can allow us to better understand the changes in consumption and trade in those regions. In particular, the confiscation of musk in which the Jesuits were involved in the Philippines around 1648, and which opened a dispute that lasted several decades, indicates that it was not something "exceptional" but rather a habitual practice in which the members of the Society of Jesus were frequently involved with in Asia throughout the seventeenth and eighteenth centuries.

Notes

1. Courses, seminars and conferences, monographs and books, plus a whole series of articles and dossiers in scientific journals in recent years show us this trend. Among the journals we highlight the *Journal of World History* (published since 1990 by the University of Hawai'i Press), the *Journal of Global History* (published since 2006 by the London School of Economics and Political Science and Cambridge University Press), and the *Journal of Global Slavery* (published since 2016 by Leiden University and Brill).
2. See Conrad, *What is Global History?*; Hausberger and Pani, "Historia global. Presentación."
3. A first attempt to summarize the numerous works within this historiographic trend can be seen in Di Fiore and Meriggi, *World History*.
4. See Gruzinski, *Les quatre parties*; and Subrahmanyam, "Connected Histories."
5. Pomeranz, *The Great Divergence*.
6. Brown, "The Global History of Latin America"; Hausberger, *Historia mínima*; and Campbell, "Africa, the Indian Ocean World." I believe that the case of Africa still needs to be the subject of further theoretical reflection.
7. No doubt the studies of Italian microhistory by Giovanni Levi and Carlo Ginzburg initiated this perspective. Today they are taken up by some authors under the notion of Global Microhistory. See Andrade, "A Chinese Farmer … "; Trivellato, "Is There a Future"; Ghobrial, "The Secret Life of Elias … " and "Introduction"; Betrand and Calafat "La microhistoure globale." In recent works, Levi in particular reflects on global history and microhistory. See Levi, "Microhistoria e Historia Global"; and "Frail Frontiers?"
8. See De Vries "Playing with Scales"; Torre, "Micro/macro: ¿local/global?"
9. See, for example, the articles in Vol. 242, Issue Supplement (November 2019) referring to the "Global History and Microhistory" in which historians such as John Paul A. Ghobrial, Jan de Vries, Giovanni Levi, Maxine Berg, Romain Bertrand, Giorgio Riello and others, discuss these theoretical-methodological proposals.
10. My translation from original Spanish. Levi, "Microhistoria e Historia Global," 22.
11. I refer here to the methodological proposal of Revel, *Jeux d'echelles*.
12. See the different chapters in Perez-Garcia and de Sousa, *Global History*.
13. Yun-Casalilla and Aram, *Global Goods*. An essay that brings together works that analyze the reverse perspective, that is, the influence of European products on the American societies of the period is currently forthcoming in 2022: Yun-Casalilla, Berti and Svriz-Wucherer, *American Globalization, 1492–1850: Trans-cultural Consumption in Spanish Latin America*.
14. Gasch-Tomas, *The Atlantic World and the Manila Galleons*; Miyata, "Comercio entre Asia y América"; Perez-Garcia, "Global Goods, Silver and Market Integration."
15. Alden, *The Making of an Enterprise*.

16. Oka, "A Memorandum by Tçuzu Rodrigues," and Loureiro, "Navios, mercadorias e embalagens."
17. In this article, the concept "Iberian Empires" refers to the Portuguese and Spanish Empires. See Yun-Casalilla, *Iberian World Empires*; Perez-Garcia and de Sousa, *Global History and New Polycentric*; Díaz de Seabra and Manso, "Macau e as Filipinas"; Cardim et al., *Portugal na Monarquia Hispânica*; Subrahmanyam, "Connected Histories"; Boyajian, *Portuguese Trade*; and many others.
18. These Jesuit activities are analyzed in Alden, *The Making of an Enterprise*; Beites Manso, "Missionários ou ricos mercadores?"; Blumers, *La contabilidad en las reducciones guaraníes*; Mörner "Un procurador jesuita del Paraguay," among others.
19. At the same time, this route coincides with another that has received greater attention in historiography, namely the so-called "Manila Galleon" that linked the Philippines with Latin America until the second decade of the nineteenth century. See Chaunu, *Les Philippines*; Alfonso Mola and Martínez Shaw, *El Galeón de Manila*; Bonialian, *El Pacifico Hispanoamericano*; Giraldez, *The Age of Trade*; Bernabeu Albert and Martínez Shaw, *Un océano de seda y plata*; Gasch-Tomas, *The Atlantic World and the Manila Galleons*, and others. It is important to note that the combination of both routes allowed the Jesuits to connect Macau, the Philippines, and New Spain.
20. Videira Pires, *A viagem do comércio Macau-Manila*, 15. An indirect route must be added to this trade, uniting these territories through other regions such as Nagasaki, Malacca and Portuguese India, especially during the first decade of the seventeenth century. Ibid., 15. There was also indirect trade via Macassar after the end of the Portuguese war of independence around 1668. Cf. Souza, *The Survival of Empire*, 87–123.
21. Sena, "In Search of Another Japan."
22. De las Cortes, *Viaje de la China*, 97. In the introduction to this edition, Beatriz Moncó notes that the father De las Cortes does not specify what he refers to as a "business of consideration." Some authors interpret this phrase from a commercial point of view, others from a religious perspective, and still others hold an "intermediate" view that this Jesuit made that journey between Manila and Macau with evangelizing and commercial objectives. I consider this to be the most appropriate interpretation, given the context in which this mission is carried out. See De las Cortes, *Viaje de la China*, 20–21.
23. Bruxo et al., *Portugueses no Oriente*, 268.
24. Yun-Casalilla, *Iberian World Empires*, 354–355.
25. Bruxo et al., *Portugueses no Oriente*, 174.
26. De las Cortes, *Viaje de la China*, 97. See the definition of *Fidalgo* in Yun-Casalilla, *Las redes del Imperio*; and Perez-Garcia, *Blood, Land and Power*.
27. Quoted by Videira Pires, *A viagem do comércio Macau-Manila*, 5.
28. Quoted by Videira Pires, *A vida marítima de Macau*, 11.
29. Bruxo et al., *Portugueses no Oriente*, 267. Etsuko Miyata notes that Asian porcelain was found in excavations in the Zócalo of Mexico City dating from the period 1550–1575, showing that these were most probably exported from Macau and/or brought by the Portuguese to the New Spanish territory. Miyata, "Comercio entre Asia y América," 117–118. This opens up the need to analyze new and even more complex trade routes between Asia and Latin America, long before the Manila Galleon.
30. See references in note 19. At the same time, the smuggling activities that were taking place in parallel to this route should be noted. See Suárez "Sedas, rasos y damascos"; Bonialian, "Acapulco."
31. Videira Pires, *A vida marítima de Macau*, and *A viagem do comércio Macau-Manila*.
32. Murillo Velarde, Pedro. *Geographia Historica de las islas Philipinas, del Africa, y de sus islas adyacentes. Tomo VIII*. Madrid: Oficina de D. Gabriel Ramírez, 1752, 52.
33. García Abásolo, "La vida cotidiana de los vecinos de Manila," 79.
34. Fechner and Wilde, "Cartas vivas."
35. "Oficio de Juan Bautista Sáenz Navarrete a Francisco Zapata sobre que se ha concedido a los jesuitas el embarcar cuatro cajones de medicinas y regalos de Acapulco a Manila, sin pagar

derechos." Madrid, 15 June 1646. Archivo General de Indias (hereafter AGI), Filipinas, 81, N.8. Shortly afterwards, a Real Cédula was issued granting the request. AGI, Filipinas, 347. L.3, f.145-f.146v.

36. "Informe de la Casa de la Contratación sobre la pretensión del memorial anterior," Seville, 16 May 1646. AGI, Filipinas, 81, N.8.
37. In this paragraph we refer to the concept of "normal exceptional" proposed by Edoardo Grendi and used by the exponents of Italian microhistory such as Ginzburg and in their analyses. Ginzburg, Microhistoria, 41.
38. Luke Clossey mentions that ten years earlier, in 1638, a ship called *Nuestra Señora de la Concepción*, "the largest ship ever built in the Philippines, was wrecked on Saipan … ," but in that case all the cargo was lost. Clossey, "Merchants, migrants, missionaries," 45.
39. "Caja de Filipinas, 1648–1649." AGI, Contaduría 1227, f.182- f. 182 s/n v.
40. "Caja de Filipinas, 1648–1649." AGI, Contaduría 1227, f.183 s/n- s/n v. The term *almoneda* was defined at the time as: "The sale of things that are publicly made with the intervention of justice through the voice of the town crier, who publishes the thing that is sold, and the price that they give for it, so that the buyers may bid against one another, and the price is increased, and it is remitted." Furthermore, " … this voice can be composed of the name *Monéda*, and of the article *Al*, because what is sold there becomes money and monéda." Finally, this is used in "the market of the things that are won in war, is appreciated for money, each one as much as it is worth." See "Almoneda," *Diccionario de Autoridades*. Volume I (1726).
41. "Expediente sobre confiscación de almizcle a Martín Martínez." AGI, Filipinas, 22, R.10, N.55. It should be noted that, according to the Philippine crate, the official judges of the Royal Treasury are charged with 54,454 pesos, 5 tomines, and 11 grains of gold that different persons placed in the royal crate from 21 April to 15 October 1648, resulting from the value of the goods that were auctioned off in the royal treasury of the goods seized from the said Portuguese "as recorded in 285 interpolated entries of the common book, and general of the royal caxa of the said year." "Caja de Filipinas, 1648–1649." AGI, Contaduría, 1227, f.95.
42. "Expediente sobre confiscación de almizcle a Martín Martínez." AGI, Filipinas, 22, R.10, N.55. Cate is a weight measure used in the early modern Philippines; it was equal to one thenth of 1 *chinanta*, to 1 pound and 6 ounces, and to 632.63 grammes. See Gasch-Tomas, *The Atlantic World and the Manila Galleons*, 230.
43. "Consulta sobre confiscación de almizcle a jesuitas." AGI, Filipinas, 2, N.156.
44. Ibid. The Emperor spoke since the musk had been sent to the Jesuits by the German ambassador, Count de Lamberg. "Carta de Bolívar y Cruz sobre licencia para comerciar a Pedro de Vargas." AGI, Filipinas, 22, R.7, N.24.
45. "Expediente sobre confiscación de almizcle a Martín Martínez." AGI, Filipinas, 22, R.10, N.55.
46. Ibid.
47. Ibid.
48. "Copia de orden de pagar alimizcle al jesuita Martín Martínez." AGI, Filipinas, 296, N.3.
49. "Petición del jesuita Manuel de Villabona sobre pago de almizcle." 27 February 1672, AGI, Filipinas, 82. N.30.
50. My translation from original Spanish. García Abásolo, "La vida cotidiana de los vecinos de Manila," 79. "Bienes de difuntos: Pedro de las Alas Marrón," 1603. AGI, Contratación, 266A, N.1, R.3.
51. My translation from original Spanish. Loyola [1585] 2002: 173.
52. Sebastían de Covarrubias Orozco. *Tesoro de la lengua castellana o española*. Madrid, 1611. f.38v.
53. De las Cortes, *Viaje de la China,* 94–95.
54. Kawamura, "Manila, ciudad española y centro de fusión," 7–8.
55. Boxer, *O grande navio de Amacau,* 158. *Pico* is a measure of weight used in East Asia equivalent to just over 60 kilograms or about 100 *cates* (one *cate*, catty in English and *Jin* in Chinese equals 625 grams). *Pico* comes from the Malay form *píkul*, meaning "a man's burden." My translation from original Spanish. Ollé, *Estrategias Filipinas*, 200, Note no. 233.

56. Two *picos* of musk are equivalent to 120 kg. Loureiro, "Navios, mercadorias e embalagens," 37. A transcript of all the goods transported by the Jesuits on that journey in Boxer, *O grande navio de Amacau*, 163–168.
57. Ibid., 159.
58. Aresta and Viega de Oliveira, *O Senado*, 97.
59. Olivan Santaliestra, "Del almizcle al agua de Colonia."
60. *Dissertacion Historica Phisico-chimica, y analysis del cacao, su usso, y dosis, que para beneficio común da al publico Don Manuel Navas de Carrera, Maestro Boticario en el Reyno de Aragon, y Regente de la Botica del Real, Militar, y General Hospital de Nuestra Señora de Gracia de la Ciudad de Zaragoza*. Zaragoza, Impreso por Francisco Moreno, 1751, 42. A question to ask, but one that remains outside of the objectives of this article, is what other use musk was used for at this time?
61. Alden, *The Making of an Enterprise*, 531.
62. Boxer, *Francisco Vieira de Figueiredo*, 33–34.
63. Father Manuel Queirós Pereira owned the boat with Francisco Xavier Doutel, who was the owner of several boats. Born in Bragança, he arrived in Macau in 1698, and married Francisca Pereira (sister of the said Jesuit and of the merchant Francisco Leite Pereira, who captained the boat). Videira Pires, *A vida marítima de Macau*, 127 and 142.
64. Teixeira, *Macau no séc. XVIII*, 121.
65. Videira Pires, *A viagem do comércio Macau-Manila*, 44–45.
66. "Carta que o Senn.º mandou em Siao ao M. R.do P.e Antonio Soares Rellig.º da Comp.ª de Jesus." 28 January 1721, in *Arquivo de Macau* 1, no. 3. August 1929, 155–156.
67. "Problemas de los barcos para salir hacia Filipinas," México, 24 April 1716, Archivo Histórico Nacional, Diversos-Colecciones, 43, N.21.
68. The carracks were the *Santa Catarina* of 1603 and *Santo António* of 1605. Borschberg, "The European Musk Trade," 6.
69. Ibid.
70. Ibid.,7.
71. Oka, "A Memorandum by Tçuzu Rodrigues," 96.

Acknowledgements

I am grateful to comments and suggestions made by professors Manuel Perez-Garcia, Bartolome Yun-Casalilla, Teresa Sena, and Rocío Moreno-Cabanillas. I thank the reviewers and editors of this journal for their comments on improving this paper. Any errors are my own.

Disclosure statement

No potential conflict of interest was reported by the author(s).

Funding

This research has been sponsored and financially supported by the GECEM Project (Global Encounters between China and Europe: Trade Networks, Consumption and Cultural Exchanges in Macau and Marseille, 1680–1840), a project hosted by the Pablo de Olavide University (UPO) of Seville (Spain). The GECEM Project is funded by the European Research Council (ERC) Starting-Grant, ref. 679371, under the European Union's Horizon 2020 Research and Innovation Programme (www.gecem.eu). The principal investigator (PI) is Professor Manuel Perez-Garcia (Distinguished Researcher at UPO). This work was supported by H2020 European Research Council and has also been part of the academic activities of the Global History Network in China (www.globalhistorynetwork.com). This research is developed within the research group Historia de la Globalización: violencia, negociación e interculturalidad (HUM-1000), funded by the Junta de Andalucía. Grupo PAIDI HUM-1042 "Dinámicas sociales e identitarias en la historia de América Latina y el Caribe", financed by Junta de Andalucía, Spain.

Bibliography

Alden, Dauril. *The Making of an Enterprise: The Society of Jesus in Portugal, Its Empire, and Beyond. 1540–1750*. Stanford, CA: Stanford University Press, 1996.

Alfonso Mola, Marina, and Carlos Martínez Shaw, eds. *El Galeón de Manila*. Madrid: Aldeasa, 2000.

Andrade, Tonio. "A Chinese Farmer, Two African Boys, and a Warlord: Toward a Global Microhistory." *Journal of World History* 21, no. 4 (2010): 573–591.

Aresta, António, and Celina Veiga de Oliveira. *O Senado. Fontes documentais para a história do Leal Senado de Macau*. Macau: Leal Senado de Macau, 1998.

Beites Manso, Maria de Deus. "Missionários ou ricos mercadores? O comercio da seda entre o Japão e Macau nos séculos XVI e XVII." *Revista de Cultura / Review of Culture. Edição Internacional / International Edition* 42 (2013): 105–113.

Bernabeu Albert, Salvador, and Carlos Martínez Shaw, eds. *Un océano de seda y plata: el universo económico del Galeón de Manila*. Sevilla: CSIC, 2017.

Bertrand, Romain, and Guillaume Calafat. "La microhistoure globale: affaire(s) à suivre." *Annales HSS* 73, no. 1 (2018): 3–18.

Blumers, Teresa. *La contabilidad en las reducciones guaraníes*. Asunción: Centro de Estudios Antropológicos, Universidad Católica, 1992.

Bonialian, Mariano. "Acapulco: puerta abierta del Pacífico, válvula secreta del Atlántico." In *Relaciones intercoloniales: Nueva España y Filipinas*, edited by Jaime Olveda, 127–146. Zapopan: El Colegio de Jalisco, 2017.

Bonialian, Mariano. *El Pacifico Hispanoamericano. Política y comercio asiático en el imperio español*. La centralidad de lo marginal. México: El Colegio de México, 2012.

Borschberg, Peter. "The European Musk Trade with Asia in the Early Modern Period." *The Heritage Journal* 1, no. 1 (2017): 1–12.

Boxer, Charles R. *Francisco Vieira de Figueiredo: A Portuguese Merchant-Adventurer in South East Asia, 1624–1667*. Leiden: Brill, 1967.

Boxer, Charles R. *O grande navio de Amacau*. 4th ed. Translated by Manuel Vilarinho. Macau: Fundaçao Oriente; Museu e Centro de Estudios Maritimos de Macau, 1989.

Boyajian, James C. *Portuguese Trade in Asia Under the Habsburgs, 1580–1640*. Baltimore, MD: Johns Hopkins University Press, 1993.

Brown, Matthew. "The Global History of Latin America." *Journal of Global History* 10, no. 3 (2015): 365–386.

Bruxo, Jorge, Leonor Diaz de Seabra, and Lourdes Escaleira. *Portugueses no Oriente: Uma Narrativa dos Séculos XV a XIX*. Macau: Instituto Politécnico de Macau, 2017.

Campbell, Gwyn. "Africa, the Indian Ocean World, and the "Early Modern": Historiographical Conventions and Problems." *Journal of Indian Ocean World Studies* 1, no. 1 (2017): 24–37.

Cardim, Pedro, Leonor Freire Costa, and Mafalda Soares da Cunha, eds. *Portugal na Monarquia Hispânica. Dinâmicas de integração e de conflito*. Lisboa: Universidade Nova de Lisboa, 2013.

Chaunu, Pierre. *Les Philippines et le Pacifique des Ibériques*. 2 volumes. Paris: Sevpen, 1960.

Clossey, Luke. "Merchants, Migrants, Missionaries, and Globalization in the Early-Modern Pacific." *Journal of Global History* 1, no. 1 (2006): 41–58.

Clossey, Luke. *Salvation and Globalization in the Early Jesuit Missions*. Cambridge: Cambridge University Press, 2008.

Conrad, Sebastian. *What is Global History?* Princeton, NJ: Princeton University Press, 2016.

De las Cortes, Adriano. *Viaje de la China [1625–1626]*. Edition, Introduction and Notes by Beatriz Moncó. Madrid: Alianza Editorial, 1991.

Descalzo Yuste, Eduardo. "La Compañía de Jesús en Filipinas (1581–1768): realidad y representación." PhD diss., Universidad Autónoma de Barcelona, 2015.

De Vries, Jan. "Playing with Scales: The Global and the Micro, the Macro and the Nano." *Past and Present* 242, no. Issue Supplement no. 14 (2019): 23–36.

Díaz de Seabra, Leonor, and Maria de Deus Manso. "Macau e as Filipinas no século XVI-XIX: A Rota Marítima da Seda." *Revista Dos Puntas* 14 (2016): 176–199.

Di Fiore, Laura, and Marco Meriggi. *World History. Le nuove rotte della storia*. Bari: Laterza, 2011.

Fechner, Fabian. "Las tierras incógnitas de la administración jesuita: toma de decisiones, gremios consultivos y evolución de normas." *Histórica* 38, no. 2 (2014): 11–42.

Fechner, Fabian, and Guillermo Wilde. "'Cartas vivas' en la expansión del cristianismo ibérico. Las órdenes religiosas y la organización global de las misiones." *Nuevo Mundo Mundos Nuevos* (2020). doi:10.4000/nuevomundo.79441.

Friedrich, Markus. "Government and Information-Management in Early Modern Europe: The Case of the Society of Jesus (1540–1773)." *Journal of Early Modern History* 12, no. 6 (2008): 539–563.

García Abásolo, Antonio. "La vida cotidiana de los vecinos de Manila a través de sus testamentos e inventarios de bienes." *Estudis. Revista de Historia Moderna* 45 (2019): 69–92.

Gasch-Tomás, José Luis. *The Atlantic World and the Manila Galleons: Circulation, Market and Consumption of Asian Goods in the Spanish Empire, 1565–1650*. Leiden: Brill, 2019.

Ghobrial, John Paul A. "Introduction: Seeing the World Like a Microhistorian." *Past and Present* 242, no. Issue Supplement no. 14 (2019): 1–22.

Ghobrial, John Paul A. "The Secret Life of Elias of Babylon and the Uses of Global Microhistory." *Past and Present* 222, no. 1 (2014): 51–93.

Ginzburg, Carlo. "Microhistoria: dos o tres cosas que sé de ella." *Manuscrits* 12 (1994): 13–42.

Giraldez, Arturo. *The Age of Trade: The Manila Galleons and the Dawn of the Global Economy*. New York: Rowman & Littlefield, 2015.

Gruzinski, Serge. *Les quatre parties du monde. Histoire d 'une mondialisation*. Paris: La Martinière, 2004.

Hausberger, Bernd. *Historia mínima de la globalización temprana*. México: El Colegio de México, 2018.

Hausberger, Bernd, and Erika Pani. "Historia Global. Presentación." *Historia Mexicana* 68, no. 1 (2018): 177–196.

Kawamura, Yayoi. "Manila, ciudad española y centro de fusión. Un estudio a través del inventario del gobernador de Filipinas Alonso Fajardo de Tenza (1624)." *e-Spania* 30 (2018). http://journals.openedition.org/e-spania/27950.

Levi, Giovanni. "Frail Frontiers?" *Past and Present* 242, no. Issue Supplement no. 14 (2019): 37–49.

Levi, Giovanni. "Microhistoria e Historia Global." *Historia Crítica* 69 (2018): 21–35.

Loureiro, Rui. "Navios, mercadorias e embalagens na rota Macau-Nagasáqui." *Revista de Cultura / Review of Culture. Edição Internacional / International Edition* 24 (2007): 33–51.

Miyata, Etsuko. "Comercio entre Asia y América durante los siglos XVI y XVII: intervención portuguesa en el galeón de Manila." In *Nueva España. Puerta americana al Pacífico asiático, siglos XVI-XVIII*, edited by Carmen Yuste López, 109–128. México: Universidad Nacional Autónoma de México, 2019.

Mörner, Magnus. "Un procurador jesuita del Paraguay ante la corte de Felipe V." *Historiografía y Bibliografía Americanistas* 15 (1971): 367–443.

Oka, Mihoko. "A Memorandum by Tçuzu Rodrigues: The Office of Procurador and Trade by the Jesuits in Japan." *Bulletin of Portuguese-Japanese Studies* 13 (2006): 81–102.
Olivan Santaliestra, Laura. "Del almizcle al agua de Colonia: perfume, olores y percepción olfativa en la España del siglo XVIII." In *Vida cotidiana en la España de la Ilustración*, edited by Inmaculada Arias de Saavedra Alías, 207–222. Granada: Universidad de Granada, 2012.
Ollé, Manel. "Estrategias Filipinas respecto a China: Alonso Sánchez y Domingo de Salazar en la empresa de China (1581–1593)." PhD diss., Universidad Pompeu Fabra, 1999.
Perez-Garcia, Manuel. *Blood, Land and Power. The Rise and Fall of the Spanish Nobility and Lineages in the Early Modern Period*. Cardiff: University of Wales Press, 2021.
Perez-Garcia, Manuel. "Global Goods, Silver and Market Integration: Consumption of Wine, Silk and Porcelain Through the Grill Company via Macao-Canton and Marseille-Seville Trade Nodes, 18th Century." *Revista de Historia Económica/ Journal of Iberian and Latin American Economic History* 38, no. 3 (2020): 449–484.
Perez-Garcia, Manuel, and Lucio de Sousa, eds. *Global History and New Polycentric Approaches Europe, Asia and the Americas in a World Network System (XVI-XIXth Centuries)*. Singapore: Palgrave-Macmillan, 2018.
Pomeranz, Kenneth. *The Great Divergence: China, Europe, and the Making of the Modern World Economy*. Princeton, NJ: Princeton University Press, 2000.
Revel, Jacques. *Jeux d'echeles. La micro-analyse à ĺexpérience*. Paris: Hautes Études, Gallimard Le Suil, 1996.
Sena, Teresa. "In Search of Another Japan. Jesuit Motivation Towards Continental Southeast Asia in the Early 17th Century." *Revista de Cultura / Review of Culture. Edição Internacional / International Edition* 52 (2016): 23–45.
Souza, George Bryan. *The Survival of Empire. Portuguese Trade and Society in China and the South China Sea, 1630–1754*. Cambridge: Cambridge University Press, 1986.
Suárez, Margarita. "Sedas, rasos y damascos: Lima y el cierre del comercio triangular con México y Manila en la primera mitad del siglo XVII." *América Latina en la Historia Económica* 22, no. 2 (2015): 101–134.
Subrahmanyam, Sanjay. "Connected Histories: Notes towards a Reconfiguration of Early Modem Eurasia." *Modern Asia Studies* 31, no. 3 (1997): 735–762.
Teixeira, Manuel. *Macau no séc. XVIII*. Macau: Imprensa Nacional de Macau, 1984.
Torre, Angelo. "Micro/macro: ¿local/global? El problema de la localidad en una historia espacializada." *Historia Crítica* 69 (2018): 37–67.
Trivellato, Francesca. "Is There a Future for Italian Microhistory in the Age of Global History?" *California Italian Studies* 2, no. 1 (2011). Accessed March 29, 2021. https://escholarship.org/uc/item/0z94n9hq.
Vermote, Frederik. "Financing Jesuit Missions." In *The Oxford Handbook of the Jesuits*, edited by Inés G. Zupanov, 128–149. Oxford: Oxford University Press, 2019.
Videira Pires, Benjamin. *A viagem do comércio Macau-Manila nos séculos XVI a XIX*. Macau: Museo Marítimo de Macau, 1994.
Videira Pires, Benjamin. *A vida marítima de Macau no século XVIII*. Macau: Instituto Cultural de Macau, Museu Marítimo de Macau, 1993.
Yun-Casalilla, Bartolomé. *Iberian World Empires and the Globalization of Europe 1415–1668*. London: Palgrave, 2019.
Yun-Casalilla, Bartolomé, dir. *Las redes del Imperio. Élites sociales en la articulación de la monarquía hispánica, 1492–1714*. Madrid: Marcial Pons, 2009.
Yun-Casalilla, Bartolomé, Ilaria Berti, and Omar Svriz-Wucherer. *American Globalization, 1492–1850: Trans-Cultural Consumption in Spanish Latin America*. London: Routledge, 2022.

Overseas flows in Cartagena de Indias: the circulation of information in the Spanish empire during the eighteenth century

Rocío Moreno-Cabanillas

ABSTRACT

In the eighteenth century, all European colonial empires undertook the task of institutionalising their postal systems. Within the framework of the Bourbon reforms, the Spanish monarchy embarked upon reforming the postal system within the Spanish America with the aim of making transatlantic communications more reliable and regular. These plans, however, were hampered by an ongoing power struggle between all agents with a stake in the circulation of information. This is clearly reflected in the postal office in Cartagena de Indias, which was a key node for the Crown and a point of confluence for the strategies and interests of different local and global powers; the office, therefore, represented the polyhedric reality of postal communication. This paper shows that the institution had its own agency by constituting one of the main power tools, which is a reflection of the close relationship that exists between empire and communication.

Introduction

Fernand Braudel said that in the Early Modern Age the greatest concern for politicians was the arrival of the mail.[1] It was crucial that the postal service be well organised and functional in order to ensure a fast and efficient flow of information and knowledge between overseas colonies and imperial governments. The mail was essential for empires to exercise their dominance and power more effectively under the conditions imposed by colonial rule. It was a matter of maintaining a dynamic link between the need for information, the act of informing and the order issued, with the essential action of tangled procedures and mediators controlling the possibilities of communication. Therefore, knowledge was understood as a means of socio-political and economic control of imperial spaces. The aim was to overcome the blindness of the sovereign and acquire ideal models of total domination.[2]

European empires, such as France, Britain, Spain, and Portugal, wanted their governments to exercise control in their respective postal systems through increased bureaucracy and reorganisation.[3] The French Empire promoted postal reform starting from the second half of the seventeenth century, and a new system was in place by the eighteenth century.[4] The British Empire established direct administration of the postal system between 1660 and 1711. After numerous failed attempts, temporary measures, and resistance, in 1711 the *Post Office Act* was passed and the American colonies were incorporated into the British imperial postal system with England, Ireland, and Scotland.[5] After the Seven Years' War, the British government intensified all reform plans, including postal reform. It introduced a new regulatory framework: The *Post Office Act* of 1765. This act introduced the idea of a postal monopoly in its territories. The reform sought to establish an organised and efficient flow of postal communication and came to serve as a model for other imperial states. In Spain, postal reforms included the creation of a maritime postal system in 1764 and a land postal system in the interior of Spanish America in 1769, both under the supervision of the Crown.[6] In the Portuguese Empire, the establishment of the overseas posts between Portugal and Brazil occurred in 1798 with the enactment of the *Regulation for the creation of the Maritime Post Office between Portugal and Brazil* which followed the pattern of the British and Spanish states.[7]

This shows that, in postal matters at least, there were no differences between the various models of sovereignty, since whether the state was under an absolute monarchy or a parliamentary system, they were pursuing the same goal: a government postal monopoly.[8] Moreover, the models of postal institutionalisation circulated from one empire to another through emulation. Here, the European imperial states improved themselves through reciprocal imitation, for example, each one carefully monitored the actions of the others in order to benefit from the usefulness of their ideas and inventions.[9] This strategy was used to improve the postal service in order to be able to compete with their rivals.

These postal services increasingly became an intricate network with a large number of agents and communication channels. By the eighteenth century, the imperial postal communication networks were highly complex and had an extraordinary geographical scope.[10] The different strategies and spheres of power had an essential human and material support in the postal system to implement the communicative process that established connections between the different imperial spaces.

This paper analyses the postal system reform projects that took place in the colonial empires during the eighteenth century and the role they played in cementing the imperial-colonial relationship. Specifically, it focuses on the Spanish Monarchy which, under the paradigm of the Bourbon reforms, promoted reforms to the Spanish-American postal system with the aim of making colonial communications more organised and regular. These plans for postal renovation were developed in practice with a deployment of different strategies and agents that participated in the circulation of information. This is reflected in the administration of the Cartagena de Indias post office, which was a fundamental nucleus for the Crown where strategies and interests of the different local and global powers converged to form a polyhedral reality of postal communication. Therefore, this study reveals how the polycentric monarchy continued to be the main key to the stability of the empire in the eighteenth century. And it also shows that the postal service had its own agency in the configuration of these European empires.

The historiographical debate on Bourbon reformism is long and complex, ranging from a more traditional to a more critical and revisionist approach.[11] The perspective of this research is based on the ideas of the latest historiography of the Bourbon reforms, which emphasise the importance of analysing how the reforms were applied to

Spanish-American territory, and the reaction and resistance that they caused, in order to understand how in these spaces local autonomy clashed with the attempts at direct action by the Crown and the limits that existed.[12] It also adopts the perspective of current approaches that recognize the multi-territoriality of modern European states, in which government action was based on hierarchies and asymmetric connections between the different spaces of power in a complex political structure that was solid and durable, as well as malleable and changing.[13]

Forging the postal project as an economic network between Spain and Spanish America

Under the Bourbon Monarchy, the postal reform project materialised with the establishment of the Maritime Post Office to Spanish America during the second half of the eighteenth century. This confirmed the role of the Atlantic Ocean as a unifying corridor and transmitter of information, culture, and economic products.

Pedro Rodríguez de Campomanes, like many other enlightened political agents, considered in his reports that in order to achieve the objective of improving and consolidating the economy of the Spanish monarchy, it was necessary to facilitate the transfer of trade between Spain and Spanish America through the postal service; traders needed a secure, fast, and reliable mode of communication.[14] This approach culminated in the postal reform which proposed a monopoly by the Crown of the right to transport all correspondence and the attempt to extinguish parallel systems, reflected in the legislation enacted during the reforms.[15] On 24 August 1764, the *Provisional Regulations of the Maritime Post Office of Spain to its West Indies* were published.[16] These regulations contained the necessary provisions for the establishment of the new postal system and detailed the procedures for the organisation, management, and transport of overseas correspondence.

One of the key decisions of the project was the choice of ports which would serve as the hubs of the overseas postal service. On the one hand, the port of Havana was chosen as the centre for the redistribution of mail in Spanish America because of its geostrategic position. Havana was one of the great enclaves of the Atlantic that had a relevant infrastructure and organisational framework for maritime traffic, with a strong dynamic interaction of the forces of the hinterland and foreland, was a mediator of its links with Spain and other European empires, and had been vector of a global information flow since the sixteenth century.

On the other hand, Corunna was chosen as the main port of the overseas communications system in Spain. The purpose was to integrate Galicia into the Spanish-American maritime and commercial traffic. Furthermore, Corunna was less exposed to attack by enemy vessels than Cadiz, whose proximity to Gibraltar continually threatened its security. Moreover, it had alternative ports nearby, such as Ferrol, which were safe havens for ships in the event of storms or persecution. And its geostrategic position between Britain and Portugal could threaten the traditional connection between the two allied powers. Another main reason for this choice was that Corunna had great experience in being the head of the postal communication circulation. In this respect, the port of Corunna had served as a postal link with England, specifically with Falmouth, from 1689 to 1815, with some interruptions in periods of war between the two empires.[17] The so-called

Corunna boats or Spanish packets operated in this line of maritime mail, transporting official and commercial correspondence from England to Spain and to Portugal.[18]

The selection responded to geographical and political issues. This decision gave the port of Corunna the privilege of being the only official port, together with Cadiz, to have its own overseas exchange line. However, one of the main aspirations of the Bourbon monarchy was to break the Andalusian commercial monopoly. Paradoxically, the reform of the control of communications ran in parallel with the break-up of the monopoly. At this point, it should be noted that the desired monopoly with Spanish America really had very different profiles. In practice, it acted as a platform for the participation of a multiplicity of agents who had a high degree of autonomy with respect to central power and who, despite operating from Cadiz, and not from Madrid, did not act to the detriment of the high degree of autonomy of the multiple centres of power in Spanish America.

The packet boats that left the port of Corunna were an effective commercial route.[19] These ships entered into competition with Cadiz's trade. This was due to the fact that the improvement of the postal system was not only intended to channel communication flows, but also commercial ones through an official channel imposed by the Crown. In these packet boats, goods were introduced on behalf of the captain, the pilot, the postmaster of Corunna or private individuals, who had to pay the appropriate fee to be able to transport their goods.[20] The private ships could carry letters as long as they passed through the post office, paid the corresponding fees, had their licence, and were carried in a closed suitcase. The Crown was tolerant in the transport of correspondence, as long as postage was paid, and mail and goods were kept under control.[21] Therefore, the major problem with letters and goods being transported illegally was the failure to pay the transport fee, which should be collected by the Royal Treasury because this financial issue was an important part of the reason for postal reform.

However, some merchants took advantage of this situation to introduce goods illegally onto private vessels without paying the fees and without a licence.[22] A similar situation occurred in the British and Portuguese maritime postal services, which were also authorised to transport goods and passengers in compliance with their legal frameworks. The illegal introduction of mail, goods, and passengers was thus a common practice that took place on the ships of these European colonial empires.

In the Spanish postal service, Álvaro de Castro, captain of the packet boat *El Cortés*, was accused of transporting goods in a hidden and clandestine manner. For this reason, his goods were confiscated, and he was imprisoned, although he escaped.[23] Other cases include those of three sailors from the packet boat *El Gallego,* who were imprisoned on 15 September 1768 for trying to transport seven barrels of wine and eighty-six shirts in a fraudulent manner; and those of five other sailors from the packet boat *El Rey*, who illegally transported thirty-four boxes of tobacco in September of the same year.[24]

Continual fraud on the packet boats led to cases where the cargo of clandestine letters significantly exceeded the registered one. This was the case of a packet boat that arrived on 10 April 1765 at the port of Ferrol from Havana. The ship's report showed that it was carrying nine boxes of letters when in reality it was carrying fifteen.[25] These fraudulent practices were so common that the postmaster of Corunna, José Antonio López, informed the Postmasters General located in Madrid that it was common for packet boats from or to Spanish America to be fraudulent.[26] In addition, it was common for the authorities to be involved and complicit in these frauds.

The relationship, both legal and illegal, between trade and mail is essential to understanding the socio-political and economic dynamics of the Spanish Empire. Thus, the postal reform enacted in 1764 opened the way for the free trade regulations of 1765. In fact, the postal project already reflected the proposals for more flexible trade with the opening of various commercial routes that broke the Cadiz monopoly, such as the configuration of the port of Corunna as a competing centre of communication, trade, and navigation to Spanish America, and the transport of goods in the packet boats that were outside the control of the Consulate of the Indies and the Council of the Indies. For these reasons, both organisations – the Consulate and the Council – were vehemently opposed to the Spanish-American postal reform project.[27]

Flows and routes of Atlantic postal exchange

The *Provisional Regulations* determined the maritime postal route: the packet boat would depart from Spain, specifically from the port of Corunna, on the first of each month, to La Habana. This route was called *Carrera de La Habana*. Once it arrived in La Habana, two ships would be dispatched from there: one to Veracruz that would carry the correspondence to the viceroyalty of Nueva España (*Carrera de Veracruz*), and another from the port of Trinidad in Cuba to Cartagena de Indias that would transport the correspondence through the interior of the south of Spanish America (*Carrera de Cartagena*).[28] The implementation of this postal route was motivated by the government's desire to expand its control of priority areas of the empire, such as the Caribbean, because of the urgency of domination that had caused the Seven Years' War. Another route called *Carrera de Buenos Aires* was added in 1767. A packet boat went from Corunna to Montevideo to carry the letters from there to Buenos Aires on the fifteenth of every other month.[29]

These routes had their spatial expression in lines of navigation that aimed to redefine the links between Spain and Spanish America, with an organisation of the space according to the communicational nodes and their respective administrative units.[30] This distribution and diversification of postal routes also took place in the British Empire where packet boats, from 1764 onwards, departed from England for three communication axes in the colonies: New York, Charleston, and the West Indies.

For imperial governments, the idea and need for a scheduled postal service was their main concern. The intended acceleration of postal communications through a monthly organisation of the maritime mails made it possible to improve the course of the postal system. The frequent and methodical dispatch of packet boats was the main incentive for the desired regularity in the flow of information between the two continents. However, the timetable, imposed by the *Provisional Regulations*, was hardly ever respected by the packet boats. This was due to delays or loss of mail caused by adverse weather conditions or human error.

The following graphs show the maximum and minimum times it took a packet boat to run the *Carrera de la Habana* in the period between 1765 and 1777. They confirm a degree of irregularity and inequality in the packet boat's schedule. One the one hand, Graph 1 shows that the longest journey was made in 1765 with 142 days, and the shortest in 1770 with 34 days. On the other hand, Graph 2 shows that the longest journey took place in 1766 with 77 days, and the shortest in 1771 with 25 days.

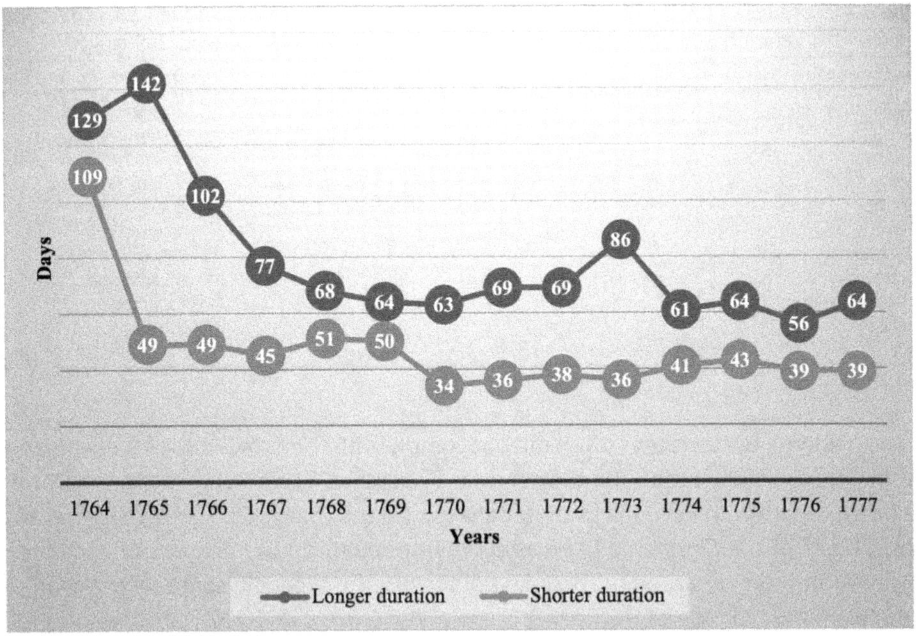

Graph 1. Travel time of the packet boats from Spain to America between 1764 and 1777. Sources: My own elaboration based on data from AGI, Correos, 469 B and AGI, Correos, 269 A – 276 B.

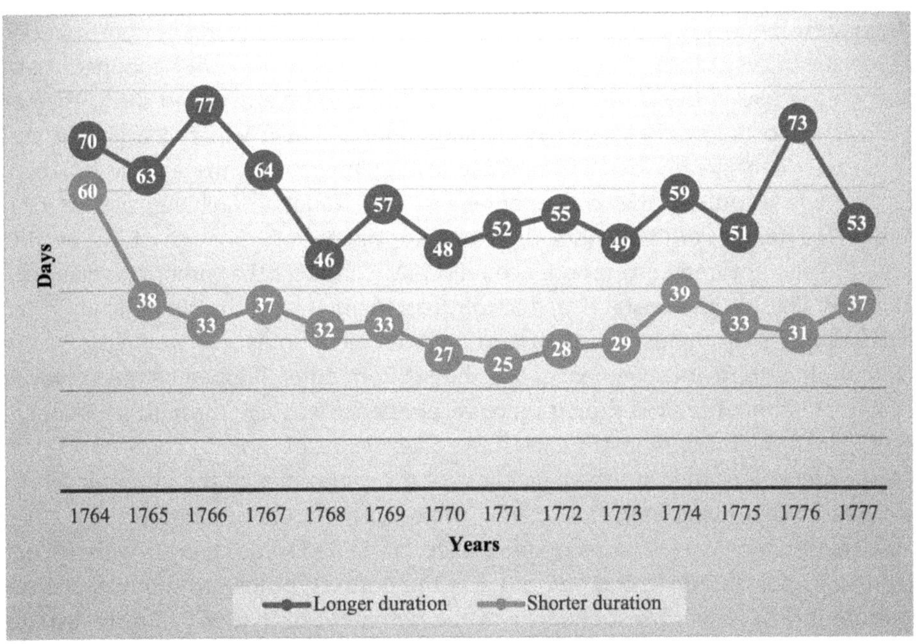

Graph 2. Travel time of the packet boats from America to Spain between 1764 and 1777. Sources: My own elaboration based on data from AGI, Correos, 469 B and AGI, Correos, 269 A – 276 B.

Table 1. Departures of the packet boats from La Coruña to La Habana during the year 1765. Sources: My own elaboration based on data from AGI, Correos, 469 B and AGI, Correos, 269 A – 276 B.

Packet boat name	Departure from La Coruña
El Magallanes	3 January 1765
El Gallego	3 February 1765
El Quirós	8 March 1765
El Rey	7 April 1765
El Príncipe	3 May 1765
El Colón	1 June 1765
El Grimaldi	2 August 1765
El Cortés	1 September 1765
El Magallanes	11 October 1765
El Gallego	3 November 1765
El Rey	17 December 1765

The maritime postal routes often did not comply with the provisions of the regulations, causing irregular fluctuations on the overseas dispatches. Table 1 shows the departures of the packet boats from Corunna to La Habana during the year 1765. This reveals that all the packet boats of the *Carrera de la Habana* did not depart on the first day of each month. However, they did depart on the first days of the month, except in some cases. An analysis of the annual circulation of the packet boats of the *Carrera de La Habana* shows a certain regularity, as these packet boats sailed monthly, except in July. This reflects the fact that official correspondence increased, enhancing contacts between Spain and Spanish America, through the flexible dynamism of the new postal communication network.

Inclement weather conditions were one of the main reasons for the delay in the departure of the ships. On numerous occasions the ships had to face strong storms at sea. These storms caused serious damage to the ships, sometimes resulting in shipwrecks where passengers, goods, and correspondence could be lost.[31] Additionally, in the European colonial empires, there was a regulation that provided for the throwing of correspondence into the sea in case of a sighting of an adversary ship. Sometimes it happened that the sailors on the packet boats saw a vessel that seemed to be a rival and threw the correspondence into the sea.[32] Later, they would confirm that it was not a hostile vessel, but the mail had already been completely lost.[33] Other times the enemy intercepted the ship and captured the correspondence. The National Archives of the United Kingdom contain a large number of letters captured from Spanish ships by British vessels.[34] This captured correspondence reflects the interest that other colonial powers had in destabilising the postal dynamics of their enemies, and the strategic importance of capturing the information and cargo of other empires' ships.

The result of these inconveniences and threats from other European empires was that, on many occasions, the most significant correspondence was sent through different channels, either through Corunna or Cadiz. These successions of sending correspondence by different procedures indicate the awareness of the authorities of the importance of the correspondence arriving at its destination, whatever the route or method.

The Spanish Monarchy's postal reform project contained some changes with respect to the previous postal service: the fitting out of the port of Corunna as the main centre of departure for overseas correspondence to the detriment of that of Cadiz; the establishment of post offices located in the main Spanish American cities, which acted as intermediary institutions between the imperial and the local; and, the creation of new posts in Spanish America as administrators, financial controllers, and officers, who were responsible for coordinating the mail service.

Establishing post offices in strategic cities reflected the idea of a decentralised network of interconnected post offices throughout the territory of the Spanish monarchy. These provisions constituted the postal system in a tentacular apparatus that extended throughout the Spanish American territory. Spain was able to draw on the British model of establishing post offices on the North American continent in the early seventeenth century; the first post office in the colonies was established in Boston in 1639. The intercolonial mail in British America was not expanded until the 1750s, however, when post offices multiplied and roads were improved and routes diversified, thanks to the work of Benjamin Franklin and William Hunter, appointed by the British Crown in 1753.[35] From 1757, they transformed the colonial postal system, making the postal service faster, more frequent, and covering a larger area.[36]

Similarly, the new line of maritime posts for the Spanish maintained some features of the previous postal operation, such as the use of already consolidated maritime routes and points of destination previously used. This was the case with the port of Cartagena de Indias, which in the sixteenth and seventeenth centuries had already been considered as a preferred point on the commercial and postal routes of the Spanish Empire.

Cartagena de Indias as a polycentric postal node

The sea and its shores held a very important strategic value for the imperial states. The maritime area was a space for global interactions.[37] This research focuses on an Atlantic area where a large number of polycentric overseas connections operated.[38] These connections were not only unidirectional, with a trajectory from the metropolis to the colonies, but were also multidirectional, as they also took place between different areas, whether inter-colonial or extra-imperial.[39]

In this overseas context, ports were spaces of contact between land and sea. They constituted an essential part of the development of these connections which took place on different scales. The ports were economic axes, military bases, communication hubs, and points of articulation, in which regional, imperial, and global economies were interconnected. Communication was a distinctive and intrinsic feature of port spaces. It promoted contact between the domains of land and maritime circulation interwoven by local and global powers. It was also a transmitter of knowledge from different parts of the world. In fact, port cities were places where information was collected, used, debated, and redistributed. They became areas of political and socio-economic geostrategy that were essential for imperial power.

The Caribbean was at the centre of European political and economic rivalries and assumed a key role in geopolitical and trade strategies. This space was formed as a meeting place for global production and was configured as a fundamental space in the world economy.[40] From this point of view, Cartagena de Indias was a crucial city in the Caribbean space. Cartagena de Indias had been an organised space for the circulation of information since the establishment of the Carrera de Indias in the sixteenth century, since it was an obligatory stop in the Fleet and Galleon system.[41] The Cartagena area was largely dominated by the development of Atlantic trade, which promoted the flow of news that was fundamental to the progress of the city.

The decision to place Cartagena de Indias as an authorised port in the Carrera de Indias, promoted by the Crown, conditioned its evolution and development. The commercial, financial, transport, and communication flows placed this city at the crucial node in the navigation routes between Europe and Spanish America and turned it into a fluid space of interaction.[42] However, this system encountered different obstacles such as the lack of compliance with the regulations because the departure schedule of the ships was almost never respected, and there were even years in which no fleet set sail.[43] The insecurity caused by successive attacks by enemy ships and the increase in smuggling made contact between the two sides of the Atlantic increasingly difficult. For these reasons the government considered modifying the transport system to Spanish America.

The complex network that operated in the city of Cartagena de Indias explains why it became one of the main centres of operations within eighteenth-century Bourbon reformism. The goal behind state intervention was to revalue the geostrategic position of its ports through ideas and projects to improve the military infrastructure and to secure advances in communication and the progress of trade.

Once the postal reform project had been drawn up and regulated, it was consistently shaped and reshaped for application in the Spanish American space. The postal renovation project was not organised and did not have the same implications in all Spanish possessions in the Indies due to the plural and different constitution of Spanish American spaces. Consequently, the multiplicity and heterogeneity of peculiar features triggered diverse adaptations and configurations in each place where they were mutually constructed, in a constant imperial-local dialogue. In this context, the Cartagena de Indias post office, with its own characteristics, constituted an essential node in the imperial postal network and a space for negotiation of Bourbon policy.

In February 1765, the post office of Cartagena de Indias was established. It organised the circulation of multi-directional postal communication, this means, with the Peninsula, Havana, Cuba, the interior of South America, and even with the foreign powers that were in the Caribbean area. The postal institution became an essential pillar in the socio-economic and communication fields of postal reform.

The post office of Cartagena de Indias had a number of subordinate or aggregated post offices, which depended on it. They were in charge of the correspondence for the Spanish-American interior. This led to a planning of the postal territory establishing numerous post offices throughout the Spanish-American space. This implied a hierarchization of the land because the important thing was the space where the correspondence was distributed.

The Spanish Empire articulated the circulation of information on different scales. The aim was to integrate the territories into the imperial frameworks through the installation of fixed postal routes that communicated with different spaces. In this way, the postal service drew up postal routes, with departure and arrival points selected according to their geostrategic importance for the political and economic powers, with the intention of integrating various spaces in the Spanish-American interior around the articulation of imperial networks. These postal communication systems played a key role in the configuration of the territories.[44]

The organisation of the post was structured, therefore, around established time intervals and spaces for postal coordination and organisation at different levels, imperial and local. The aim was to achieve these in order to establish a regularity in which the two rhythms were merged. However, local circumstances did not allow the times regulated by the instructions to be met, resulting in a continuous variation of travel times on the same routes.

From this point of view, it is necessary to think about distance and time in colonial society as a question of relative and flexible perspective, framed in certain socio-economic and political-cultural contexts that conditioned the governability of colonial empires. Distance depended on economic, social, and political needs that were changing and responded to particular circumstances and characteristics of the moment. In fact, the actors, their social interactions and attitudes and their practices were those that involved the dynamics of time. Therefore, the notion of efficiency and speed of the mail must be questioned, since these would be subordinated to the circumstances of the moment and the perception of time that the agents had.[45]

Agents and strategies in the Cartagena postal network

The implementation of postal reform on the local Spanish-American territory presented different challenges that required agents to use diverse strategies for the consolidation of the new postal model. The agents who participated in the transport of the mail on an official basis were the employees of the post offices: the drivers, who were in charge of transiting the postal routes, linking the key points of these routes, and carrying the mail under the licence of the postmaster; and the sailors who were in charge of the maritime postal service. They were agents of change that carried out the postal dynamics and were also intermediaries between the social and political spaces and the local and imperial ones.

The subordinate agents actively participated in the postal service. They mobilised the correspondence with the aim of achieving maximum efficiency and fluidity. This was the case with the postal drivers, who were generally the indigenous people who served as messengers, known as *chasquis*, in the Spanish-American interior.[46] The *chasquis* transported the mail and packages in an official or unofficial way, because they had excellent knowledge of the Spanish-American territory.[47] For this reason, the postal employees acted jointly with these agents to ensure the distribution of correspondence. Therefore, there was a strategy of integrating the natives to make the postal service more efficient in the interior regions. Other agents involved in the circulation of information were local authorities, merchants, the military, and religious orders. As a result, communication flowed through various channels, often unknown to the postal administration itself.[48]

The geographical expansion of trade in the eighteenth century led to an increased demand for information from distant places on the part of traders.[49] This was the case in Cartagena de Indias, which was a strategic commercial hub. The merchants had an enormous need to establish fluid communication with Spain because of their economic interests. They needed to have precise market information, not only to master the supply and demand of European goods, but also to feed the interpersonal confidence required in long-distance trade.[50] Consequently, the Atlantic trade networks were dependent on the letters that guaranteed the good progress or failure of their business.[51]

From this point of view, trust between the agents emphasised the role of solidarity links in social and economic networks due to the risk and uncertainties of colonial trade. Therefore, trust occupied a key place in the mentality of traders, who depended upon the action of trusted mediating agents to obtain information from long-distance markets.[52] In this context, the postal network in Cartagena de Indias had access to privileged information about colonial markets. This allowed it to know the commercial circuits that were produced at short, medium, and long distance and to have a certain flexibility to adapt to the different economic situations.

Consequently, merchants often sought other means of circulating postal communication away from the official. They used their private boats, called registration ships, which had a direct connection between Cartagena de Indias and Spain. In this way these merchants did not have to stop in Cuba or comply with a rigid schedule like that of the Maritime Post Office. They were managed by an immediate postal service, with direct links to the ports, which could accommodate their commercial needs as dictated. These circumstances made their postal exchanges more efficient and explain why merchants preferred to send letters from Cartagena de Indias to Cadiz in their own ships where they anticipated a quicker response.[53] They established dense and fluid commercial channels and networks over which postal communication circulated. These postal networks were based on the needs, flexibility, speed, and trust between the different commercial agents installed in the multiple global mercantile nodes, all forming complex networks at a global level.[54] This reflects the close link between colonial trade and transatlantic communications.

To summarise, many agents did not use the official postal system, preferring to send their mail through private agents without a licence. These various unofficial communication options, driven by particular interests, tended to be broader and more far-reaching. This situation was also found in other overseas empires where, as in the Spanish one, the transport of mail in private boats was cheaper and evaded government control. For example, two parallel communication networks coexisted in the overseas domains of the British Empire: the formal British postal service oriented towards a monopoly of the circulation of information; and an informal postal system that eluded the official one and operated through a huge network of connections in multiple spaces and through various agents.[55] Similarly, in the Portuguese Empire, many letters were sent by private vessels, such as the merchant ships.[56] This shows that these agents did not see positive advantages in an organised and regular structure established with state intervention.

The need to communicate according to each agent's own interests generated multiple channels and parallel actors to the official position. Most official correspondence was vertical. This means that communication was hierarchical, where local agents, especially postmasters and officials, reported to their superiors on postal matters.[57] This permanent flow of information to the political centre was not an indicator of increased power but, on the contrary, was a compensation for dominance, not a command in itself.[58]

An examination of the horizontal communication reveals the role played by other actors in the flow of information. This was the case with local authorities, such as the governor and royal officials of the Royal Treasury of Cartagena de Indias. The Viceroy of New Granada, José Alfonso Pizarro, put them in charge of the postal order in 1750. An analysis of the documentation indicates that they continued to manage the circulation of information during the postal reform.[59] Thus, multiple agents competed for the control of postal information flows at different local and global levels.

In short, there was a multidirectional communication with horizontal relations, between peninsular authorities and their local employees, and vertical relations, between authorities and other local agents, reflecting the existence of different communication modalities and situations in the postal network of Cartagena de Indias. The establishment of interpersonal postal links between multiple actors had a strong impact on the configuration of political spaces at a global and local level. This demonstrates the interplay between the different levels of authority within the postal system, where groups and institutions with different interests converged with a common objective: to establish effective postal communication.

Conclusion

"All ages have been the information age and, each in its own way, communication systems have always shaped events."[60] With this concept, Robert Darnton presents communication systems as agents that shape societies in every historical period. Humans have always had the need to communicate with one another and, for this reason, governments have felt the need to organise the circulation of written information. The articulation of these postal needs by the European empires in the Early Modern Period allows reflection on a complex postal network.

Eighteenth-century projects to reform postal systems are related to the process of structuration and construction of imperial states. Colonial states required well-organised, fast, and efficient channels of communication to keep a tight hold over their possessions. An efficient postal system was key to compiling information, to ensuring that orders were enforced, and that commercial operations were not interrupted – the post was the basis of trade. In the eighteenth century, governments enacted numerous measures in order to control communication systems and institutionalise the post. In this regard, the postal system became a veritable agent of change, insofar as it consolidated the political authority of the empires and paved the way to the implementation of different policies in their territories through the consolidation of official communication channels.

However, these measures were different from place to place, and had to adapt to local circumstances. This undermined the idea of imperial control and made the ultimate aim, political centralisation, harder to achieve. This process rarely resulted in a direct and progressive increase of central power, leading instead to a widening of the margins for local action.

This research highlights processes in which the power and authority of the Bourbon monarchy were not imposed by force, but through negotiation with the interested parties in different decisional nodes throughout the empire. This is not to argue that the monarchy was weak, but that negotiation was part of normal government practice, including the reform of the postal system. As such, the alleged central model of the Bourbons was in fact dispersed throughout the complex polycentric mosaic of the Empire, resonating and proliferating in the multiple spaces into which the Empire was divided.

The terms of negotiation and conflict were the primary axes of the Spanish American postal system. This case study has emphasised the fact that this process did not take place along the classic lines of single centre and periphery, but that it was constructed of multiple power nodes. These not only included the administrative centres created by the Crown, but others as well, economic, military, cultural, and religious, which often shaped the decisions adopted with regard to the postal system.

Cartagena de Indias was one of those political nodes, and it soon turned into one of the most important information hubs in colonial Spanish America. In this space there were different actors who, in various situations, mobilised information through different dynamics and strategies, originating a process of re-articulation and decentralisation of the polycentric spheres of power.

The postal structure that revolved around Cartagena de Indias not only involved local but also global agents. These social groups faced the challenge of creating communication networks, or thwarting them, as the circulation of information was one of the main population and territorial control tools. The Bourbon government did not control postal flows but was merely one agent among many. As such, the route to Cartagena de Indias did not act solely as an official route, but as an additional crank in a system, already complex, in which official and unofficial channels intermingled. This research shows the multi-layered power plays involving all the agents that tried to shape the direction of the postal reform project.

This paper thus argues for a polyhedric postal reform, that is, a reform with multiple interrelated faces in which a wide variety of agents operated, each one with their own strategy. The postal system in Cartagena de Indias was populated by different powers and interests, and included areas of convergence, conflict, and cooperation. Postal officials, whose task was to organise the distribution of the mail, involved the local authorities, such as the governor and royal officials, navy and army officers, and other social groups such as the clergy, the merchants, and the indigenous population groups. All of them had a stake in the distribution of the post, leading to points of confrontation and cooperation. The postal service was formed by different layers that interacted and overlapped at the local, regional, imperial, and global levels.

I also argue that the postal system played a central role in the configuration of imperial spaces, exercising its own agency. The postal administration was an autonomous agent capable of changing the socio-political and economic face of the empire. The postal system activated different actors and strategies that mobilised information, giving rise to a process of re-articulation of the spheres of power, which shaped the structure of the monarchy. The very dynamic local practices of the postal system, such as the routes and networks and connections, gave it a certain character of its own that differentiated it from the intentions of the Crown.

The idea of ascribing agency to institutions, specifically to the postal system, is original and controversial. Bruno Latour proposed the idea of agency to refer to the capacity for action of non-humans, for example, machines, institutions, buildings, and organisms. From this approach, Latour suggested the existence of a plane of material relations between various aspects of the world, functioning as a whole. Therefore, he proposed the presence of many forces interacting and forming the state.[61]

Accordingly, Patrick Joyce stated the need to think about the state in terms of connectivity and one of the main elements that provides this connectivity are forms of communication, specifically the postal system that participates in the nature of the state. He argues that the daily operation of the postal system reflected the ordinariness of both the everyday state and daily life in the empire.[62]

This research shows that this concept of agency can be usefully applied to state institutions, such as the postal system, since it can help to explain the role played by these institutions in the state's framework and the relationship between power, society, and empire. As such, this case study regards the postal services as agent. The idea is supported by the analysis of the postal administration in Cartagena de Indias, which included multiple entanglements of things and persons with human and non-human agency.

Notes

1. Braudel, *El Mediterráneo*, 314.
2. Brendecke, *Imperio e información*, 43–103.
3. See Le Roux, *Post Offices of Europe*; Raymond, *News Networks.*
4. See Banks, *Chasing Empire.*
5. See Steele, *English Atlantic*; Dierks, *In My Power*; Dubcovsky, *Informed Power.*
6. See Alcázar Molina, *Historia del correo*; Garay Unibaso, *Correos marítimos españoles*; López Bernal, *El correo marítimo colonial*; Moreno Cabanillas, *Cartas para gobernar.*
7. See Sobral Neto, *As comunicaçoes*; Guapindaia, "Comunicação e poder"; Guapindaia, "Regulações centrais, práticas regionais."
8. Zilliacus, *From Pillar to Post*, 78.
9. Paquette, "Enlightened Narratives," 63.
10. See Brandtzaeg et al., *Travelling Chronicles.*
11. See Vives, *Historia social y economía*; Domínguez Ortiz, *Carlos III y la España*. Pietschmann, *Las reformas borbónicas*; Guimerá, *El reformismo borbónico.*
12. See Paquette, *Enlightenment, Governance and Reform*; Kuethe and Andrien, *The Spanish Atlantic*; McFarlane, *War and Independence.*
13. See Eissa-Barroso, *The Spanish Monarchy*; Herrero Sánchez, "Spanish Theories of Empire."
14. Report by Pedro Rodríguez Campomanes to the Postmasters General. Madrid, 10 July 1762. Archivo General de Indias (hereafter AGI), Correos, 462 B.
15. This monopoly of the postal service by the Crown would be confirmed by the legislation enacted during the reforms, especially the *Provisional Regulations of the Maritime Post from Spain to its West Indies*, and the *Royal Ordinance of the Maritime Post*. See Regulations of the Maritime Post from Spain to its West Indies. Madrid, 16 December 1764. AGI, Estado, 86, n. 8.; and Royal Ordinance of the Maritime Post. El Pardo, 26 January 1777. AGI, Correos, 430 B.
16. Letter from the Marquis of Grimaldi to the Postmasters General. San Ildefonso, 24 August 1764. AGI, Correos, 428 A.
17. After the suspension of the postal service between England and Spain, merchants continued to press for its re-establishment. They considered it essential for their trade relations with Spain and Portugal. Report by the postmasters-General Ja [James] Craggs [the elder] and [Charles] Cornwallis to [Secretary James] Craggs [the younger; Secretary of State, Southern Department], 20 March 1719. National Archives of the United Kingdom (hereafter TNA), State Paper Office, 35/15/111.
18. See Beck, *A History of the Falmouth*; Mejide Pardo, *Correos marítimos.*
19. The packet boats were the ships in charge of the postal maritime service for the transport of correspondence, but they could also carry passengers and goods. They originated in the seventeenth century, on a ship carrying mail between Calais (France) and Dover (England), which was named Packet-Boat, and which was transferred to Spain under the name *Paquebote*. Garay Unibaso, *Correos marítimos españoles*, 57.
20. Some of the goods transported by the ships from Spain to Spanish America were wine from Catalonia, flour, nuts from Asturias, socks, hats, olives, hemp, glass glasses, shoes, boots, crockery, iron, and many others of different kinds. Conversely, the ships that went from the Indies to Spain brought goods such as mahogany, cocoa from Guayaquil, logwood

from Campeche, leather, tobacco, and sugar. News of goods transported from Corunna to Havana and viceversa, 1766. AGI, Indiferente General, 1586.

21. Regulations of the Maritime Post from Spain to its West Indies, 1764. Archivo General de la Nación de Colombia (hereafter AGNC), Colonia, Correos, Cundinamarca, Tomo 1, Documento 65.
22. For example, Manuel de Zulueta and Juan Ángel de Olavarrieta's merchant company signed a contract with the postal service on 22 January 1768, to introduce a specific amount of flour in each monthly mail to Havana. However, these merchants shipped flour on private vessels whose cargoes they arranged themselves. Manuel de Zulueta and Juan Ángel de Olavarrieta to the Postmasters General. Madrid, 7 August 1770. AGI, Correos, 429 A.
23. The Royal Officers to the Marquis of Grimaldi. Campeche, 4 May 1765. AGI, Indiferente General, 1587.
24. The postmaster of Corunna José Antonio López to the Postmasters General. Corunna, 6 December 1769. AGI, Correos, 464.
25. The Postmaster General to the Marquis of Croix. Madrid, 10 April 1765. AGI, Correos, 390 B.
26. The postmaster of Corunna José Antonio López to the Postmasters General. Corunna, 12 November 1768. AGI, Correos, 464.
27. For the opposition, in both Spain and Spanish America, to the postal reform, see Moreno Cabanillas, "A Global Postal Service," 94–111.
28. The Postmasters General to the Marquis of Grimaldi. Madrid, 1764. AGI, Correos, 428 A.
29. The Marquis of Grimaldi to the Postmasters General. San Lorenzo, 21 October 1767. AGI, Correos, 429 A; The Postmasters General to the Marquis of Grimaldi. Madrid, 1 February 1771. AGI, Correos, 429 B.
30. Araneda Riquelme, *Un gobierno de papel.*
31. The Viceroy of New Spain Antonio Bucareli to Julián de Arriaga. Mexico, 30 October 1771. AGI, Indiferente General, 1587.
32. Instruction to the Packetboats destined for the Post Service. Madrid, 24 August 1764. AGI, Estado, 86 A, n. 6.
33. José Antonio Pando to the Viceroy of New Granada Pedro Mesía de la Cerda. Cartagena de Indias, 20 November 1769. AGI, Correos, 69 A.
34. Captured ship: San Francisco Xavier alias La Perla, Don Josef Perez Muente master (José Pérez de Muente) (former master Don Melchor de Alarcón), 29 October 1779. TNA, High Court of Admiralty, 30/275.; and Captured ship: San Francisco Xavier alias La Perla, Don Josef Perez Muente master (José Pérez de Muente) (former master Don Melchor de Alarcón), 29 October 1779. TNA, High Court of Admiralty, 30/276. The correspondence intercepted was generally private letters related to the commercial sphere. Xabier Lamikiz analyses this correspondence captured by the British Empire through the case of the Spanish merchant ship called *San Francisco Xavier La Perla*. See Lamikiz, 2010.
35. Benjamin Franklin and William Hunter designed instructions on the convenient method of operation of the postal service for postmasters. These regulations were circulated to post offices in the British colonies in America, for example, *Post Office Instructions and Directions, 1753*. See Labaree, *The Papers of Benjamin Franklin*, 161–177.
36. Lemay, *Life of Benjamin Franklin*, 627.
37. Martínez Shaw, "La historia marítima," 71.
38. For a discussion of the history and an extended analysis on polycentric monarchies see Cardim et al., *Polycentric Monarchies*; Herrero Sánchez, "The Business Relations"; Grafe, "Polycentric States"; Pérez García and De Sousa, *Global History and New Polycentric Approaches.*
39. Gruzinski, *Las cuatro partes del mundo*, 81.
40. Vidal Ortega, *Cartagena de Indias,* 20.
41. Haring, *El comercio y la navegación,* 251–254.
42. See Meléndez, "Negotiating Subjectivities."
43. From 1697 to 1721 only three fleets arrived in Spanish America. In fact, from 1697 to 1706 no fleet arrived in Cartagena de Indias. Castillo Mathieu, *Llave de las Indias*, 16, and 92.
44. For the overland routes from Cartagena de Indias, see Stangl, "Los correos terrestres."

45. Uribe, *Las dinámicas del tiempo*, 110–114.
46. The origin of the *chasquis* is in the culture of the Incas. The *chasquis* were the messengers who moved through Inca territory carrying messages in the pre-Hispanic postal system. Vega, *Antología de los comentarios reales*, 249–251. The word *chasqui* evolved into a generalization since after the postal reform this concept was used to designate any indigenous, black, or mestizo mail driver until the first years of the nineteenth century.
47. See González Martínez, "De los chasquis."
48. The Postmasters General to the Marquis of Grimaldi. Madrid, 16 March 1774. AGI, Correos, 213 A.
49. Trivellato, "Merchants Letters," 81.
50. Lamikiz, *Trade and Trust*, 95.
51. Rueda Ramírez, "La Cultura Escritura," 63.
52. See Lamikiz, *Trade and Trust*; Lamikiz, "Social capital, networks and trust."
53. The Postmaster of Cartagena de Indias Manuel de Valbuena to the Postmasters General. Cartagena de Indias, 15 December 1765. AGI, Correos, 69 A.
54. On commercial networks in the Iberian empires at a transnational and global level, see Hausberger and Ibarra, *Redes y negocios globales*; Herrero Sánchez, "The business relations."
55. Adelman, "A Constitutional Conveyance," 714.
56. See Guapindaia, "Entre correios marítimos."
57. Letters, files and accounts of the Post Office of Cartagena de Indias, 1764–1770. AGI, Correos, 69 A–74 A.
58. Brendecke, *Imperio e información*, 489.
59. Notes on the movement of the mail. Cartagena de Indias, 1751–1782. AGNC, Colonia, Correos, Bolívar, Tomo 2, Documento 8.
60. Darnton, "Una de las primeras sociedades," 371.
61. See Latour, *Reassembling the Social.*
62. See Joyce, *The State of Freedom.*

Acknowledgments

We are grateful to comments and suggestions made by professors Manuel Herrero Sánchez, Antonio J. López Gutiérrez, Manuel Pérez García, and Pedro Miguel Omar Svriz Wucherer. We thank reviewers and editors of this journal for their comments to improve this paper. Any errors are our own.

Disclosure statement

No potential conflict of interest was reported by the author(s).

Funding

This research has been sponsored and financially supported by the GECEM Project (Global Encounters between China and Europe: Trade Networks, Consumption and Cultural Exchanges in Macau and Marseille, 1680–1840), a project hosted by the Pablo de Olavide University (UPO) of Seville (Spain). The GECEM Project is funded by the European Research Council (ERC) Starting-Grant, ref. 679371, under the European Union's Horizon 2020 Research and Innovation Programme (www.gecem.eu). The principal investigator (PI) is Professor Manuel Perez-Garcia (Distinguished Researcher at UPO). This work was supported by the H2020 European Research Council. This research has also been part of the academic activities of the Global History Network (GHN) in China (www.globalhistorynetwork.com). This study was developed within the research project called Res Pública Monárquica. La

Monarquía Hispánica, una estructura imperial policéntrica de repúblicas urbanas (PGC2018-095224-B-I00), funded by the Ministerio de Ciencia, Innovación y Universidades of Spain and within the research group Estudios sobre Europa, el Mundo Mediterráneo y su difusión Atlántica (HUM-680), funded by the Junta de Andalucía. The PI is Professor Manuel Herrero Sánchez.

The publication is part of the grant FJC2021-046538-I, funded by MCIN/AEI/10.13039/501100011033 and by the European Union "NextGenerationEU"/PRTR.

ORCID

Rocío Moreno-Cabanillas http://orcid.org/0000-0001-5579-3712

References

Adelman, Joseph M. "A Constitutional Conveyance of Intelligence, Public and Private: The Post Office, the Business of Printing, and the American Revolution." *Enterprise & Society* 11, no. 4 (2010): 709–752.

Alcázar Molina, Cayetano. *Historia del correo en América: notas y documentos para su estudio*. Madrid: Rivadeneyra, 1920.

Araneda Riquelme, José. *Un gobierno de papel. El correo y sus rutas de comunicación en tiempos de la reforma imperial en Chile (1764–1796)*. Santiago de Chile: Biblioteca Nacional de Chile y Centro de Investigaciones Diego Barros Arana, 2020.

Banks, Kenneth. *Chasing Empire Across the Sea: Communications and the State in the French Atlantic, 1713–1763*. Montreal: McGill-Queen's University Press, 2006.

Beck, John. *A History of the Falmouth Packet Service, 1689–1850: The British Overseas Postal Service*. Exeter: South West Maritime History Society, 2009.

Brandtzaeg, Siv Goril, Paul Goring, and Christine Watson. *Travelling Chronicles: News and Newspapers from the Early Modern Period to the Eighteenth Century*. Leiden: Brill, 2018.

Braudel, Fernand. *El Mediterráneo y el mundo mediterráneo en la época de Felipe II. Tomo 1*. México D.F.: Fondo de Cultura Económica, 2016.

Brendecke, Arndt. *Imperio e información. Funciones del saber en el dominio colonial*. Madrid: Iberoamericana/Vervuert, 2012.

Caplan, Jay. *Postal Culture in Europe, 1500–1800*. Oxford: Voltaire Foundation, 2016.

Cardim, Pedro, Tamar Herzog, Gaetano Sabatini, and José Javier Ruiz Ibáñez. *Polycentric Monarchies: How Did Early Modern Spain and Portugal Achieve and Maintain a Global Hegemony?* Eastbourne: Sussex Academic Press/Fundación Séneca/Universidade Nova de Lisboa – CHAM/Red Columnaria, 2012.

Castillo Mathieu, Nicolás del. *Llave de las Indias*. Bogotá: Ediciones El Tiempo, 1981.

Darnton, Robert. In *El coloquio de los lectores: ensayos sobre autores, manuscritos, editores y lectores*. México: Fondo de Cultura Económica, 2003.

Dierks, Konstantin. *In My Power: Letter Writing and Communications in Early America*. Philadelphia: University of Pennsylvania Press, 2009.

Domínguez Ortiz, Antonio. *Carlos III y la España de la Ilustración*. Madrid: Alianza, 2005.

Dubcovsky, Alejandra. *Informed Power: Communication in the Early American South*. Cambridge, MA: Harvard University Press, 2016.

Eissa-Barroso, Francisco A. *The Spanish Monarchy and the Creation of the Viceroyalty of New Granada (1717–1739): The Politics of Early Bourbon Reform in Spain and Spanish America*. Leiden: Brill, 2017.

Garay Unibaso, Francisco. *Correos marítimos españoles*. Mensajero: Bilbao, 1996.

Martínez González, Nelson Fernando. "De los 'chasquis' de Nueva España: la participación de los indios en la movilización de correo y la reforma del aparato postal novohispano (1764–1780)." *Indiana* 34, no. 2 (2017): 85–109.

Grafe, Regina. "Polycentric States: The Spanish Reigns and the Failures of Mercantilism." In *Mercantilism Reimagined: Political Economy in Early Modern Britain and its Empire*, edited by Philip J. Stern, and Carl Wennerlind, 241–262. Oxford: Oxford University Press, 2013.

Gruzinski, Serge. *Las cuatro partes del mundo. Historia de una mundialización*. México: Fondo de Cultura Económica, 2010.

Guapindaia, Mayra. "Comunicação e poder: a implantação do Correio Marítimo de 1798 e as respostas dos governos da América Portuguesa." *Nuevo Mundo Mundos Nuevos* (2017). Accessed 22 March 2021. https://journals.openedition.org/nuevomundo/71539

Guapindaia, Mayra. "Entre correios marítimos e embarcações de comércio: envio de cartas entre Portugal e América Portuguesa no período das reformas postais (1798–1822)." *Paper presented at the V Encontro Internacional de Jovens Investigadores em História Moderna*, Coimbra, 2017. Accessed 22 March 2021. https://ejihm2017.files.wordpress.com/2017/06/mayra-guapindaia-texto-completo.pdf

Guapindaia, Mayra. "Regulações centrais, práticas regionais: a provisão dos oficiais de correio na América Portuguesa." *Revista Brasileira de História* 40, no. 85 (2020). Accessed 22 March 2021. https://www.scielo.br/scielo.php?pid=S0102-01882020000300057&script=sci_abstract&tlng=pt

Guimerá, Agustín. ed. *El reformismo borbónico: una visión interdisciplinar*. Madrid: Alianza Editorial, 1996.

Haring, C. H. *El comercio y la navegación entre España y las Indias en época de los Habsburgo*. Paris: Desclée de Brouwer, 1939.

Hausberger, Bernd, and Antonio Ibarra. *Redes y negocios globales en el mundo ibérico, siglos XVI–XVIII*. Madrid: Iberoamericana/Vervuert, 2011.

Herrero Sánchez, Manuel. "The Business Relations, Identities and Political Resources of Italian Merchants in the Early-Modern Spanish Monarchy: Some Introductory Remarks." *European Review of History: Revue européenne d'histoire* 23, no. 3 (2016): 335–346.

Herrero Sánchez, Manuel. "Spanish Theories of Empire: A Catholic and Polycentric Monarchy." In *A Companion to Early Modern Spanish Imperial Political and Social Thought*, edited by Jörg Telkamp, 17–52. Leiden: Brill, 2020.

Joyce, Patrick. *The State of Freedom. A Social History of the British State Since 1800*. Cambridge: Cambridge University Press, 2013.

Kuethe, Allan J., and Kenneth J. Andrien. *The Spanish Atlantic World in the Eighteenth Century: War and the Bourbon Reforms, 1713–1796*. New York: Cambridge University Press, 2014.

Labaree, Leonard W. ed. *The Papers of Benjamin Franklin*. New Haven, CT: Yale University Press, 1962.

Lamikiz, Xabier. "Social Capital, Networks and Trust in Early Modern Long-Distance Trade: A Critical Appraisal." In *Merchants and Trade Networks in the Atlantic and the Mediterranean, 1550–1800: Connectors of Commercial Maritime Systems*, edited by Manuel Herrero Sánchez, and Klemens Kaps, 39–61. London: Routledge, 2017.

Lamikiz, Xabier. *Trade and Trust in the Eighteenth-Century Atlantic World: Spanish Merchants and Their Overseas Networks*. Woodbridge: Royal Historical Society/Boydell Press, 2010.

Latour, Bruno. *Reassembling the Social: An Introduction to Actor-Network-Theory*. Oxford: Oxford University Press, 2008.

Lemay, J.A. Leo. *Life of Benjamin Franklin*. Philadephia: University of Pennsylvania Press, 2008.

Le Roux, Muriel. *Post Offices of Europe 18th–21st Century. A Comparative History*. Brüssel: P.I.E. – Peter Lang, 2014.

López Bernal, José Manuel. *El correo marítimo colonial (1764–1824). Rutas y tarifas Postales*. Madrid: Real Academia Hispánica de Filatelia, 2011.

Martínez Shaw, Carlos. "La historia marítima como historia total." *Historia a debate* 3 (2009): 65–72.

McFarlane, Anthony. *War and Independence in Spanish America*. New York: Routledge, 2014.

Mejide Pardo, Antonio. *Correos marítimos entre Falmouth y La Coruña (1689–1815)*. La Coruña: Instituto José Cornide de Estudios Coruñeses, 1966.

Meléndez, Mariselle. "Negotiating Subjectivities on the Fringes of the Empire: The Port City of Cartagena de Indias as Site of Social and Political Convergence." In *The Routledge Companion to the Hispanic Enlightenment*, edited by Elizabeth Franklin Lewis, Mónica Bolufer Peruga, and Catherine M. Jaffe, 142–156. London: Routledge, 2020.

Moreno Cabanillas, Rocío. *Cartas para gobernar. El establecimiento de la administración de correos de Cartagena de Indias (1764–1769)*. Saarbrücken: Editorial Académica Española, 2017.

Moreno Cabanillas, Rocío. "A Global Postal Service: Empire, Reform and Conflict in the Spanish Atlantic in the 18th Century." *Ciencia Nueva. Revista de Historia y Política* 3, no. 1 (2019): 94–111.

Paquette, Gabriel. "Enlightened Narratives and Imperial Rivalry in Bourbon Spain: The Case of Almodóvar's Historia Política de los Establecimientos Ultramarinos de las Naciones Europeas (1784–1790)." *The Eighteenth Century: Theory and Interpretation* 48, no. 1 (2007): 61–80.

Paquette, Gabriel. *Enlightenment, Governance, and Reform in Spain and its Empire, 1759– 1808*. London: Palgrave Macmillan, 2008.

Pérez García, Manuel, and Lucio de Sousa. eds. *Global History and New Polycentric Approaches: Europe, Asia and the Americas in a World Network System*. Singapore: Palgrave Macmillan, 2018.

Pietschmann, Horst. *Las reformas borbónicas y el sistema de intendencias en Nueva España: un estudio político administrativo*. México: Fondo de Cultura Económica, 1996.

Raymond, Joad. *News networks in early modern Europe*. Leiden: Brill, 2016.

Rueda Ramírez, Pedro. "La Cultura Escrita en el mundo Atlántico Colonial: Claves historiográficas, retos y perspectivas." *EREBEA. Revista de Humanidades y Ciencias Sociales* 2 (2012): 53–76.

Sobral Neto, Margarida. *As comunicaçoes na Idade Moderna*. Lisboa: Fundação Portuguesa das Comunicações, 2005.

Stangl, Werner. "Los correos terrestres de Cartagena de Indias en tiempos de la renta (1768– 1810): Itinerarios, cartografía, un «mapa en relación topográfica», GPS y un SIG." *Revista de Indias* 80, no. 278 (2020): 199–250.

Steele, Ian K. *English Atlantic, 1675–1740: An Exploration of Communication and Community*. New York: University of Oxford Press, 1986.

Trivellato, Francesca. "Merchants' Letters across Geographical and Social Boundaries." In *Cultural Exchange in Early Modern Europe. Vol. III: Correspondence and Cultural Exchange in Europe, 1400–1700*, edited by Francisco Bethencourt, and Florike Egmond, 80–104. Cambridge: Cambridge University Press, 2007.

Uribe, Ricardo. *Las dinámicas del tiempo. Relojes, calendarios y actitudes en el virreinato de la Nueva Granada*. Medellín: La Carrera Histórica, 2016.

Vega, Garcilaso de la. *Antología de los comentarios reales*. Madrid: M. Aguilar Editor, 1929.

Vidal Ortega, Antonino. *Cartagena de Indias y la región histórica del Caribe, 1580–1640*. Sevilla: Secretariado de Publicaciones de la Universidad de Sevilla, 2002.

Vives, Vicens. *Historia social y económica de España y América*. Barcelona: Editorial Teide, 1957.

Zilliacus, Laurin. *From Pillar to Post: The Troubled History of the Mail*. London: William Heinemann, 1956.

Index

Note: Endnotes are indicated by the page number followed by 'n' and the endnote number e.g., 20n1 refers to endnote 1 on page 20.

For Product Safety Concerns and Information please contact our EU
representative GPSR@taylorandfrancis.com
Taylor & Francis Verlag GmbH, Kaufingerstraße 24, 80331 München, Germany

www.ingramcontent.com/pod-product-compliance
Lightning Source LLC
LaVergne TN
LVHW082343011026
849160LV00025B/1592
* 9 7 8 1 0 3 2 4 5 9 9 4 3 *